UNDERSTANDING AFFORDABILITY

The Economics of Housing Markets

Geoffrey Meen and Christine Whitehead

BRISTOL
UNIVERSITY
PRESS

First published in Great Britain in 2020 by

Bristol University Press
1-9 Old Park Hill
Bristol
BS2 8BB
UK
t: +44 (0)117 954 5940
www.bristoluniversitypress.co.uk

British Library Cataloguing in Publication Data
A catalogue record for this book is available from the British Library

ISBN 978-1-5292-1186-3 hardcover
ISBN 978-1-5292-1185-6 paperback
ISBN 978-1- 5292-1189-4 ePub
ISBN 978-1- 5292-1188-7 ePdf

Cover design by blu inc, Bristol
Front cover image: iStock/kelvinjay

Printed and bound by CPI Group (UK) Ltd, Croydon, CR0 4YY

Contents

List of Figures and Tables

Figures

Tables

Preface

In October 1918, a British soldier, Jim Coote, fighting on the Western front wrote home to his sister that he was surprised she was getting married, but realized the decision was based on the need to obtain a good home while they could since 'things will not be half as good and double the price later on'.[1] He was right, and problems of housing affordability – the subject matter of this book – have never fully disappeared. Despite strongly held views, there are no simple solutions, since housing outcomes are the result of sets of interrelated complex forces. Yet, an understanding of the underlying causes is a prerequisite to any improvement in housing conditions.

The book is based on our academic research conducted over many years but includes new ideas as well. It has also been stimulated by frequent contact with those working within government and in the housing sector in order to address 'real world' problems; these interactions have kept our work grounded. Policy makers often ask questions that are difficult to answer and that do not always fit easily within the scope of readily available models; economists are good at building elegant models that are analytically tractable, but are not necessarily relevant to the interests of the policy community. Nevertheless, we believe strongly that policy should be evidence-based.

The book does not attempt to cover all areas of housing economics and policy but concentrates particularly on those issues which are the most important to an understanding of housing affordability. Both authors recently worked together as Specialist Advisors to the House of Lords Economic Affairs Select Committee and this experience was one (of the many) influences on the work. A further influence was our research for the Barker Review of Housing Supply, published in 2004: research which is still used within the English Ministry of Housing, Communities and Local Government.

Among economists who study housing issues, there are loosely two groups; first, there are those who treat housing as a specialist subfield. For this group, the life blood of the subject includes market imperfections, spatial differences, tenure, externalities, taxation and subsidies, distribution problems and the role of institutions. Although housing is a market, under this view, it typically does not adjust smoothly in the same way as, for example, non-durable goods. Housing markets can remain out of equilibrium for long periods of time and distributional issues may be as or more important than economic efficiency.

By contrast, the major expansion in housing economics in recent years has come mainly from the macro-finance community. As a generalization, this approach applies more standard economic models to housing, paying less attention to the distinguishing characteristics of housing. For example, some research applies models of financial asset valuation directly to house prices without fully recognizing the underlying differences. These differences are, to simplify, seen as a nuisance that can be assumed away and mainstream techniques applied.

While there have been valuable insights generated by this second approach, in our view, the essence of housing studies is to recognize the fundamental attributes of housing and how these impact on behaviour and outcomes.

A further important distinction is between those who believe that freely operating private markets are the best way to improve affordability and those who advocate government intervention. Advocates of each view can be found among both housing specialists and macroeconomists. Just as in economics more generally, support for each position has varied over the years. For example, direct rent controls were introduced during the First World War with building subsidies after the war to mitigate the effect of the housing shortages which worried Jim Coote; public sector building expanded strongly after the Second World War as well; from the 1970s policy shifted from the provision of supply subsidies towards individual support for households, partly reflecting the free market economic and political stances of the time. For similar reasons, deregulation of mortgage markets took place in the 1970s and 1980s. Particularly since the Barker Review, the government priority has been on expanding private housing supply, notably through the easing of planning controls, under the view that private expansion will not only improve aggregate affordability, but also filter down to benefit those on low incomes. But neither financial deregulation nor the easing of planning regulations is without problems.

The book is not just about looking back at our earlier work, but also asks whether there are new directions for policy. As noted, in recent years, policy concerned with improving affordability has concentrated heavily on ways to increase housing supply. Much less attention has been paid to the demand side of the market; one reason is that changing demand – for example through the tax system – is difficult and politically sensitive. Economists have long advocated reform but there is little evidence that policy makers will undertake reform on the required scale and there are good reasons why this should be the case in a property-owning democracy. But, arguably, the roots of housing economics lie in an understanding of the demand side of the market; in the UK, housing demand appears to be highly sensitive to changes in income, but relatively unresponsive to changes in house prices. Using more modern approaches in economics, one explanation is in terms of social norms and the interactions with peer groups. But, more generally, concentrating on just one side of the market – currently supply – hampers improvements in affordability and there is a need for a more balanced approach.

The book is written by two economists, but one of the pleasures of researching in housing is that it is an inter-disciplinary subject and, therefore, the book is not just written for other economists, but for a wider housing audience in both academia and policy circles. Although the book explores economic concepts, except occasionally in appendices, there are no mathematical equations and our hope is that the book is accessible. Most of the concepts discussed in the book are applicable to a range of developed economies but, perhaps inevitably given the differences in institutional structures, the majority of the examples come from our own country, England. Even within the UK there are significant differences in policy since housing is a devolved function across the constituent countries. Nevertheless, in many chapters, we have also included international comparisons.

Just as this book was ready for publication, COVID-19 hit the world. In England, a number of housing measures were immediately implemented, including the opportunity to postpone mortgage payments, banning evictions for tenants, increases in the local housing allowance for private renters, and government calls for house moves to be delayed. But these are short-term initiatives, although, especially in the case of the housing allowance, very welcome. As the book shows, housing market outcomes are far more heavily influenced by broader developments in the macroeconomy and longer-term pressures on income inequality than by most housing specific measures. No one can possibly know the full extent of the damage that is likely to be caused to the economy; but, remembering that housing in Britain has still not fully recovered from the 2008 Global Financial Crisis, the housing effects are likely to be long-lasting and severe. Moreover, we can expect that the new build market will be particularly badly affected because it is much easier to stop building than to get back to pre-crisis levels.

Some research, including our own, has shown that, over history, it requires large shocks – including wars, plagues or natural disasters – to produce permanent structural changes in society and the virus, as seen today, is certainly a large shock. But, even then, change is not guaranteed. Indeed, there is currently discussion throughout the world about 'getting back to normal'. In this new normality there will be some parts of the housing system which will have to be propped up; notably, the cross subsidy model by which the provision of social housing is paid for out of market development will have to change. But, on past evidence, it would be optimistic to predict significant positive structural policy changes. Therefore, our expectation is that the core theme of affordability discussed in the book will continue to remain relevant well after the worst of the effects of COVID-19 have passed.

In housing markets across the world, since house prices are highly sensitive to changes in economic activity, house prices, and indeed rents, may well decline and one view might be that this will be good for first-time buyers and renters; we would caution against this view. In recessions, the young and those on low incomes are more vulnerable to income and job losses and it is these groups – the focus of the book – who are most likely to suffer.

Finally, to be a little less pessimistic, at the present time, there is considerable talk of community and mutual support. In this context, the book sets out some of the ways in which improving affordability and reducing inequality in housing could be achieved not just through large scale structural changes but more immediately through better regulatory frameworks especially in the private rented sector and modifying the housing welfare system to reduce the burden of housing costs.

Too many people have influenced our thinking over the years to thank them all individually but one person we would like to mention is the late Alan Holmans who both made a direct contribution to many of the topics in the book but also supported academic research in the field for over 40 years. We have also gained enormously from our academic colleagues across the world even when they have disagreed with us. In addition, we would like to highlight the contributions of successive generations of housing economists working within government (although they bear no responsibility for the views expressed here). In England, the name of the government department responsible for housing has changed many times since we became involved in housing research – the Department of the Environment; the Department of the Environment, Transport and the Regions; the Office of the Deputy Prime Minister; the Department of Communities and Local Government; and at the time of writing the Ministry of Housing, Communities and Local Government. Furthermore, the revolving door of housing ministers has often been criticized – there have been approximately 40 housing ministers since 1951.

But, in our experience, the economists in these departments have been a pleasure to work with, even when we have not always been able to answer their questions fully. Geoff Meen would also like to thank the Economic and Social Research Council (UK) (ESRC), the Arts and Humanities Research Council (AHRC) and the Joseph Rowntree Foundation for support for the project through their financing of the UK Collaborative Centre for Housing Evidence (CaCHE). Thanks also are due to the staff of the UK Data Service at the University of Essex, who have provided access to the English Housing Survey used in this book.

Crisis, What Crisis?

Introduction

Problems of housing affordability are not new. Many ordinary households a hundred years ago would recognize some of the issues to be discussed in this book. Rent controls had been introduced in 1915 because of housing shortages, but house prices still rose sharply in 1919 and 1920. As we shall see, the problems and the proposed solutions remain similar today. However, it would be wrong to conclude that there have been no improvements over the long term: nationally, at the time of the 1911 census, there were, on average, approximately five persons in each property, but this had halved a hundred years later.[1] On this measure, overcrowding has declined enormously. Furthermore, even in the immediate aftermath of the Second World War, 64 per cent of households were without piped hot water to a bath, sink and hand basin. Now we no longer bother to measure shortages of this type.

The majority of households now enjoy generally good housing conditions and affordability problems primarily concern groups excluded from these wider improvements. Some groups benefit from rising house prices and low outgoings, notably those who have already paid off their mortgages, and there are now more households who are outright owners than those with mortgages, in part because of an ageing population. But two groups – those on low incomes and those at early stages of their housing careers – continue to lag behind. Furthermore, an increasing proportion of outright owners with high incomes are likely to own a second home, whereas low-income households are unlikely to own even one, widening the dispersion of wealth, which depends heavily on property ownership. The affordability crisis, therefore, has strong distributional elements. The market has generally worked adequately for the majority, but not for the poor and the young.

So why do we care so much about housing affordability? There are, after all, many goods that certain groups in society are unable to obtain, given their incomes and the prices of those goods. Part of the explanation, as noted, arises from the effect on wealth distribution. But, more fundamentally, successive governments have accepted that all households should have the opportunity to achieve a decent standard of housing and have provided subsidies to support that standard. Also, low-quality housing generates externalities and may contribute, for example, to poor educational performance and health, adding to future costs for society. There are also wider macroeconomic effects: for example, volatility in house prices adds significantly to volatility and risk in the economy as a whole. Central banks now pay more attention to housing and mortgage market conditions than was once the case because of concern about macro stabilization.

The objective of this book is not, however, to advocate a particular set of policies – there are plenty of other publications that take this approach. Rather, the aim is to consider the balance of policies; the constraints under which housing policy operates governed primarily by the macroeconomy and politics; what can realistically be achieved; the structural changes that would need to occur; and the significant sacrifices that would have to be made by some sections of society if we are to make real improvements in affordability for the young and those on low incomes. Affordability is the result of a complex process, and the modest policy initiatives that have been undertaken in recent years are unlikely to be adequate. But to appreciate this, we need to understand first how changes in affordability occur over time and between different households. One of our concerns is that housing policy is insufficiently coherent across the government departments that have a housing function and this leads to conflicting objectives. The analysis reveals that there are no silver bullets or costless solutions, but there are new policy directions that can be explored in addition to those that have dominated in recent years.

Recent policy issues

At the time of writing, housing is high on the political agenda. In 2017, the government issued its White Paper, *Fixing Our Broken Housing Market*.[2] The recommendations of the White Paper have been reflected in a revised National Planning Policy Framework and in many other initiatives. In addition, in 2016, the House of Lords conducted an inquiry into building more homes,[3] whereas the Housing, Communities and Local Government Select Committee of the House of Commons consistently reviews aspects of housing in England including, latterly: affordable homes, housing for older households, homelessness, issues around leasehold, and the private rented sector. Furthermore, there have been independent studies, including for example the Lyons and Redfern Reviews, the Affordable Housing Commission, the Institute of Public Policy Research and Shelter, all dealing with questions directly or indirectly related to affordability.[4]

In the White Paper, the need to promote more house building is the central feature for addressing affordability. This continued a policy theme dating back well before the important 2004 Barker Review of Housing Supply.[5] Internationally, higher rates of construction have also been promoted as the solution to affordability problems. With exceptions, rather less attention has been paid to the demand side of the market in recent years, although this was certainly not the case in the past. But there are important questions concerning the feasibility of stabilizing affordability by supply increases alone, and the relative recent neglect of the demand side of the market is, at best, controversial and limits the range of policy options. An alternative view is that housing problems mainly arise from the distribution of homes rather than from an absolute shortage in terms of numbers: the tax system, mortgage finance and changes in the income distribution have all favoured older or richer households. If the distribution were more equal, the UK's housing affordability issues would, on this view, disappear. Arguably, the tax system supports home ownership while the low returns on financial assets provide a stimulus to the Buy to Let market where returns are higher. In fact, supply and demand policies are not alternatives but complements in a more integrated policy framework.

Methods of analysis

Even though the problems are persistent, the methods of economic analysis have developed over time. During the last 20–30 years there have been considerable advances in the techniques and tools available: these include the development of large-scale micro data sets and the micro econometrics to interrogate them; advances in time-series methods for modelling housing trends and cycles; greater understanding of the interactions between housing and the wider economy; new theoretical approaches to modelling social interactions that contribute to an understanding of the spatial structures of cities and patterns of segregation; the integration of institutional approaches from economic historians, recognizing the importance of path dependence for housing outcomes; and greater emphasis on behavioural economics, a field that is now being taken seriously in housing economics. Of course, other disciplines have also made major contributions to housing studies but, as two economists, economic methods provide the main tools for our analysis. Nevertheless, housing economic forecasting has had its spectacular failures of which the inability to predict the Global Financial Crisis in 2007/08 was the most obvious. Housing markets were not the fundamental cause, but they acted as a trigger, and many have been critical – not only in the UK – with some justification, of the conventional economic models used in housing and economics more generally.[6]

Technique and understanding are, however, not the same; the latter requires us to ask the right questions, and needs careful study of market structure and the application of the most appropriate model to the policy question, rather than adopting a one-size-fits-all approach to key issues. Technical tools and models are useful but, by themselves, only provide limited guidance for policy. This book attempts to bridge the divide between technique and policy. Our core interest is in potential solutions based on a strong theoretical and empirical evidence base.

A feature of our analysis is to stress the important interlinkages between different parts of the housing system, across household types, tenures and locations. In addition, housing affects the wider economy and general macroeconomic policies – both monetary and fiscal – have a crucial impact on housing. The first part of this book is, therefore, concerned with establishing the conceptual framework, which captures the interlinkages at both micro and macro levels. This shows both the limitations of policy and the dangers of policy making without an appropriate evidence base. The developed evidence base is empirical, which allows us, in some cases, to quantify the effects of different policy initiatives. One feature that stands out is that explicit housing policies alone have only limited effects; housing outcomes are more usually the by-product of wider fiscal and monetary policies. For example, in the setting of interest rates, housing conditions are only one of a wide range of factors taken into account by the Bank of England Monetary Policy Committee, but there is no necessary reason why the required level of interest rates for general inflation targeting should be the same as that required for housing stability. Furthermore, some of the most successful policies for housing throughout history have not been aimed directly at housing.[7] These include advances in medical knowledge and improvements in sanitation in the 19th century; technological improvements to railways and roads, which in the 20th century allowed suburbanization; advances in urban design and their contribution to slum clearance; and the effects of financial deregulation in the 1980s. In addition, long-run growth in the economy has been crucial to the improvement in housing conditions.

Direct housing policies may attempt to mitigate the constraints imposed by macro policy. Recent Help to Buy initiatives, primarily aimed at first-time buyers and developers, provide an example. The predominance of macro policy over housing is not new and pervades the post-Second World War period. Nor is the issue confined to the UK, and research in Australia and Canada (among other countries) also highlights the problem.[8] It has been argued that politicians concerned with housing policy often 'look busy' without adopting policy measures that will disturb the status quo. This is partly because action is constrained by special interest groups, but also because housing is the poor relation to wider macroeconomic policies.

One of the problems in drawing international policy conclusions concerning best practice is that the institutional context matters. The institutional structure typically develops over many years and, therefore, policies that have been successful in one country cannot necessarily be transferred to another with the same degree of success. Although many of the chapters contain international comparative sections, most of the detailed examples are taken from the UK and notably its largest country, England, since housing policy is devolved and there are differences in legal structures and policy priorities. Nevertheless, we would suggest that the concepts developed in the book are relevant to a wide range of advanced economies and, indeed, are derived from a substantial international literature.

Developing the analytical framework

The book is divided into two main parts: the first developing the analytical framework and the second examining major housing policy strands and their impact on affordability. The starting point is to understand what we mean by affordability. So, Chapter 2 is concerned with different measures and their relative strengths and weaknesses. Despite the fact that the concept of affordability has a long history, there is still little agreement over the most appropriate way of measuring it. There are both conceptual and practical problems. Furthermore, there is no reason why the same measure should be appropriate to different groups and indeed different measures are needed for first-time buyers and low-income households. There is a substantial literature on this subject but, broadly, four approaches can be identified: the first, house price to earnings (or income) ratios are the most common and are the simplest – which is their main attraction – but are heavily flawed and it is worrying that the ratio, measured at the local level, is now the main way in which affordability is taken into account in English local housing assessments. Among the problems is the fact that it is an average measure, rather than addressing the issues around the distribution of outcomes across households. Households who already own benefit from rises in house prices and worsening affordability on this measure, but renters and those who are yet to form separate households are the losers.

The second approach considers household expenditures (rather than prices) relative to income. Again, the measure is widely used, but has attracted considerable criticism both on the grounds of its theoretical shortcomings and the ways in which expenditures should be measured. Some of the weaknesses are addressed by the third approach – the residual income method. This measure estimates the income each household has available for spending on non-housing consumption goods after the subtraction of housing costs. If residual income falls below the level that can finance an acceptable level of consumption, captured for example by a poverty threshold, then housing is considered unaffordable. However, practical difficulties associated with its construction have meant that no country has adopted the measure as a regularly published indicator. A fourth measure attempts to take into account the supply of housing available or the imbalance between demand and supply.

None of the measures are ideal, but some are preferable to others. The chapter shows that, despite their theoretical shortcomings, measures based on housing expenditure ratios for low-income renters are correlated with wider measures of financial stress at least in England and, therefore, are useful in practice. But affordability for potential first-time buyers needs a different approach, and a new method is suggested which looks at the distribution of incomes, the distribution of house prices in each location and the constraints that households face both in terms of mortgage repayments and access to credit – in other words it incorporates both demand and supply elements – summarized in a version of the Lorenz curve and Gini coefficient. These are both widely used measures in the inequality literature and can be easily constructed and understood.

Whatever measure of affordability is employed, house prices and rents play a central role and Chapter 3 turns to the factors that determine these variables. Even in a country as small as the UK, housing markets are not entirely national in character, although there are some common trends across space, and, therefore, sub-national markets need to be considered in addition. Although house prices have, at times, been highly volatile, we argue that both the volatility and long-run trends can be explained by a fairly small number of variables and that these variables and the size of their effects on prices have changed little over the last 50 years. The problem has been that house prices are very sensitive to changes in this small number of variables, notably income, interest rates and credit conditions. We establish a condition that explains the rise in real prices in the long run, which begins to cast doubt on the ability of increases in housing supply alone to stabilize affordability. The chapter also argues the case for paying greater attention to measures of housing market risk, an issue taken up in more detail in Chapter 8. At the regional level, the chapter reexamines the nature of the ripple effect, which is widely used to explain an international phenomenon: house prices in a lead region or city tend to rise first and, then, other areas within the country gradually catch up over time to reestablish a long-run relationship between locations.

Chapter 3 is also concerned with the determination of market rents and links with house prices. At least in the UK there is less empirical evidence on the factors affecting rents as opposed to house prices. This is partly because freely operating private rental markets on a large scale have been a fairly recent development, although the market has doubled since the late 1990s. In addition, research has been hampered by the absence of adequate data on market rents until new indices were introduced in 2005. The information now available suggests that rents have grown at a slower rate than house prices. One explanation lies in the fact that landlords are typically reluctant to raise the rents of established tenants, particularly if they have a good track record. Additionally, the level of rents (rather than the growth rate) is determined by demand as well as supply and is already high as a proportion of median incomes. Nevertheless, the difference in the two growth rates also reflects the fact that housing is an asset and low interest rates are capitalized into house prices.

The next two chapters address issues around affordability for the different groups. Chapter 4 concentrates on household formation and the tenure choices of younger age groups. Not only have current cohorts experienced lower rates of home ownership than previous generations, but they are more likely to remain with parents for longer or share with those in a similar position. The decline in aggregate home ownership in England from 71 per cent in 2003 to 62.6 per cent in 2016/17 (although the rate rose again to 63.5 per cent in 2017/18) is concentrated on younger households and the change is not unique to this country. The US, Australia and many European countries have experienced similar patterns, sometimes starting earlier.

The fall in the share in England has been more than offset by a rise in private renting (as social housing has also fallen). It is sometimes suggested that the change represents preferences – young households now value more the flexibility associated with renting. An alternative view is that younger households are constrained from entering home ownership because of high housing costs, the impact of credit market restrictions, competition with Buy to Let investors and those wanting second homes, increased job insecurity and changes in the earnings of the young relative to older households.

Chapter 5 turns to housing for low-income groups and links up later to Chapters 11 and 12. Chapter 2 had already noted the wide dispersion of costs faced by households; the data in England and many other countries show that those on low incomes are more likely to spend a high percentage of their incomes on housing in the absence of support. Some wealthier households allocate a high percentage of their incomes but, in these cases, the decision is likely to be a choice rather than a necessity. In addition, low-income households are less able to accumulate the required deposit for home ownership and generally have a greater propensity to be in the rental sectors, either social or private. This chapter, therefore, concentrates on the measures that have been implemented to support housing, including an introduction to the changes to the nature of subsidy and regulatory regimes – from the introduction of rent controls in the First World War, to the expansion in public housing and later income-related subsidies. Since total government expenditure on income-related housing support has increased sharply over time, it is unsurprising that governments have looked for areas of cuts, both in terms of eligibility and the quality, location and price of housing that is supported. But low-income affordability cannot be considered in isolation from other parts of the housing market and, indeed, from the economy more widely, and policy has generally taken insufficient account of the interlinkages.

Whereas the emphasis of the early chapters is on housing demand, Chapter 6 turns to supply and the constraints it faces. It constructs a clear analytical framework, but is best read in conjunction with Chapters 9 and 10, which look in more detail at the key policy measures that have been implemented to support housing investment. Housing policy is heavily concerned with ways of increasing supply and, in terms of analysis, the responsiveness of housing construction to changes in house prices is one of the key parameters and has been heavily researched internationally. If the response is strong then increases in housing demand are primarily met by an increase in supply; if the response is weak then demand increases lead to worsening affordability. Therefore, any constraints on the ability to raise output in response to price signals are detrimental to affordability. The literature finds that supply responses are weaker in the UK than in many other countries. New private housing supply has, in fact, shown no permanent upward trend since the 1920s, which provides one measure of the extent of the problem. In fact, some other countries have also experienced no upward trend, although the *levels* of construction differ.

In addition, in conjunction with Chapter 10, the chapter discusses the structure of the house building industry, notably its current dominance by a small number of large developers and continuing low rates of productivity. Finally, the chapter quantifies the effects of increases in housing construction on measures of affordability. Simulations reaffirm findings originally highlighted in the Barker Review of Housing Supply that increases have to be large and sustained in order to induce a significant improvement in affordability.

Chapter 7 considers fiscal and monetary policy and their effects on the demand for housing. The chapter pays particular attention to structural changes in mortgage finance markets, which have distributional as well as aggregate consequences. From the early 1980s, the UK experienced two periods of strong mortgage growth: the first lasted until the recession of the early 1990s and the second started in the mid-1990s and ended with the Global Financial Crisis (GFC). These periods coincided with a boom in house prices although credit expansions were not necessarily the main cause (an issue discussed further in Chapter 8). Indeed, a major post-war hike in house prices took place in the early 1970s, when mortgages still faced greater controls but incomes were rising rapidly. A distinguishing feature of the GFC period was the fall in the *stock* of mortgages as a percentage of household incomes – this had not happened during the recession of the early 1990s – and even greater falls occurred in the US. However, the decline in the *flow* of mortgage advances was much more dramatic than in the stock. Indeed, expressed relative to average house prices, net advances still remain below the levels of the early 1980s.

Since the vast majority of current owners have equity in their existing properties, which they can use to finance future purchases, credit shortages are less of a problem than for first-time buyers. Therefore, the decline in availability has had important distributional effects. Similarly, the stress tests that borrowers now have to undertake fall primarily on aspiring first-time buyers and those with volatile incomes. Accumulated equity also provides an advantage for existing owners entering the expanded Buy to Let market. The chapter also considers non-neutralities in the property tax system which can discriminate against first-time buyers.

Housing and policy

The second part of the book is concerned with housing policy and how it affects affordability. As noted earlier, more emphasis is given to the position in the UK (and particularly England, since housing is a devolved responsibility), but the book also draws on international experience. Our focus is on policies that attempt to improve affordability, but housing sits within a wider macroeconomic framework and the opening chapter (Chapter 8) of this part deals with how housing affects the macroeconomy, an issue of concern to the stabilization policies of central banks. The 'financialization' of housing, where dwellings are treated as a store of wealth, as well as a place to live has attracted increasing attention as both an economic and a social issue and means that risks associated with housing are transmitted to the wider economy as well as vice versa.[9]

Although the GFC provided an additional impetus, research on housing and the economy had been increasing before then. The rise in consumers' expenditure in the late 1980s had led to research on the relationship between consumption and house prices, since the latter were also rising sharply at the time. However, although the correlation between the two variables was well-established, causality was disputed. Proponents argued that housing provided wealth that could be used to support consumption; opponents suggested that the rise in both variables was caused by a common third factor, notably improved labour productivity, and disputed the underlying theoretical relationship. More recently, however, views have moved towards convergence and greater attention has been paid to the role of housing in providing collateral for loans. A further development has been the attempt to move away from partial analysis – for example simply looking at the relationship between consumption and house prices – to a general equilibrium approach, where housing is integrated into a full model of the economy. In this case, although housing investment only comprises a modest percentage of GDP directly, its total effect is much greater because of the indirect linkages, notably through what are known as financial accelerators.

International comparisons suggest those countries that have undergone the greatest degree of financial deregulation have experienced the highest levels of house price volatility; the expansion of mortgage advances to the US sub-prime market prior to the GFC is but one extreme example. Furthermore, a long history of research on mortgage default indicates that the size of the mortgage loan relative to the value of the property is an important factor (but by no means the only influence). Consequently, central banks in many countries have tightened controls on the size of loans relative to household incomes and/or loans relative to the value of the property as part of macro stabilization policy. The UK is among these countries and, indeed, lenders had already begun to tighten the criteria well before the formal controls. As noted, the controls have distributional consequences particularly for first-time buyers. However, it is not the case that volatility in prices can be entirely attributed to financial liberalization and the chapter also discusses additional explanations, notably the role of expectations and animal spirits, which introduce a different approach to modelling.

In addition to the wider macroeconomic constraints, the land use planning system is frequently seen as a key constraint on increasing housing supply and this is discussed in Chapter 9 in conjunction with an analysis of the development and use of household projections in this context. Household projections had, and continue to have, very real impacts on how land supply and prices are determined and therefore on how many new homes are provided. They, thus, ultimately affect the cost and affordability of housing across the country. The chapter discusses the development of the regulatory system which was instituted at a time when the state saw it as both possible and desirable to substitute administrative allocation for market methods (including much of new housing supply as well as planning) on the principle that this would increase social welfare and ensure a more equitable distribution of resources. Starting from the 1947 Town and Country Planning Act and post-war shortages, the chapter moves on to examine the development of concerns about the negative impacts of planning from the 1970s which were seen particularly by economists as resulting in restrictions in land supply and increases in the cost of land in the face of demand-determined house prices.

The question arises whether this approach remains relevant in a market-led economy where there is limited willingness for government directly to provide housing for those unable to afford market prices and where there is concern with the reliability of household projections as the basis for decisions about housing need. The chapter also considers alternatives to the English land use planning model, notably through the use of zoning, although the alternatives do not provide a panacea.

Chapter 10 returns to the question of raising the level of private housing construction, continuing the discussion in Chapters 6 and 9. Although the restrictions on construction arising from land use planning policies are frequently stressed, there are many other constraints. These arise from the behavioural responses and incentives structures facing local authorities, builders and landowners, particularly in the context of large sites, which favour large developers rather than smaller building firms. Output is, therefore, influenced by the structure of the housebuilding industry, notably the business model among larger speculative builders; the skills base and productivity in the industry; and the extent to which demand (as opposed to need) is there to maintain increasing output levels. The chapter then discusses new models for speeding up development, including the role of off-plan sales for private developers and the increasing incentives to housing associations to develop market housing as a way of cross-subsidizing their core activities. In addition, the chapter considers attempts to simplify and limit the negative impacts of planning controls through permitted development and planning in principle as well as the core role of planning obligations.

Chapter 11 is concerned with subsidies to the supply of rental housing. The traditional approach to affordability has been to subsidize first local authorities and then housing associations to produce additional social housing. Historically, it was seen as the main means of increasing total housing supply, by providing cheap land and planning permission, and importantly through the new town development corporation framework. Later, the emphasis shifted to introducing private finance into social housing provision and recycling past subsidy to provide a range of affordable housing products, but also to reduce public expenditure. Additionally, the planning system was modified to make it possible to require the provision of affordable housing on residential development sites. Allocation principles have also changed, moving away from accommodating lower income working households to emphasizing provision for vulnerable households of all types. Here, we examine the impact of changing financing mechanisms on the capacity to add to the housing stock, the types of provision and the rents that are charged across the country. We also consider the impact of Right to Buy and other approaches to transferring accommodation within the social rented sector as well as to owner occupation and latterly recycling realized finance to add to the social sector stock. Finally, we look to comparable international experience.

Chapter 12 turns to tenant subsidies. Since the introduction of income-related housing subsidies to tenants in the early 1970s there has been continuing debate about the relative weight to be given to demand side and supply side subsidies. The starting point here is that the numbers helped by the second is limited by available supply while in the UK the first provides an as of right benefit to all eligible households in both the social and private rented sectors. Other elements of policy choice relate to the efficiency and capacity to target assistance across the two very different tenures, the relative public expenditure costs of the approaches to subsidy and their impact not just on the effective allocation of affordable housing but on work incentives.

In this chapter there is particular emphasis on the private rented sector, since one of the most important and unpredicted structural changes in the housing market has been in the growth of this sector, particularly since the turn of the century. It now accommodates more than 20 per cent of all households in England and more than one in four in London, where many of the worst affordability problems are to be found. Importantly, until this century, most of the increase in supply of privately rented housing had been transferred from either owner occupation or the social sector, rather than coming directly from new supply. Benefit payments to private tenants who are paying market rents now exceed those made to social sector tenants where sub-market rents pertain. Here we clarify the nature of these tenure shifts and the households being accommodated in the different sectors. We examine how austerity and recent changes to welfare policy have impacted on households and their capacity to afford the other necessities of life. Particular policies that have been introduced to ensure greater flexibility, targeting and lower public expenditure are discussed.

Chapter 13 is concerned with owner occupation and discusses both the long history of tax reliefs for this sector and the scope for enabling increases in ownership among younger cohorts in future years. Support has always been closely related to political as much as economic objectives, notably the desire to promote a property-owning democracy which dates back to the 1920s. As a consequence, some policies – particularly those concerned with taxation – have been off limits politically. Nevertheless, many economists are highly critical of the current tax system as it relates to housing and have advocated thorough reform. This includes changes to the current Council Tax system, which is regressive, and in many cases those living in high-value properties located in the most expensive parts of the country face relatively low Council Tax burdens.

The chapter shows, therefore, that a tax regime where the local tax is proportional to the value of the property is less regressive than the current Council Tax and leads to an increase in payments by older households and those living in the South of England. Since the taxes are capitalized into house prices, younger aspiring first-time buyers are likely to benefit from their decline but there are significant losers among existing owners, and these impose constraints on policy that cannot be ignored.

Falling home ownership rates among the young and indeed the early middle aged are an international phenomenon; nevertheless, the decline has been greater in the UK than in most other developed economies. The chapter also argues the need for home ownership to be sustainable and that *maximizing* home ownership is not a suitable goal. This raises the question of the benefits from additions to the standard debt financing model. Greater use of equity finance potentially has benefits and Help to Buy schemes and shared ownership provide examples, but the question remains as to whether there is scope for an expansion of equity finance more widely across the private sector.

Chapter 14 highlights the key themes of the book and discusses the substantive implications for policy of what has been discussed in the earlier chapters, including possible new directions for policy. In fact, there is considerable agreement among economists with regard to the range of required policy reforms to improve affordability. These include changes to land use planning, taxation, social housing provision, rents and subsidies, and to financial markets. But there are external constraints, both political and economic, that impose limitations on even the most positive reforming governments. Responsibility for housing is spread over a number of different agencies and government departments where housing is not necessarily the priority. Housing is constrained by, and affects, monetary policy, fiscal policy, welfare policy, health, and education, and the shared responsibility means that the full importance of housing is underestimated. This suggests that the reforms advocated by economists are unlikely to be implemented at least on a sufficient scale, especially while the emphasis on new supply remains the core element of political debate. But the absence of positive policy change implies that the worsening affordability and volatility that have often typified housing markets in the past are likely to continue into the future. Even so, it should be stressed that, over the longer term, despite policy inadequacies, housing conditions have improved for the vast majority of households, making it particularly frustrating that we seem unable to ensure adequate housing for all.

Our understanding of how housing markets work has improved, and the book highlights what we now suggest can and cannot be achieved by different policies. We argue that affordability can be explained mainly by four central market-based parameters in addition to income distribution. These parameters are: the responsiveness of housing demand to changes in income (the income elasticity of housing demand); the responsiveness of demand to price changes (the price elasticity of housing demand); the responsiveness of demand to changes in the cost of capital (the cost of capital elasticity) and the responsiveness of housing supply to changes in house prices (the price elasticity of housing supply).

In many developed countries, recent policy has concentrated heavily on the last of these factors as a means of improving affordability and housing conditions. But the book shows the need to extend housing policy beyond this current concentration on expanding supply. Of particular importance in this context is that, since demand for housing is strongly responsive to changes in incomes but fairly unresponsive to changes in prices, while, at the same time, incomes among younger cohorts have grown at a slower rate than older households, there is inevitably a distributional problem arising in a market system. This is reinforced by the mortgage market which favours existing owners with accumulated equity. Moreover, it is undoubtedly true that low levels of interest rates have made housing attractive as an asset and have contributed to the rise in house prices. However, the affordability problem is not purely one of distribution arising from the treatment of housing as an asset. Rather, there is inherently both a distribution problem and a shortage of homes – a high income elasticity of demand and rising incomes will ensure this.

Recent research in behavioural economics may, tentatively, indicate a new direction for policy, which, nevertheless, returns to early roots of housing economics. The book suggests that the long-run growth of house prices has arisen primarily from consumption demand rather than housing's role as an asset and this depends on the factors that affect the income and price elasticities of that housing demand. But why is the income elasticity so high in the UK and may be higher than in some other countries (although the evidence base is thin)? A possibility is that owner occupied housing reflects social norms and housing's role as a positional good. If housing demand is affected by social interactions with peer groups, then modest changes at the individual level can have much larger effects at the economy-wide level. But increases in housing provision, under this view, may not necessarily lead to improvements in aggregate wellbeing.

In summary, the book argues for a more balanced approach to housing policy, which places greater emphasis on the factors that affect housing demand as well as supply. Although important, increases in housing supply alone are unlikely to stabilize, let alone improve, affordability. Furthermore, taxation and mortgage markets are crucial to understanding affordability and we also argue that risk is, typically, inadequately taken into account in many formal housing forecasting models. But, additionally, there are fundamental issues of what determines household preferences for housing and the influences on the income and price elasticities of housing demand, including the possible role of social peers.

2

Is Housing Really Unaffordable?

Introduction

This chapter is concerned with the conceptual bases and measurement issues associated with different affordability indicators that have been proposed. At one level, at least in the private market, housing cannot be unaffordable in aggregate or the price of dwellings would simply fall. But this does not mean that the outcomes are acceptable either to individuals or to government. The outcome may be damaging especially for those on lower incomes because they cannot then live what we, as a society, regard as a reasonable life or indeed realize their economic potential. Some would argue that this simply means income should be supplemented. But there are both practical reasons and matters of principle which make it more usual to approach the problem directly. In this context, in the literature, adequate housing is often regarded as a 'merit good' – one that government, as our agent, should address by ensuring people can afford to be adequately housed. But this raises the issue of how affordability is to be measured and different measures relate to different ways of achieving that objective. This chapter considers the options that might be used, including new approaches.

There is a widespread perception that housing in the United Kingdom is unaffordable, but unaffordable by whom? The issue is one of distribution. Perhaps the most widely quoted statistic – not only in the UK – is the ratio of house prices relative to earnings or incomes, despite the fact that fewer than two-thirds of households are owner occupiers. In 2018, house prices in England, according to official statistics, were on average eight times earnings and, for many, this simple summary indicator epitomizes the extent of the housing crisis; it does not appear plausible that prices relative to earnings could be sustained at these levels. But, in fact, there is very little support for the use of price to earnings ratios in the academic literature and, indeed, for any measure that concentrates on averages alone, because different groups experience different conditions. Furthermore, different affordability measures are required for households in each tenure. More generally, there is a recognition that affordability consists of a set of interrelated elements, which include not only price, but also physical adequacy and overcrowding,[1] and expenditure indicators alone can be highly misleading.

Two related problems are, therefore, addressed in the chapter: the measurement of affordability and the groups in society most affected by affordability problems. This is unrelated to the policy definition of 'affordable housing', which is addressed in later chapters. The next section looks at the historical use and development of affordability indicators, particularly in the UK and the US. In the former, this was associated with a switch in policy priorities away from the emphasis on housing need as a social objective towards a more market-based approach, where affordability was used as a basis for providing assistance to lower-income households. Until the 1970s, policy did not explicitly take into account affordability in the sense of defining an acceptable relationship between housing expenditure and income, although it was implicit in public and private rental policies.[2] The problem also became more acute as an affordability crisis emerged for owners in the late 1980s and early 1990s.[3] In the US, the development of affordability indicators occurred earlier but, by the early 1990s, concern with affordability had risen towards the top of the housing policy agenda, associated with the decline in home ownership rates and affordability problems for middle and lower-class owners.[4] This displaced more traditional policy concerns with sub-standard housing, neighbourhood decay and racial discrimination.

The following section discusses the strengths and weaknesses of four approaches to affordability measurement – price to earnings ratios; housing expenditure as a share of income; a residual income approach; and methods that take greater account of housing supply.[5] The shortcomings, both conceptual and practical, of each method are brought out for both owners and renters. We then examine the empirical validity of the expenditure share approach by directly testing its relationship to indicators of housing stress, using information from the English Housing Survey (EHS); the tests are particularly relevant for low-income renters. However, it is not necessarily the case that the same indicators are appropriate for different household groups and, so, again using EHS information, we examine the position for potential first-time buyers as well. For this group, it is important to distinguish between affordability problems arising from access to finance and problems meeting mortgage repayments.[6] This leads to two new indicators which are targeted on the main groups of policy concern, have intuitive plausibility, and are straightforward to construct and update using regularly published data.

Affordability measurement: some background issues

Before discussing the different affordability measures that have been proposed, a number of issues arise that are common to most of the indicators used in practice. First, the emergence of affordability problems is not recent, and the development of indicators can be seen against a background of 19th century research on household expenditure shares. However, these early studies, and all subsequent work, have suffered from serious conceptual and measurement problems when applied to housing and these problems remain to be resolved. Secondly, the relationship between housing expenditure shares and income differs between cross-section and time-series data; the two need to be reconciled since the relationship is important in explaining changes in house prices over time. Thirdly, even if indicators can be constructed, their validity as a descriptive device does not necessarily imply that they can be used for policy. Finally, we need to understand why simple measures of affordability continue to be widely used in the media and in policy practice despite their clear shortcomings.

In the early years of the 20th century, when most households were still private tenants, an investor return on working-class dwellings of 5 per cent in England would have required on average a rent, including rates, of between six and eight shillings per week,[7] or approximately 23 per cent of average earnings.[8] In practice, at that time, rents and rates typically comprised between one-sixth and one-fifth of earnings. Substantial numbers of low-income households could not afford housing of a decent standard without subsidy and privately constructed homes (or those built by philanthropic organizations) were, therefore, not occupied by the lowest strata of society; overcrowding was commonplace.

Modern affordability concepts have their roots in 19th century studies of household budgets,[9] and the turn-of-the-century expression used in the US, 'one week's pay for one month's rent', was an early example of the 25 per cent rule, later to be used by both mortgage lenders and in housing policy. Housing expenditure to income rules of thumb arose from Ernst Engel's and Herman Schwabe's 19th century work on the relationship between categories of household expenditure and income (known as the Engel Curve). Following Engel and Schwabe's 19th century research, a large number of empirical studies were conducted in the first half of the 20th century but continued to suffer from both conceptual and practical difficulties, including the appropriate definitions of housing costs and income. Therefore, definitive conclusions on the relationship between the two variables have never been reached. Moreover, even if it were possible to derive an expenditure 'law' from the data, this cannot necessarily be extended to a statement of what households *should* spend for policy purposes. Nevertheless, rules of thumb are still widely used.

As an illustration, Figure 2.1 shows the relationship between the percentage share of housing expenditure in income (including both owners and renters) and the level of household incomes in 2017/ 18 in England.[10] The values are averaged across households in each income band; this produces fairly smooth, downward-sloping curves. In fact, expenditure proportions exhibit a high degree of variation across individual households *within* the bands, reflecting the fact that other variables influence expenditure in addition to income. The data problems are immediately apparent; information is taken from the EHS – a key source for policy – based on a survey of more than 13,000 households. In the case of renters, information is available on the actual rent due to the landlord and the subsidized rent paid by the tenant after the receipt of housing benefits. The figure shows, as might be expected, that the relationship differs considerably according to whether benefits are treated as an addition to income or as a reduction in rent. In the case where rents are measured net of benefits, the curve is much flatter. Owner occupier costs are measured by mortgage payments, although now more owners have paid off their mortgages than have mortgages outstanding and, so, have no measured housing costs (and, therefore, are excluded from the figure). For both groups, there is no information on property tax payments, fuel costs or other elements such as service charges which can be argued to be part of wider housing costs. Importantly, income is measured by actual income in the current year; it might be suggested that permanent income, which excludes temporary fluctuations, provides a better measure should it be available. Furthermore, income estimates are collected for the head of household, the head and a partner, and for all household members; it is not immediately clear which is the more appropriate. Additionally, income could be measured on a gross or net of tax basis; in practice, more information is available on gross incomes. So, Figure 2.1 is

Figure 2.1: Housing expenditure to income ratios, England, 2017/18

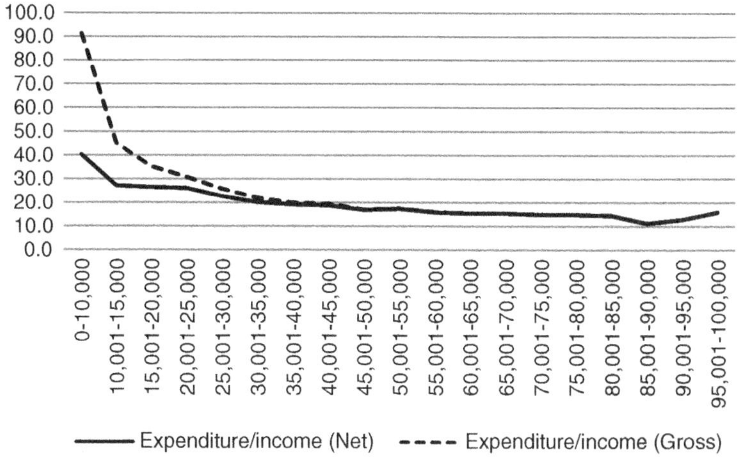

Note: Horizontal axis: household income. Vertical axis: housing expenditure as percentage of income.

Source: Authors' estimates derived from the English Housing Survey, 2017/18

compiled primarily on the basis of data availability. Different sources could lead to different conclusions and international comparisons become particularly complex.

Even if the data problems could be overcome, considerable care is needed in using such indicators; notably, we cannot necessarily use information on a sample of households at a point in time to infer implications for the long-run aggregate relationship between housing demand and income. The survey data show how housing expenditures differ as income differs between households; aggregate time-series studies show how expenditure changes as aggregate income changes. To move from one to the other requires information on whose income changes – for example, those at the top or bottom of the income distribution – since the effects differ. A further international finding is that the relationship between housing expenditure and income is flatter on cross-section data than on time-series data; formally, this suggests that the income elasticity of housing demand (the responsiveness of housing demand to a change in income) is lower on the basis of the former. As we show in the next chapter, the income elasticity of housing demand is extremely important for understanding long-run changes in affordability and, therefore, we need to be able to reconcile cross-section and time-series estimates.

In fact, similar issues arose in the 1950s in studies of aggregate consumers' expenditure; again, surveys indicated a smaller response of consumption to current income than time-series studies. A particularly influential explanation (although not the only one) – the permanent income hypothesis – was associated with Milton Friedman.[11] As noted previously, observed income in a survey for any household may not represent its long-run (or permanent) income; it simply represents income achieved in a given year and includes temporary (or transitory) positive or negative shocks to income. Those households observed to be at the bottom of the current income distribution are more likely to have been subject to negative shocks, whereas those at the top end are more likely to have experienced temporary positive gains. But under the Friedman hypothesis, consumption is based only on permanent income; since permanent income of those at the bottom end may be understated and those at the top end overstated, a plot of the relationship between consumption and current income will be flatter than the true relationship between consumption and permanent income. Since time-series data deal with the long run (as well as the short run), the income measure is more closely related to permanent income. More formally it can be shown that estimates of the responsiveness of consumption to current income, known as the marginal propensity to consume (MPC), depend positively on the variance of permanent income relative to transitory income. In cross sections using individual data, the transitory component is expected to be large and, therefore, the marginal propensity to consume low. By contrast, on time-series data, the permanent income component dominates and so the MPC becomes larger.

The same point holds with respect to housing expenditure; housing demand is based on permanent or long-run expected future income rather than current income, and mortgage markets help households to borrow (although in an imperfect way) against future incomes and thus increase housing demand. This can help to explain why, in the EHS, some households appear to devote a huge proportion of their current income (in some cases more than 100 per cent) to housing; current income mis-measures permanent income. It may appear that we are labouring the point, but the distinction is important for affordability policy. If changes in income are permanent, they have larger effects on housing demand and house prices than if the changes are purely transitory.

David Hulchanski[12] considers the validity of six uses of affordability rules of thumb – in his case housing expenditure to income ratios: (i) as a *description* of household expenditures; (ii) *analysis* of trends and comparison of different household types; (iii) *administration* of public housing by defining eligibility criteria and subsidy levels; (iv) *definition* of housing need for public policy purposes;[13] (v) *prediction* of the household ability to pay a rent or mortgage; and (vi) as part of the *selection criteria* in the decision to provide a rental or mortgage. He suggests that the first three uses are valid, assuming that the indicators can be adequately measured and the appropriate methodologies developed, but the final three – definition, prediction and selection – represent inappropriate uses of the indicator. For example, performance indicators derived from averages do not generally provide good predictors of the ability to pay or the likelihood of default by an individual household. We examine the relationship between financial stress and the expenditure ratio later. Nevertheless, it remains common practice for simple rules to be used for all six purposes.

Finally, it might be asked why rules of thumb and heuristics are so widely used in policy and the media as measures of affordability, in preference to the more complex approaches advocated in the academic literature. A heuristic is 'a simple procedure that helps find adequate, though often imperfect answers to difficult questions'.[14] By contrast, the construction of complex models is characteristic of what some psychologists call System 2 modes of thinking, which require careful and deliberate analysis, whereas System 1 modes are intuitive, rather than analytical, and include our automatic responses to difficult situations or problems. In many instances, the latter responses are perfectly adequate and, indeed, crucial to our daily lives, but decisions characterized by System 1 methods of thinking are subject to biases and systematic errors, are not strong on statistics and may lead to the substitution of easier heuristic approaches. One problem, however, is that rules can be learnt and, by regular exposure perhaps through the media, become part of our intuitive beliefs and we do not necessarily appreciate their weaknesses. Our intuitive response to news that house price to earnings ratios have risen is that this must be bad; we do not automatically ask why the ratio has risen – for example, it might be because of a fall in mortgage interest rates – or who are the losers by the rise. Moreover, in some circumstances, high house price to earnings ratios are an indicator of economic success and an indicator of the strength of the economy.

Commonly used measures of affordability

Price to earnings or income ratios

Most housing market forecasters do not use detailed models of the form to be discussed in the next chapter. Rather, they rely on rules of thumb of which house price to earnings (or income) ratios are the most common measures of affordability chosen. The choice of denominator often varies. In England, for example, the median house price to earnings ratio is used in housing needs assessments, but price to income ratios are commonly employed in Europe and income is used in the formal models in Chapter 3. In fact, the central message in this chapter is generally not dependent on the precise measure. The idea is that if house prices relative to earnings or income are above the long-run trend, then they should fall. However, it is straightforward to show that this ratio is a poor guide to prediction and as a measure of affordability. So why do price to earnings ratios continue to be used, not least as a guide to housing shortages in policy decisions? Both New Zealand and more recently the UK have advocated the use of the ratios in land use planning.[15] There are, in fact, a number of practical advantages to house price ratios; first, the underlying data are regularly published and are available on a broadly comparable basis internationally. For example, the United Nations developed a set of internationally comparable urban indicators, which included house price to income and rent to income ratios.[16] Secondly, there are no regular, published assessments of the accuracy of the forecasts produced by different methods and, so, the weaknesses of the ratio approach are not immediately apparent. Thirdly, it is possible to tell an intuitively plausible story about why there should be a constant long-run affordability ratio to which the economy returns; for example, mortgage lenders impose limits on borrowing in relation to incomes, which particularly affect demand by first-time buyers. Fourthly, predictions on this basis are cheap to construct and require few technical skills. Finally, simple rules of thumb fit more with System 1 modes of thinking, which are reinforced by familiarity with the concept arising from regular media attention.

Figure 2.2 illustrates the issues in the UK case.[17] Here, average house prices are measured relative to household disposable income – as noted previously, measurement relative to average earnings as an alternative does not change the conclusions. The graph shows the aggregate position for the economy as a whole, but changes in the ratio are limited in their usefulness as indicators of the position of different groups in society (although it is possible to construct similar graphs, for example, for different quartiles of the earnings distribution). The graph also shows the average ratio constructed on the data between 1969 and 2000. Over this period, there is, in fact, only limited evidence of an upward or downward long-run trend[18] and this forms the basis of the view that affordability must return to the long-run level. Possible

Figure 2.2: Ratio of UK house prices to household disposable income (2015=100), 1969–2017

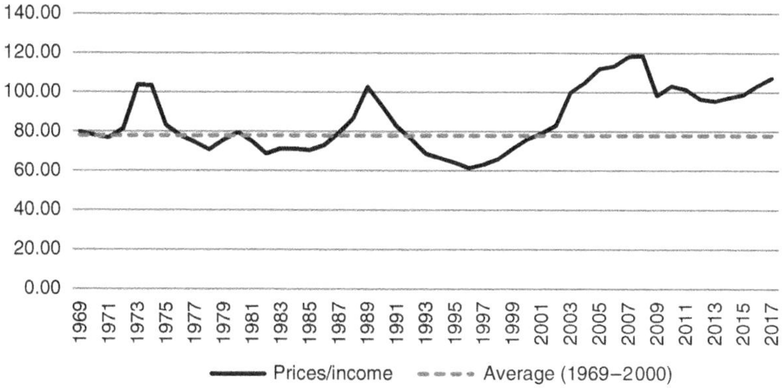

Prices/income – – – Average (1969–2000)

Source: Office for National Statistics

over-valuation during the booms in the early 1970s, the late 1980s and post-1996 particularly stand out, along with under-valuation in the first half of the 1990s. But it is also clear that the cycles have been very different in nature and certainly not regular; the 1970s and 1980s booms were relatively short and sharp, whereas the post-1996 boom was longer-lasting. The ratio, therefore, provides no basis for short-term forecasting. More importantly, the ratio has remained above the trend even after the GFC which occurred between approximately 2007 and 2010. The reason is simply that nominal interest rates have been very low, so that households can afford to purchase higher-priced dwellings for a given level of income. Low interest rates are capitalized into house prices and, consequently, price to income ratios are misleading at times of low interest rates and over-state affordability problems. At the very least, housing expenditure, rather than prices, relative to income is more appropriate.

The rise in the ratio in recent years is not limited to the UK. The Organisation for Economic Co-operation and Development (OECD) data show that similar rises have occurred in at least some other countries, for example, Australia, Canada and Sweden, but the increases have not been universal: the US, Germany and Japan have experienced a long-run decline since the early 1980s. In summary, there is no necessary reason why price to income ratios should be constant in the long run; indeed, economic theory suggests that in conditions where increases in housing supply match demand, house prices should rise in line with construction costs rather than incomes.

Housing expenditure to income ratios

Housing *expenditure* may, under some circumstances, provide a better guide to affordability changes over time since owner occupier expenditure at least includes the effects of changes in interest rates. Thus, while Figure 2.2 implies worsening affordability in recent years, a measure that takes into account explicitly lower interest rates would show less evidence of a decline.[19] In addition, measures based on expenditure ratios have paid more attention to the distribution of outcomes across household types. Nevertheless, some of the weaknesses have already been outlined in the last section.[20] It is helpful to introduce the budget constraint, widely used in consumer theory to illustrate the issues. In any year, a household is faced with the constraint on its expenditure, given by relationship (2.1):

Consumers' expenditure (excl. housing) + housing costs + saving from current income = post-tax household earned income + post-tax income from net financial assets or welfare (2.1)

This is a simple accounting identity; for a given level of income – either earned or from investments/welfare benefits – shown by the right-hand side, the household can decide how much to spend on housing, other consumer goods, or to save. Savings can be negative if the household borrows to finance its expenditure. Therefore, the relationship demonstrates that there is a trade-off and an opportunity cost, where the true measure of housing expenditure is in terms of the non-housing goods which must be foregone. However, at this level of abstraction, households can *choose* between housing and other consumption goods; households may choose a low level of housing if they prefer a higher level of non-housing goods or may choose to live in a low-priced area.[21] As a result, some studies attempt to look at the cost of a minimum standard of housing.[22] In practice, there are constraints on free choice; first, there may be binding government-imposed minimum housing standards so that households cannot consume housing below a given level. These may be imposed because inadequate housing is associated with poor health and low educational outcomes or because housing is seen as a merit good. But (2.1) stresses that there is a cost associated with standards (unless the housing is subsidized as in Figure 2.1) in terms of lower levels of non-housing consumption and reduced saving (or higher borrowing). Indeed, it is possible that minimum housing standards reduce non-housing consumption below poverty levels.

Secondly, households may not be able to achieve their desired levels of housing consumption and, indeed, choice of tenure because of insufficient access to credit markets given their incomes; this particularly affects potential first-time buyers. The constraints typically arise because of lender-imposed deposit requirements and limitations on loan repayments.[23] The proportion of high-value loans in relation to income in the UK has fallen since the GFC and borrowers are now required to pass stress tests in terms of their ability to meet loan repayments. A consequence is that housing expenditures expressed relative to incomes appear more affordable than the true position, because such measures do not take into account credit market constraints and the fact that households are forced to consume sub-optimally in terms of quality of housing and location. The effects on non-housing consumption are ambiguous; households may either reduce consumption in order to save more to raise the deposit or give up on owner occupation and increase non-housing consumption and/ or spend more on better quality housing in the rented sector. A further consequence is that they may remain with parents for longer or share with others in a similar position. However, the point for this chapter is that housing expenditure to income ratios do not necessarily reflect optimal household choices and some measure of credit restrictions has to be taken into account.

In practice, rather than measuring housing expenditures in absolute terms as in (2.1), affordability is usually measured relative to incomes – in other words the budget constraint, (2.1), can be divided through by income so that the sum of the expenditure and savings shares adds to one. Although scaling so that affordability is measured as a percentage can be useful, for example, in international comparisons, it also has disadvantages. From (2.1) in the ratio form, the budget constraint is independent of the *level* of income. This implies that it is possible that those on low incomes can consume low *levels* of both housing and non-housing goods, but housing still appears affordable, whereas those on larger incomes consume higher levels, but housing appears unaffordable in percentage terms.[24] More generally, questions of housing affordability cannot be divorced from questions of housing standards;[25] those households observed to live in homes considered to be affordable may be experiencing unacceptable standards, but some of those households experiencing measured housing stress may have more housing than they need.

The fact that high-income households can spend a large percentage of their income on housing, without incurring shortages in non-housing consumption, has sometimes led to the use of a 30:40 rule, which considers only the proportions or number of households in the bottom two income quintiles who are spending more than 30 per cent of their income on housing.[26] The measure has commonly been used in Australia.[27] Although the parameters are arbitrary, in Australia it is the case that affordability problems for those in private rentals are not confined to those on the lowest incomes and exist for those in the lowest two income quintiles at least.[28] But the choice of 30 per cent is not fully based on objective evidence; 25 per cent has often been employed in other countries in the past and 40 per cent is regularly used in Europe and now in the US. Nevertheless, some care is required in comparisons since housing expenditures are not always measured in the same way; fuel costs, for example, may be included in some instances.

In Australia, the 30:40 rule is sometimes used as a measure of housing stress and attempts have been made to assess the extent to which housing stress is associated with wider indicators of financial stress and wellbeing. In fact, the relationship appears to be modest, at least in the Australian case, once standardization for other demographic factors is taken into account. As might be expected, there is a significant positive relationship with the ability to pay the mortgage or rent on time,[29] but the relationship is weaker for other indicators of financial deprivation and health outcomes. Furthermore, the relationships become even weaker when the dynamics are taken into account by using longitudinal data; there is little evidence that *changes* in measured housing stress over time are associated with an improvement in financial wellbeing.[30] We examine the extent to which financial stress and housing affordability are related for England later.[31]

Residual income approaches

Despite the widespread use of ratio-based indicators, there is a general appreciation of their shortcomings; a rule that housing expenditures should not exceed 25 per cent, 30 per cent or 40 per cent of incomes implies that non-housing expenditures including savings should not be less than 75 per cent, 70 per cent, or 60 per cent irrespective of the level of income or household type. These percentages are largely arbitrary. We also noted that observed historical percentages cannot be used as an indication of the adequacy of housing or non-housing consumption standards. This has led some authors[32] to advocate the use of measures that show the *difference* between incomes and housing costs rather than the ratio. Alternatively, ratio approaches can be combined with difference or residual income methods to construct a hybrid indicator.[33] The residual income approach subtracts from disposable income the monetary value of a predefined standard of non-housing needs; this, therefore, determines how much is affordable for housing. If the amount actually paid for housing exceeds affordable housing costs, then the residual income left over for non-housing consumption will be inadequate.[34] Since actual housing costs reflect the quality and location as well as price, an alternative is to consider only the cost of basic physical housing in order to abstract from the issue of over- or under-consumption.[35]

This approach can also be seen in terms of a simplified version of relationship (2.1), ignoring savings and borrowing, and again shows the opportunity cost of housing expenditures; for a given non-housing budget standard (generally related to poverty or social security indicators), which determines the first element on the left-hand side of (2.1), affordable housing is determined by the constraint. However, the non-housing budget standard requires the specification of a basket of goods of essential items that have to be priced and which varies between households; in general, larger households have greater non-housing needs. It also follows that housing affordability will decline with household size but will increase with income. Importantly, even if *aggregate* indicators of affordability show limited differences between ratio and residual income approaches, the *distributional* outcomes are typically very different.[36]

The general principle that affordability should be household specific is appealing, but also implies that the method is more demanding in terms of data and construction, although the problems are not insurmountable. The approach requires the use of household specific budget standards, which are regularly updated. Perhaps because of the greater complexity, there are few examples where the residual income method has been applied consistently over time so that changes in conditions can be traced.[37] In recent years, the approach has attracted greater attention in Australia, but there are no recent applications in the UK except as part of the welfare system more generally. Also, arguably, the residual income approach is more consistent with current mortgage lender practice and regulatory requirements, which take into account the amount borrowers have available to cover their mortgage repayments if interest rates increase after allowing for other outgoings.

Finally, the standard approach to residual income measurement underplays a central feature of the budget constraint, (2.1) – the ability to borrow; as noted previously, current income may over- or under-state permanent income,[38] and the ability to save or dis-save can be used to smooth consumption patterns.

Housing supply

Each of the previous approaches concentrates primarily on housing demand and pays little attention to the supply of homes available to the lowest income groups or to the imbalance between demand and supply. These could be measured by vacancy rates for units at low rentals or the total number of properties available at different rent levels. However, many of the same problems observed in the demand indicators remain. For example, the measures provide little information on the quality, size or location of the units; furthermore, although there have been applications in the US,[39] regularly available data are inadequate for the task in the UK.

Alternatively, measures can be constructed that incorporate both demand and supply elements by comparing the distribution of available housing by costs with the distribution of household incomes. These attempt to compare the number of housing units potentially affordable by different income groups with the total number of households in each income group. In principle, the measures can be applied to both rental housing and to ownership. Under the latter, the distribution of house prices in any location can be compared with the proportion of households in each income band that can afford those prices under assumptions about interest rates, the mortgage loan length and the required deposit. If the market 'matches' – and the definition of the housing market area is important – we might expect, for example, households in the bottom income decile to be able to afford properties in the bottom price decile.

Renter financial stress and affordability measures

A fundamental reason for interest in affordability is its potential impact on stress and wellbeing. But the fact that a significant proportion of households are spending more than a certain proportion of their income on housing even after allowing for benefits cannot necessarily be taken as an indication that households are facing wider financial stress. As noted earlier, in the Australian case, the relationship is modest, although there does appear to be some relationship in England.[40]

The EHS does not provide longitudinal data, which would allow an analysis of the length of time that households have been in stress; this appears to be important in Australia, but some key features of the Australian studies and earlier English studies based on the British Household Panel Survey can be replicated.[41] We are interested in the probability that a household paying more than a threshold level of housing costs will face financial stress. The EHS asks three relevant questions:[42]

• How easy is it to pay your rent after benefits?
• Are you up to date with rent payments?
• Have you fallen behind with rent payments over the last 12 months?

If the household answers either 'fairly difficult' or 'very difficult' to the first; or 'No' to the second; or 'Yes' to the third, we take this to be an indicator that the household faces stress. Similar questions are asked for owners, but at least recently, high levels of outright ownership and low interest rates for those with mortgages have meant that few owners reported stress, although this was not necessarily the case in earlier years.[43] But 29 per cent of the sample of renters under the age of 60 experienced stress based on this definition in 2015/16.

The key variable used to explain financial stress is whether the household is spending more than a threshold percentage of income on housing after the subtraction of housing benefits. Since the threshold is arbitrary, we experimented with different values and, in fact, found that a value of 25 per cent provided a slightly better explanation than 30 per cent or 40 per cent.[44] The expectation is that those in the lowest income quintiles are more likely to experience stress than those on higher incomes, who are more likely to *choose* to spend a high percentage of their incomes on housing; this is tested directly. Furthermore, demographic controls are explicitly incorporated, since a failure to allow for such factors may distort the relationship between stress and affordability. The demographic variables considered are ethnicity, household size, the number of dependent children, age, length of residence at the current address, whether the household was homeless before entering into renting, whether there is a disabled or long-term sick member of the household, and the number of unemployed members of the household. In addition, stress might differ between tenures (local authority, housing association and private tenants) and location. Each household's location is captured by the Government Office Region in which it resides and the 2015 Index of Multiple Deprivation decile ranking for its location.

The important results concern the relationship between financial stress and whether the household is spending more than 25 per cent of its income on housing and the details appear in Appendix 2.1. The coefficients from the appendix are scaled in Table 2.1 for the different income quintiles, where a value of one is set for the top quintile. In this form they cannot formally be interpreted as probabilities and,

Table 2.1: The effects of affordability on renter financial stress by household income quintile

Income	Relative effects
Quintile 1	1.97
Quintile 2	1.69
Quintile 3	1.58
Quintile 4	1.27
Quintile 5	1.00

Table 2.2: Housing benefit and financial stress

Income	Probability of stress (2015/16 benefits)	Probability of stress (No benefits)
Quintile 1	0.29	0.48
Quintile 2	0.31	0.39
Quintile 3	0.31	0.34
Quintile 4	0.28	0.28
Quintile 5	0.24	0.24

as explained later, more information on the probabilities is given in Table 2.2. Nevertheless, the value of one for the highest quintile implies that affordability has no significant influence for this group, but the effect of affordability on stress declines sharply as income rises. Furthermore, the results are not as straightforward as the simple 30:40 rule suggests: renters facing high housing costs in the bottom quintile are more likely to undergo stress than renters in the second quintile, but even those in the third quintile on moderate incomes with high housing costs have a significant probability of stress. Therefore, in fact, in the English case, expenditure ratios provide a better predictor of financial stress than might have been expected given their theoretical shortcomings. But the indicator needs to be more nuanced than the basic 30:40 rule.

There is an important related question; households with high net housing costs are more likely to face stress if they are in the lower income deciles, but the values in Table 2.1 do not imply that, on average within each quintile, those in the bottom quintile have a higher probability of stress than those in the top quintile. Housing benefit reduces housing costs particularly for those on low incomes and Figure 2.1 hinted at this, showing that, net of benefits, housing costs as a percentage of income do not differ dramatically across the income classes. Table 2.2 demonstrates the point. The second column shows the estimated probability that households in each quintile will be in stress, averaged over the households in that quintile, if households each receive the appropriate level of benefits. These differ little over the quintiles because housing benefit flattens the cost distribution. But the third column simulates the effects of removing benefits which, unsurprisingly, have a disproportionate effect on the lower-income groups; for those in the lowest quintile the probability of being in stress rises by almost 20 percentage points. Those at the top end of the income distribution are unaffected. The differences reflect the distribution of housing benefits since those on higher incomes typically do not receive benefits.

Affordability for first-time buyers

The last section suggested that traditional housing expenditure ratios provide a useful representation of the stress faced by low-income renters at least in England. But a different approach is required for our second focus group – first-time buyers – because their problems are rather different. Whereas, in the case of renters, the differences are between high- and low-income groups, for owners the problems are also intergenerational and spatial. Once first-time buyers are able to achieve ownership, there is little evidence from the EHS that, after the early years of a loan, owners face significant stress. Given low interest rates, their housing costs are typically low and they accumulate capital gains if house prices are rising. Furthermore, at times of high general inflation, the real value of mortgage debt is reduced quickly, although these benefits have been more modest at the lower inflation rates of recent years. For first-time buyers, two elements of affordability need to be distinguished: *purchase affordability* (whether the household is able to borrow sufficiently to buy a house) and *repayment affordability* (which considers the proportion of income spent on repaying the mortgage).[45] Both differ around the country. Therefore, affordability indicators have to take into account the required deposit and location. In addition, indicators need to capture quality differences; we saw earlier that some approaches have attempted to measure the affordability of a minimum standard of housing. Furthermore, indicators should capture the supply of different classes of accommodation as well as demand. Therefore, overall, we need a measure that summarizes the ability (or otherwise) of households at different income levels to become home owners; the measure needs to capture the distribution of outcomes. A variant of the Lorenz curve can achieve this.

Consider relationship (2.1) again, which holds for both renters and owners, although housing costs differ between the two groups; in the case of renters it is the market or subsidized rent and mortgage payments for owners. For the same quality of accommodation, we might expect households to choose the cheaper, which allows higher levels of non-housing consumption. But the direct cost of ownership hides the fact that potential first-time buyers may face credit market constraints through an inability to raise the required deposit. Deposits are necessary to meet the requirements of lenders and the regulations imposed by the central bank designed to limit high loan to income lending. It is possible to show that actual housing demand will deviate from the unconstrained desired level and the length of time spent in disequilibrium will be positively related to the required deposit percentage.[46]

To demonstrate, these principles can be applied to currently renting households – these are potential future first-time buyers – under the age of 60 living in the South East of England outside of London and also to those living in the North East region, sampled in the 2017/18 EHS. Arguably, age should have a lower cut off point than 60, but further exclusion reduces the already modest sample size and the key results are unaffected. Similarly the use of regions is, perhaps, not optimal since they do not correspond to housing market areas but only limited information on incomes is available at finer spatial scales.[47] The sample excludes non-dependent children living with their parents who are also potential first-time buyers.[48] With the exception of London, the South East is generally the most expensive region of the country and so the affordability problems are the most severe, whereas the North East is the cheapest. Using data from the Land Registry, in 2017/18 the median house price in the South East was £285,000 and £133,000 in the North East. Relative to *renter* incomes, the difference between the two locations was less extreme – the median price to earnings ratio was 10.9 in the South East and 7.7 in the North East. Note also that restriction of the samples to renters under the age of 60 in only two regions limits the sample sizes, to 603 households in the South East and 258 in the North East. Renters cover private, local authority and housing association tenants.

Household incomes and house prices are divided into deciles; the latter provides information on the supply of and demand for homes of different types. Consequently, it is possible to calculate the proportion of the house price distribution a potential first-time buyer in each income decile could purchase under differing assumptions concerning deposits and mortgage interest rates, if mortgage repayments as a percentage of income are not to exceed a threshold (assumed to be 30 per cent below although we also see the response to different values).[49]

This gives rise to a form of Lorenz curve and Gini coefficient, shown in Figure 2.3. Gini coefficients have been used before in the analysis of affordability inequality, but primarily in order to summarize the distribution, across households, of house price to income ratios.[50] Our approach is rather different. A restriction should be noted; we are interested in properties that are realistically achievable by first-time buyers, whereas, in fact, in the South East, the highest-priced property sold in 2017/18 was £21 million. Therefore, in the South East the price distribution has been curtailed at £500,000 and £350,000 in the North East. These are approximately the highest valued dwellings that a renting household at the 10th income decile could afford under the assumptions concerning deposits and mortgage interest rates. It should also be noted that this approach does not attempt to match the *numbers* of households and properties, because of the concentration on first-time buyers; matching is concerned with the stock of owners and properties, whereas first-time buyers are only one segment.

Figure 2.3a shows the Lorenz curve for the South East assuming a 2.5 per cent mortgage interest rate (the average mortgage rate in 2017/18), a 25-year repayment mortgage and a required 5 per cent deposit and the results are striking. Under these assumptions, a household with an income at the median could not afford to purchase a property at any point in the truncated property distribution without paying more than the 30 per cent of its income in housing costs. The Gini coefficient is 0.70, reinforcing the high degree of inequality obvious from the figure. Simulations under alternative values can also be conducted; if the required deposit is 20 per cent, the Gini coefficient falls to the still high value of 0.58, but, of course, most aspiring first-time buyers would struggle to raise 20 per cent without help. The results are, however, sensitive to the 30 per cent threshold; increasing the maximum proportion to 50 per cent reduces the Gini coefficient to 0.24. Comparisons can also be conducted for earlier years; in fact, in 2008/09 the value of the Gini coefficient for the South East was only slightly lower than that in 2017/18. At first sight this might appear surprising since house prices between the two years rose faster than renter incomes so we might have expected the coefficient to have increased. But the constancy is explained by the fall in mortgage interest rates from approximately 5 per cent in 2008/09 to 2.5 per cent in 2017/18.

By contrast, the position is fundamentally different for existing home owners who wish to move, because of the accumulated equity in their current homes. The EHS provides owner-based assessments

Figure 2.3a: Lorenz curve: affordability for potential first-time buyers in South East England, 2017/18

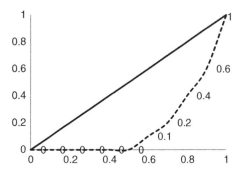

Note: Horizontal axis: cumulative percentage of households going from poorest income decile (left) to richest income decile (right). Vertical axis: cumulative percentage of house prices from lowest (bottom) to highest (top).

Figure 2.3b: Lorenz curve: affordability for potential first-time buyers in North East England, 2017/18

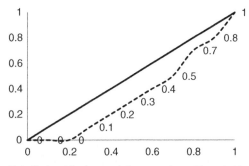

Note: Horizontal axis: cumulative percentage of households going from poorest income decile (left) to richest income decile (right). Vertical axis: cumulative percentage of house prices from lowest (bottom) to highest (top).

of equity and, using these estimates, with the exception of the most expensive properties in the (untruncated) price distributions, most owners, even in the lower income ranges, could afford higher-value properties without paying more than 30 per cent of their incomes in housing costs. The results, therefore, reinforce the nature of the intergenerational problem. Existing owners can use accumulated equity to meet the deposit on a new (or additional) home and can achieve low mortgage payments at the same time. Accumulated equity matters more than income for existing owners, a benefit not available to renters.

Figure 2.3b shows the equivalent Lorenz curve for the North East under the 5 per cent deposit, 2.5 per cent mortgage interest rate and

30 per cent repayment rules. At 0.30, the Gini coefficient is noticeably lower than in the South East, but there are still significant proportions of households who cannot afford to buy even properties at the lowest priced decile. Therefore, affordability for first-time buyers is not just a southern problem, once the full distribution of outcomes is taken into account, rather than just averages.

In conclusion

In this chapter, we have examined indicators of affordability relevant to the two main groups of interest and suggested that different indicators are required for low-income renters and potential first-time buyers. The indicators can be constructed using well-known concepts and regularly published data (although the sample sizes are smaller than we would have wished). Importantly, the measures are based on the distribution of outcomes rather than relying on averages. This is necessary because different groups face different housing conditions. The majority of households do not face affordability problems and, indeed, increasing house prices represent a capital gain for those already on the owner occupation housing ladder. Measures applicable to low-income groups and across different locations have been widely discussed in the literature but measures applicable across the generations have received less attention. We look at all three.

The chapter concentrates on a number of classes of affordability indicators. We are highly critical of the simplest – the house price to earnings or income ratio – despite the fact that it is the most widely used and is built into land use planning policies. The ratio provides no information on the distribution of outcomes across household types and income levels, it can be misleading as an indicator of changes in affordability over time even at the aggregate level, and it is worrying that it is still widely used. The second class – measures of housing expenditure (both rents and mortgage payments) relative to incomes – has also been heavily criticized in the literature on conceptual grounds; for example, ratios cannot distinguish adequately between households with different income levels. We consider, therefore, whether they provide useful information in practice and, perhaps surprisingly, in the English case, they are strongly related to direct measures of financial stress. Nevertheless, the results have to be carefully interpreted. The third approach – the residual income method – has conceptual advantages and is implicit in welfare policies more generally, but still has practical measurement problems, notably in the definitions of income and non-housing budget standards. The fourth approach recognizes that affordability needs to take into account the supply of properties as well as demand, but some of the problems of the other approaches remain.

Recognizing the importance of variations in the availability of different types of property and mortgage market conditions that particularly affect first-time buyers, the chapter provides estimates of affordability for first-time buyers based on variations of the Lorenz curve and the Gini coefficient. These incorporate both measures of access to mortgage markets, through the required deposit, and mortgage repayments. The indicator suggests that in the South East of England, a household would need an income above the median before it could afford a property in the first decile of prices. The Gini coefficient is much lower in the North East; but there are still significant numbers of households who could not afford to purchase.

These new affordability indicators can be used to assess the distributional consequences of policy changes since they are constructed from samples, mainly taken from the EHS. Examples in this chapter include the effects of changes in the benefit system (and more nuanced changes than those shown here can be simulated) or the effects of changes in deposit requirements on aspiring first-time buyers. Further reference to the indicators is made in later chapters.

3

What Factors Determine Changes in House Prices and Rents?

Introduction

Whatever measure of affordability is employed, house prices and rents play a central part and, therefore, this chapter is concerned with their main determinants at national and sub-national levels, bringing in relevant findings from different countries, but with an emphasis on house prices in the UK. The determinants play a crucial role, particularly because they begin to show the limits to policy. We refer back to the central findings in later chapters. In fact, the previous chapter has already highlighted three of the key influences on the demand for owner occupied housing and house prices: incomes, interest rates and mortgage market conditions. House price to income ratios provide a flawed indicator for prediction and for policy, but this does not imply that incomes are unimportant for house prices; incomes are, in fact, one of the most important determinants quantitatively, but they are not the *only* influence and it is the neglect of other factors that causes many of the problems, even at the national scale. Chapter 2 hinted at the importance of interest rates: from Figure 2.2 house prices relative to incomes have been above trend since the beginning of the century, despite the GFC, reflecting low interest rates, which are capitalized into prices. At low interest rates, households can afford to pay higher prices. Furthermore, the chapter began to discuss the importance of credit markets: if households face restrictions in access to mortgages, then their consumption of housing is likely to be sub-optimal with consequences for house prices. For policy, credit restrictions are particularly important since their presence reduces the effectiveness of interest rate policy, an issue explored further in later chapters.

However, nationally, there are potentially other variables that help to explain changes in house prices over time; most importantly for policy these include the influence of housing supply. Further possible influences include household formation and, given our interest in low-income households and first-time buyers, changes in the income distribution. This chapter explores in more detail the quantitative impact of all these variables. The chapter also considers rent determination. Although in principle the relationship between house prices and market rents is well-understood, the practice is more complex because of institutional features of the rental market. Furthermore, the market is segmented; at one level it caters for some high-income households and an increasing proportion of those on middle incomes, but at the other end of the spectrum, private renting now houses more lower-income households than the public sector. Empirically, we understand less about rent determination in the UK than about house prices, hindered by data weaknesses and less interest when private renting was a smaller part of total supply.

The chapter also examines sub-national markets. There is now a substantial international literature on the relationship between regional house prices, but there is general agreement that regions are not the best scale to represent housing market interactions and the chapter, then, explores what can be learnt at finer scales.

Understanding national house prices

A great deal of quantitative research has been conducted into the main factors that determine house prices.[1] A common argument is that UK house prices are unstable and difficult to model; however, instability should not be confused with volatility. Historically, there have certainly been periods when prices were highly volatile, exhibiting strong cycles, but this is not the same as instability. Instability occurs when an external event or shock causes prices permanently to diverge from their long-run equilibrium position. However, simply looking at Figure 2.2 might cause some scepticism: there appear to be forces that prevent house prices permanently moving too far away from incomes, despite the weaknesses of Figure 2.2 as an affordability indicator. The idea of instability is also sometimes linked with the view that the parameters of equations used to explain changes in house prices are not constant over time and vary either randomly or are trended.[2] We will suggest that, in fact, the parameters have been remarkably consistent over the last 30 years. With caveats, the main factors that have affected house prices are fairly straightforward. Nevertheless, this does not mean that future price movements are easy to predict.

House prices are determined by the interactions of demand and supply, but the same approaches typically used to explain outcomes in non-durable goods markets cannot be used.[3] The critical differences are the longevity of the housing stock and its spatial fixity. Longevity implies that housing is an investment as well as a consumption good, whereas spatial fixity implies that house prices do not necessarily change at the same rate in different parts of the country. Longevity and the role of housing as an investment have meant that the standard approach to explaining house prices is derived from the life cycle model. This model is closely related to the permanent income hypothesis mentioned in the last chapter and, so, some of the findings are relevant. Key elements are: (i) housing demand is determined by long-run or permanent income; (ii) households do not purchase from current income alone, but the existence of mortgage markets allows households to borrow against future income; (iii) expectations of future capital gains are central to investment demand.

One of the key concepts derived from the model is the housing user cost of capital, which measures the annual cost to the consumer of a unit of owner occupied housing services. The true annual cost is not the house price (although this is taken into account) but includes the mortgage cost – or the opportunity cost of investing in housing rather than other assets – maintenance and depreciation expenditures, property taxes and the expected future capital gain or loss. The last element reduces the potential costs faced by the household if house prices are expected to rise, but increases the cost if prices are falling.[4] The user cost also, in principle, allows for the effects of mortgage market restrictions, although this is difficult to measure in practice. Therefore, the measure attempts to capture two of the key variables mentioned in the Introduction – interest rates and credit markets – in a theoretically consistent manner.

The definition is summarized as relationship (3.1). All the terms in brackets are expressed as a percentage of the house price. The cost of capital, that is the element in brackets, is graphed in Figure 3.1, and so is also shown as a percentage.

Housing User Cost = House price * (market nominal interest rate + depreciation + maintenance + property taxes + mortgage market constraints – expected annual capital gain) (3.1)

Figure 3.1: UK cost of capital (per cent), 1970Q1–2017Q4

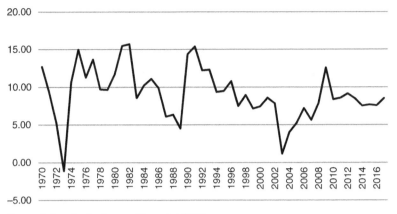

Source: Authors' estimates; see Meen et al (2016)

The cost of capital is a type of real interest rate, but rather than subtracting the expected general rate of inflation from the nominal interest rate as is usual in measures of real rates, it subtracts the rate of house price inflation. As might be expected from a *real* interest rate, the series in this form[5] has no long-run trend and so does not explain the long-run increase in real house prices. However, it is highly volatile (mainly due to changes in interest rates and price expectations) and so could contribute to an explanation of short-run volatility. The variable is also a discount rate; if house prices represent the discounted present value of a future rental stream arising from the consumption of housing services (as is often assumed in housing models), then the cost of capital is the appropriate discount rate. It has been suggested that the fact that the ratio of market rents to house prices fell from the mid-1990s until the GFC in both the UK and US is consistent with a decline in the discount rate.[6] There is some evidence to support this from Figure 3.1, but equally the graph implies that the ratio cannot fall permanently.

Further clarification is needed on the role of mortgage debt in explaining house prices since this is widely misunderstood in empirical research and has implications for monetary policy – the issues are considered in more detail in Chapter 8. The two variables are closely correlated, but this does not necessarily mean that changes in debt *cause* changes in house prices. In fact, the causation may be the other way and helps explain why house prices are important for macro stabilization policy. The stock of mortgage debt can only contribute to an explanation of housing demand and prices if there are constraints on access to credit, such as before the liberalization of mortgage markets in the 1980s and since the GFC. In other periods households have generally *chosen* how much they wish to borrow, within the bounds of prudential borrowing. Both 1980s liberalization and constraints in the GFC contributed to changes in prices, but, in both instances, the effects were partly offset by accompanying changes in mortgage interest rates.[7]

There is a very large literature that has emerged in recent years on the relationship between house prices and credit (see Chapter 8). One area concerns the expansion of Buy to Let mortgages from the late 1990s. An important feature of the market was that it enabled existing owners to use equity in their current home to purchase additional properties, adding to overall demand. It can be shown,[8] theoretically, that this may increase the volatility of house prices but, rather surprisingly, there is little evidence that this has been the case and conventional models do not appear to have 'broken down'. Tenure and second homes are considered further in Chapter 4.

The cost of capital can help to explain changes in house prices, but it is, by no means, the only factor. Table 3.1 sets out the responsiveness of house prices to a set of variables, taken from a series of empirical studies conducted over a number of years.[9] The comparisons are designed to show the consistency of the findings over the studies. Each value in the table represents an elasticity; therefore, for example, in the most recent study, column (4), a 1 per cent increase in household income is expected to increase real house prices by approximately 2.5 per cent. Since house prices are determined by demand and supply, this coefficient represents the ratio of the underlying income elasticity of housing demand relative to the price elasticity. The exception in interpretation is the cost of capital where the values are *semi*-elasticities;

Table 3.1: The determinants of house prices

Study*	(1)	(2)	(3)	(4)
Estimation period	1964(Q3)–1987(Q4)	1969(Q3)–1996(Q1)	1969(Q3)–2007(Q4)	1969(Q4)–2017(Q3)
Per household real disposable income	3.00	2.40**	2.61	2.46**
Real household financial wealth	0.45	0.34	0.32	0.12
Cost of capital (*semi-elasticity*)	-0.054	-0.037	-0.061	-0.045
Housing stock/number of households	-1.81	-1.74**	-1.55	-1.78**

Notes: * The four studies are: (1) Meen (1990); (2) Meen and Andrew (1998); (3) Meen (2013); (4) an updated version on more recent data.
** Specification is slightly different because neither variable is divided by the number of households.

so, a 1 percentage *point* increase in the cost of capital, for example from 3 per cent to 4 per cent, decreases prices by 4.5 per cent. The cost of capital coefficients may appear small by comparison, but they are, in fact, large effects.

The cross-section evidence in Chapter 2 suggested that higher incomes are not necessarily associated with higher housing expenditure shares and that income elasticities of housing demand are higher on time-series than cross-section data. Table 3.1 is, indeed, consistent with a higher income elasticity of housing demand derived from time series. But, at first sight, there still appears to be an anomaly: since, an increase in income leads to a more than proportionate rise in house prices, we would expect Figure 2.2 – which shows the price to income ratio – to exhibit a strong upward trend. In the absence of a noticeable trend, the figure would suggest an income elasticity closer to one. The results are, however, consistent because the table takes into account the effects of additional factors; for example, increases in housing supply in response to a rise in demand will mitigate any increase in house prices relative to incomes.

The feature that stands out from Table 3.1, however, is the consistency of the values over studies spanning approximately 30 years, suggesting that the underlying housing demand relationship has also changed little. Since the parameters are fairly constant, the equation in the second column, estimated only up to the first quarter of 1996, is able to predict fairly successfully the subsequent time periods; 1996 is significant in that it marks the beginning of the boom period that lasted until the collapse in the GFC. On this basis, there was only limited evidence of an over-valuation of property prices between 1996 and 2008. Conventional models that did not attempt to incorporate speculative bubbles were able to explain the period fairly well.[10] Nevertheless, this does not necessarily imply that the models predicted the GFC.

The results in Table 3.1 can be used to derive a simple rule to explain the conditions under which the ratio of house prices to income rises or falls over the long run (that is abstracting from short-term cycles) given by relationship (3.2). The formal derivation is given in the endnote.[11]

Percentage change in the ratio of house prices relative to per household income $\approx$
1.5 * [percentage change in household income / percentage change in the housing stock] (3.2)

The third equation in the table is used to derive it, although similar results occur using the other versions. The price to income ratio can only be constant over the long run if aggregate household income in the economy grows at the same rate as the housing stock; the speed at which the ratio changes depends on the income elasticity of housing demand relative to the price elasticity, reflected in the coefficient 1.5. In countries, such as the UK, that have a high income elasticity of housing demand,[12] the ratio is likely to improve or deteriorate quickly. Importantly, the relationship highlights the key policy question as to whether real house prices can be reduced by further increases in new house building or changes to the existing stock. We return to this question in more detail in Chapter 6 but, historically, the housing stock has grown at a much slower rate than income.

Notice that household formation does not appear explicitly in the relationship. At first sight, this might seem surprising since household projections form the basis for the official assessments of local housing requirements. The point is, however, that household income on the right hand side of (3.2) is an *aggregate* rather than a *per capita* indicator and so demographics and household formation are taken into account in this variable. Therefore, no additional variable is required. This issue is also taken up in Chapter 14.

Nevertheless, (3.2) reveals a problem with the modelling approach; there is little evidence from Figure 2.2, despite stronger growth in income than the housing stock, that the ratio of prices to income has risen significantly over time. There must, therefore, be something missing from the model; as it stands it is unsurprising that investors are attracted to housing as an asset, since it implies that the asset price continuously rises faster than earnings. The missing ingredients become evident from further analysis of credit markets and the treatment of risk. In (3.1) the user cost does not include a risk premium, which is expected to increase at times of rapid house price inflation and, therefore, imparts downward pressure on the market. Risk and credit shortages provide in-built stabilization mechanisms. These two issues were fundamental to the housing problems that arose during the GFC and we return to them in Chapter 8.

Finally, Chapter 4 highlights the fact that intergenerational housing problems arise not only from the housing market itself, but also from differences in relative income growth rates. Over long periods of time, the incomes of young households have grown at slower rates than those of older households. Since the responsiveness of house prices to changes in income is shown to be strong in Table 3.1, this puts young households at a relative disadvantage. It also has implications for the structure of aggregate models used to explain house prices. Formally, the models are only valid if *either* the income and price elasticities of housing demand are the same across different households *or* incomes grow at the same rate for all households.[13] Neither condition holds in practice and implies that aggregate price relationships have to be modified to include a measure of changes in the income distribution, which also affects the affordability relationship (3.2).

International comparisons

House prices have also been discussed in detail in other countries. Since housing comprises a large percentage of household wealth in most developed economies, there have been a number of comparative long-run studies designed to construct international measures of house prices, typically, from the 19th century.[14] In addition, the factors that affect house prices over shorter periods have been widely analyzed. However, a problem in drawing conclusions from international studies is that the variables taken into account in models are rarely the same. For example, some studies do not include the housing stock as a measure of housing supply and, from the previous arguments, we would expect this to lead to a lower estimated response of house prices to changes in income,[15] Also, international comparisons are hampered by data inconsistencies and by institutional differences; for example, even across Europe, mortgage market structures differ very considerably. Nevertheless, it is important that an attempt is made to understand the reasons for variations in international house price trends since a significant volume of comparative research has emerged in recent years[16] and it is easy to draw incorrect policy inferences.

Based on a sample of 13 European countries, Table 3.2 sets out the growth in real house prices (that is, net of general inflation) and in house prices relative to wages. Real house prices in the major European economies have not consistently grown at the same rate over time; for example real prices in the UK grew at an annual average rate of 3.6 per cent between 1970 and 2015, whereas real prices in France grew by 2.1 per cent; in Spain by 3.3 per cent; in Italy by 1.2 per cent; in the Netherlands by 2.5 per cent; and in Germany by −0.3 per cent. These variations suggest that European markets cannot be treated as a single entity, partly reflecting tenure patterns and institutional differences in mortgage market structures. In addition, the trends may indicate international variations in housing preferences. Differences in housing supply, arising from land use planning controls have attracted particular attention and it is now widely believed[17] that countries with the strongest regulations are more likely to experience both higher long-run price growth and greater volatility. The third column of Table 3.2 further illustrates the difficulties in using price to earnings ratios as a comparative indicator of affordability; there is no international norm

Table 3.2: Long-run growth in real house prices and relative to wages, 1970–2015

Country	Annual average growth rates in real prices 1970–2015 (%)	Annual average growth rates in house prices relative to wages 1970–2015 (except where stated) (%)
Belgium	2.3	1.6 (1980–2015)
Denmark	1.7	-0.3
Finland	1.5	-0.7
France	2.1	0.1
Germany	-0.3	-1.9
Ireland	3.3	-0.6 (1990–2015)
Italy	1.2	n.a.
Netherlands	2.5	0.6
Norway	2.7	-0.4
Spain	3.3	1.2 (1995–2015)
Sweden	1.5	0.8 (1980–2015)
Switzerland	0.3	n.a.
Great Britain	3.6	1.3

Source: Derived from OECD data

and the ratio has risen in some countries and fallen in others. The UK and Germany, as extreme cases, are highlighted.

From relationship (3.2) changes in Germany relative to the UK depend on whether the ratio of income to the housing stock grows more slowly in the former and on whether the income elasticity of housing demand is lower. In fact, both are possibly the case; in Germany, since 1970, the housing stock relative to incomes has been broadly constant,[18] but has fallen sharply in the UK, by approximately 1.5 per cent per annum. But, in addition in Germany, the responsiveness of affordability to changes in income (as noted earlier, derived from the income and price elasticities of demand) may be weaker than the 1.5 shown in (3.2) for the UK. Decomposing price movements in the two countries indicates that a part of the rise in real prices (and worsening affordability) in the UK, relative to Germany, may be attributed to the demand side of the market. Although policies that aim to increase housing supply are important, the results suggest the value of measures that pay attention to the demand side of the market as well since, under high income elasticities, it is difficult to stabilize affordability through supply alone. An important question remains, however; why might it be the case that the income elasticity of demand differs internationally? Is it affected, for example, by variations in home ownership rates and the role of housing as a status or positional good?

Sub-national differences

In a country as large as the US, it is unsurprising that house prices do not evolve in a uniform manner across areas (see Table 3.3). But even outside North America, house prices within a country exhibit distinct spatial differences, but a problem is the appropriate spatial scale at which housing markets should be considered. One approach defines housing market areas but, in practice, time-series data are rarely constructed on this basis. A second approach is to construct 'clubs'. The idea of clubs is, perhaps, best known in the literature concerned with the extent to which countries or regions grow at similar rates over time. However, some of the features have been captured in the house price literature and it characterizes a situation where groups of local or regional house prices within a country converge to common levels (allowing for housing quality differences, neighbourhoods characteristics, and the environment), even though, in the short run, local price growth rates may still differ considerably.

Empirical work on clubs is often constrained by the availability of time-series data – we noted the same problems for international comparisons in the last section. Within countries, analysis typically takes place across the administrative units for which information is published; in the UK, most research has been conducted across regions – the Standard Statistical Regions until the 1990s and, subsequently, the Government Office Regions (GOR).[19] The international literature on regional house price convergence has expanded rapidly in recent years; the concept of ripple effects is often used, so that a country typically has a lead city or region, where prices change first and, then, neighbouring and subsequently more distant areas gradually catch up over time. But there is no necessary reason why all areas should exhibit common trends and so price clubs could exist.[20] Indeed, US results suggest that local or regional house prices do not converge to the national level, but rather converge to club averages. This implies a degree of segmentation.[21] In the UK,[22] a variety of different statistical approaches has been employed and the extent to which convergence has been found to exist depends on the method. But, as a generalization, we might think of three meta-regions where convergence occurs, consisting of the South, the Midlands and the North.[23]

With exceptions,[24] the emphasis of much of the literature is on the development of econometric tests of comovements,[25] rather than understanding the underlying transmission processes. But, in general, spatial price changes can be decomposed into those caused by variations in the drivers, for example, incomes or the housing supply may differ

Figure 3.2: House prices in London relative to Yorkshire and Humberside (log scale), 1969–2016

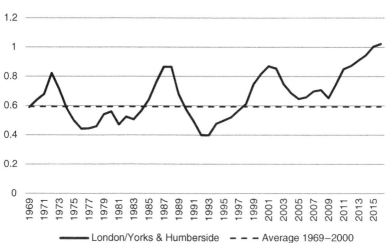

London/Yorks & Humberside – – – Average 1969–2000

Source: Office for National Statistics

across space, and those arising from variations in spatial responses to common income or supply changes.[26] Figure 3.2 shows the ratio of house prices[27] in Greater London relative to Yorkshire and Humberside; the former is often taken as the lead region, whereas Yorkshire and Humberside lies in the North of England and the region is chosen because the boundaries did not change with the move from Standard Statistical Regions to GOR and, so, consistent data exist since 1969. The vertical axis is expressed in logarithmic scale and, therefore, approximately represents the percentage difference in prices between the two areas. Because the ratio is always substantially greater than zero, London average house prices are, unsurprisingly, consistently higher than in the North. However, the cyclical pattern illustrates the so-called ripple effect. In each housing cycle, prices in London have, initially, risen relative to those in the North but, subsequently, there is some visual evidence that the ratio has returned to trend, shown by the dotted line calculated as the average ratio between 1969 and 2000. An exception has been the post-GFC period, when London prices have risen much more rapidly, although the annual growth in London prices has weakened since 2017.

There is a danger in taking this as a mechanical rule that always occurs; if that were the case, London prices could be used as a forward indicator to enable speculative returns to be made on housing investment in the North. But, in fact, the patterns have been different in each cycle. In terms of the transmission mechanisms, there are a number of possibilities: first, the patterns could arise from mobility since there is evidence that households respond to differences in relative house prices.[28] As households typically move only short distances, local house prices are more likely to change quickly in response to any initial London rise, but the subsequent induced spatial chain eventually leads to changes in areas further away from the capital. Secondly, the linkages could arise from speculative investment and spatial arbitrage of the form noted previously. Thirdly, comovements may arise from common changes in incomes across the regions. As shown in Table 3.1, the responsiveness of house prices to income is high and, so, if labour markets in an upturn expand initially in the South, before spreading to other areas, then similar patterns in house prices are expected. Although there may be some truth in all these explanations, they do not appear to be fully consistent with the data. An additional explanation is that the regions respond differently to common national events. For instance, there is evidence[29] that London and the South East are more responsive to changes in interest rates. One hypothesis is that households in these areas are more highly indebted than those in the North and are, therefore, more heavily affected by changes in interest rates. The continuing low level of interest rates is one possible reason why the South/North ratio, shown in Figure 3.2, has yet to be restored to the historical position.

Spatial variations in regional house prices are not confined to the UK and the US provides a further example. Table 3.3 sets out measures of house price volatility, calculated for each of the US Census divisions; more precisely, the table shows the standard deviation of divisional house price growth rates between 1992 and 2017, ranking each division by order of volatility. The feature that stands out is that the four divisions experiencing weaker volatility than the US average lie in the Mid-West Census Region and parts of the South, and are located away from the East and West coasts. By contrast, the West and North East Regions and the South Atlantic Division (which includes Florida) are much more volatile. Florida was, in fact, the first area of the US to experience a residential housing market crash in the 1920s.[30] Restricting the estimates to the pre-GFC period reduces volatility in all divisions but does not fundamentally affect the rankings, although New England rises to second place.

The rankings in Table 3.3 are correlated with measures of local land use regulation,[31] although the issues raised previously concerning the demand side of the market should be remembered and are also an important part of the story. Nevertheless, the Wharton Residential Land Use Regulation Index indicates that coastal areas are the most

Table 3.3: Volatility in US house prices: census divisions, 1992–2017
(Standard deviation of nominal annual house price growth rates)

Division	Volatility, 1992–2017
Pacific	9.52
Mountain	6.78
South Atlantic	5.80
New England	5.46
Middle Atlantic	4.64
USA	4.60
East North Central	3.54
West North Central	3.03
East South Central	2.82
West South Central	2.35

Sources: US Federal Housing Finance Agency and authors' estimates

heavily regulated, particularly in the North East, followed by the Pacific coast, notably California. By contrast, states in the South and Mid-West are less highly regulated than the average. The role of land use planning in restricting supply and the effects of controls on prices has generated a large literature and considerable policy debate on both sides of the Atlantic. These are discussed in more detail in Chapters 6, 9 and 10.

Local variations

It is unsurprising that the growth rates of house prices in small neighbouring areas are correlated; mobility and commuting flows ensure that convergence in growth occurs, even if not immediately. Since most household moves are short distance, at the local level, population change is dominated by migration rather than by natural increases through births and deaths and housing market areas (HMAs) are, in fact, usually defined by the strength of migration and commuting flows.[32] However, common growth rates do not necessarily imply that the *level* of house prices is the same even in adjoining locations, and this depends on whether the areas are part of the same housing sub-market.[33] Levels are determined by the physical and environmental characteristics of the area, since they are capitalized into prices. They also reflect the structure of the housing stock, which is built up over decades. These characteristics contribute to patterns of household segregation and the spatial distribution of house prices can, as a result, exhibit a high degree of persistence.

Modelling English local house price changes on the basis of commuting and migration flows is challenging and, instead, official local measures of affordability, based on price to earnings ratios, use local authority boundaries. The prices of individual properties have been published since 1995 and so, in principle, prices for any geography can be constructed, but measures of earnings cannot be obtained directly for HMAs and have to be estimated. Consequently, there are few English local house price studies[34] that use other than local authority boundaries. A consequence is that, in empirical work, we expect to observe spatial correlation in prices, because local authority boundaries do not necessarily coincide with those of HMAs. Spatial econometric techniques are often employed to capture any spill overs or spatial diffusion between the areas.[35]

Research on housing sub-markets has been extensive.[36] As the hedonic pricing literature shows, the price of any dwelling is a composite of the prices of the individual characteristics that make up the property; these include not only the size of the property and its type (the structural characteristics), but also the quality of the neighbourhood. If there is a single integrated housing market, then the price of each of the attributes should be the same across the area – migration, for example, would ensure this occurs. This does not, however, imply that the prices of all properties would be the same in the market, because each house possesses different bundles of attributes; even if two houses are physically identical, their prices may still differ if the environments vary. However, a set of sub-markets exists, rather than a unified market, if the prices of the individual attributes vary. In this case, the market forces are insufficient to ensure that attribute prices are equalized. Most empirical work has concentrated on the existence of sub-markets across location, but, equally, sub-markets can exist across product groups – different types of properties or building materials, for example.[37]

The empirical methods used to estimate sub-markets have improved considerably over the years and there is little doubt that sub-markets are common, but it remains hard to draw general conclusions. The results are place specific, there is evidence that the boundaries of sub-markets change over time and there is still only limited information on the delineation of sub-markets by property type. Nevertheless, there is still sufficient information to conclude that the markets do not adjust seamlessly even within individual cities.[38]

As noted previously, patterns of household segregation are likely to arise. Within built-up areas, there are limits to the ability to increase the supply of attributes that are in high demand and so their prices will be high. The housing stock and associated infrastructure are built up over long time periods and cannot be easily replicated. Similarly, area characteristics, such as the availability of good quality schools, are capitalized into local house prices,[39] and those households more willing and able to pay for those features are likely to live in the areas where they exist. Segregation can occur in both neo-classical residential location theory and in models that stress the importance of social interactions between households.[40] Furthermore, in social interaction models, segregated communities are the stable state to which areas tend; integrated communities, by contrast, break down and are unstable.

The determinants of rents

The previous sections indicate the large amount of research that has been conducted on house prices but, at least in the UK, empirical evidence on the determinants of private market rents is weaker. This is because the unregulated rental sector was modest in size until fairly recently, although the expansion in the Buy to Let market has doubled private tenancies since the late 1990s, and now over one in five households are private tenants. The current index of private rents, which is included as a component of the Consumer Prices Index, has only been constructed since 2005 and has grown at an annual average rate of approximately two per cent since that time – this is similar to the overall rate of inflation – and well below the rate of house price inflation. As noted earlier the differences in growth rates may be compatible if the discount rate has fallen. However, there are further reasons why rents may have grown at a slower rate, reflecting features of rental markets.

Theory suggests that house prices should be equal to the discounted present value of *imputed* (not market) rents. The imputed rent is the rent that owners would charge if the properties were to be rented to themselves. Although, in practice, we often assume that the two are the same, there are reasons why they may not grow at the same rate. First, owners have perfect knowledge about their own behaviour, but less information with regard to outside tenants. The owner has only limited knowledge as to whether they will be 'good' tenants in terms of looking after the property, paying the rent on time or how long they will remain in the property. Therefore, the owner has a strong incentive to keep good tenants in order to reduce voids and the substantial transaction costs. The evidence suggests that in 2018[41] for the most recent tenancy renewal, 70 per cent of landlords kept the rent the same (although letting agents were more likely to increase the rent), but rents were increased more frequently for new tenants. Therefore, imperfect information reduces the rate of rent increase. The EHS can be used to examine the quantitative importance of some of these issues. Appendix 3.1 shows, for a sample of 1,237 households across the country in 2017/18, the relationship between, on the one hand, annual market rent payments and, on the other hand, house prices and the characteristics of the tenants. Although rents and house prices are positively related, rents are likely to be lower for those households who have been in residence for a number of years and if the tenants are in employment. Both are characteristics that are observable to the landlord.

Additionally, even if the *rate of increase* in rents is modest, the *level* of rents may still be high relative to household incomes. Across England as a whole, for those households not in receipt of housing benefit, the median rent was £675 per month in the year to September 2017, which equated to approximately 28 per cent of gross median earnings. But median rents in the South East of England for the same period were £875 (33 per cent of earnings) and £1,433 (50 per cent) in London. At the lowest quartile, the respective values for the South East and London were £695 (37 per cent) and £1,175 (57 per cent).[42] The point is that, even if the growth rate in rents is no more than the general rate of inflation, the level will still be considered unaffordable by large parts of the population unless they are in receipt of housing benefit.

In conclusion

In conclusion, there are a number of messages that should be reinforced. First, at the national level, models of house prices are more robust than commonly believed, although this does not imply that forecasts of house prices are likely to be accurate. Table 3.1 shows that house prices are sensitive to changes in incomes and interest rates, for example. Therefore, even if the responsiveness has changed little over time, small errors in predictions of future interest rates or incomes produce even greater errors in house price forecasts. Secondly, internationally, a significant part of the differences in responsiveness of house prices to incomes and other variables found in studies appear to arise from differences in model specification: standardization of the specification often reduces the differences. Thirdly, to anticipate later chapters, those involved in modelling and forecasting house prices in the UK have paid insufficient attention to risk. Although risk measures are generally taken into account in some form in the academic literature, this is a complex area and risk is time-varying but, in its absence, models may predict that house prices rise without bound under some conditions.

At the regional scale, a criticism that can be levelled at the literature is that more attention has been paid to the statistical techniques that capture the nature of the interactions than understanding the transmission mechanisms that cause interdependencies across the markets. The simplest explanation is that the linkages are an artefact of the data because regional administrative boundaries do not coincide with those of HMAs. There is probably more to it than that, but equally it is over-simplistic to assume that the links are entirely due to mobility and migration. Furthermore, the nature of ripple effects has differed across each cycle: it is not a purely mechanical process.

Finally, this chapter has been concerned exclusively with the factors that drive house prices and rents. Equally important are the impacts that the housing market has on the macroeconomy. This issue is considered in Chapter 8. More generally, the empirical results begin to show what can and cannot be achieved by policy and results such as relationship (3.2) play a key role in the policy discussions in later chapters.

4

Influences on Household Formation and Tenure

Introduction

This chapter turns to the first of our groups – potential first-time buyers[1] – dealing with both household formation and tenure. Not only have current young cohorts experienced lower rates of home ownership than previous generations, but they are more likely to remain with parents for longer or share with others. This has been an international phenomenon. Intergenerational differences, not just in housing, have attracted considerable attention,[2] and the question, therefore, arises why the declines have taken place. Is it just a question of affordability – and Chapter 2 provided the appropriate indicators available – or have there been underlying changes in household preferences, reflecting new lifestyles or aspirations? These are the central issues for this chapter.

But new households cannot be seen in isolation from the rest of the market. Changes in demand for housing arise from two sources; first from new household formation (which is a *flow*) and, secondly, from the requirements of existing households (which is a *stock*). Since approximately 160,000 net new households were formed annually between the census dates of 2001 and 2011 in England, but there are more than 23 million existing households and, on average between the census years, approximately one million households moved each year in total, then current households are likely to have a greater impact on prices and rents than the newly forming households. There has been particular concern over the extent to which existing households – particularly older households – are deemed to under-occupy housing and the policies that might be implemented to induce so-called 'right sizing'. In addition, potential first-time buyers may face competition from Buy to Let investors and second home owners, who have advantages in terms of accumulated equity from existing homes. These issues imply that the number of first-time buyers is a *response* to market pressures as much as a *cause*. At one time it was commonly argued that sufficient numbers of first-time buyers were required to 'oil' the market. However, this is no longer obviously the case with the expansion of the investment market. Indeed, a key theme of the chapter is that household formation and tenure patterns are heavily affected not only by demographics but also by changes in economic conditions. This argument is reinforced in Chapter 7 when mortgage markets and their relationship to housing demand are discussed.

The next section looks in more detail at the changes in tenure that have taken place, including evidence for a selection of other countries – further discussed in Chapter 13 – and shows that England has not been alone in its tenure trends. The section also considers initial information on the relationship between household formation and affordability. We, then, discuss young household tenure aspirations and the evidence for changes over time. The following section considers demand by existing home owners, notably the rise in second home ownership and the evidence for housing under-occupation. The chapter is completed by the provision of further evidence on the effects of affordability on young household formation and tenure.

Changes in tenure and household formation

Table 4.1 sets out information on aggregate changes in tenure in England since the early part of the 20th century. It highlights, for most of the period, the rise in home ownership, the decline in private renting and the changes to social housing. But during the 21st century, home ownership has declined sharply, social housing has continued to fall, and both have been compensated by a rise in private renting. However, the changes in shares have eased slightly since 2013/14 and indeed ownership rose modestly in 2017/18. The long-run rise in owner occupation is, arguably, unsurprising: it reflects the various rent controls that were in operation from 1915 to 1988, which reduced the yields to renting, and rising real incomes backed up by liberalized funding. Since, from Chapter 3, the income elasticity of demand for space is high, demand is more likely to be satisfied in the owner occupier sector where the quality of the housing stock is generally superior. Further expansion occurred as a result of the Right to Buy programme introduced in 1980 (see Chapters 11 and 13). Finally, as

Table 4.1: Tenure in England (per cent), 1918–2017/18

Year	Home owners	Social renters	Private renters
1918	23.0	1.0	76.0
1939	32.0	10.0	58.0
1953	32.0	18.0	50.0
1961	43.0	23.0	34.0
1971	51.0	29.0	20.0
1981	57.2	31.7	11.1
1991	67.6	23.0	9.4
2001	70.4	19.5	10.1
2003	70.9	18.3	10.8
2005	70.7	17.7	11.7
2007	69.6	17.7	12.7
2009/10	67.4	17.0	15.6
2011/12	65.3	17.3	17.4
2013/14	63.3	17.3	19.4
2014/15	63.6	17.4	19.0
2015/16	62.9	17.2	19.9
2016/17	62.6	17.1	20.3
2017/18	63.5	17.0	19.5

Sources: 1918: Holmans (2005); 1939–1971: Holmans (1986); 1981–1991: Labour Force Survey, Housing Trailer; 2001–2007: Labour Force Survey; 2009–10 onwards: English Housing Survey

an investment, low yields on financial assets in recent years and the expansion of Buy to Let mortgages enhanced the recovery in the private rented sector evident in the table. Households in the private rented sector fell from approximately three-quarters of the total in 1918 to under 10 per cent by 1991 but the sector has subsequently doubled, with most of the growth in this century. In many ways, the growth in private renting is a success story, reversing the decline of a sector which is considered of importance for promoting labour mobility. As noted in Chapter 12, private renting had come to be seen as an inferior sector which might be expected to continue to decline. But the question arises whether the change results from household *choices* and *preferences* or reflects the *constraints* that younger households now face.

Some care is needed in the use of ratios or shares; it is possible for the home ownership rate to increase even if the absolute number of first-time buyers rises only modestly or even falls or if older owners live longer. This may occur if there are only small changes in the total number of households, which is used as the denominator in constructing the shares. As we shall see, there is evidence that new household formation has weakened and it may be the case that poorer individuals, who would usually be housed in renting, have contributed to the weakness; in this case, as a share, the proportion of households who are owners may actually rise. Therefore, information on the numbers of first-time buyers is, arguably, more relevant.

At the aggregate level, this can be seen in changes in the number of first-time buyers from the mid-1990s (Table 4.2), although the table needs to be interpreted cautiously as it refers to recent first-time buyers resident for less than three years, not the number of households who became owners in each year. On this basis, first-time buyers fell from 922,000 in 1995/96 to 654,000 in 2015/16, before rising again to 785,000 in 2017/18. The aggregate English home ownership rate peaked at 71 per cent in 2003, falling to under 63 per cent in 2016/17, but Table 4.2 suggests that a weakening had started earlier. The decline was heavily concentrated on the two youngest age groups in the table (and values for the youngest may have been affected by the expansion in higher education and student debt); indeed, the rise in buyers in the 35–44 age group suggests a delay in entering ownership.

Although the ownership share remains much lower in London than in other parts of the country (48.4 per cent in 2017/18), reflecting the lower age distribution and labour market mobility as well as the cost of housing, all regions have experienced a fall in the share since 2003. The decline has not been limited to the most expensive areas; indeed, it remains the case that the Southern and Midlands regions have home ownership rates above the average, whereas rates in the North (and London) are lower.

Furthermore, the decline in owner occupation has not been limited to England.[3] Figure 4.1 graphs the changes in owner occupation in the US and Australia as well as England – trends in other countries are discussed in Chapter 13. These three countries have experienced falls since the early years of the century and in the Australian case longer, where the decline for the younger age groups started in the 1980s if not earlier; each has cited worsening affordability as part of the explanation. In both Australia and the US, since public housing is small as a share of the total, the decline in ownership has been matched by a rise in private renting.

As noted earlier, changes in tenure *shares* are also determined by the total number of households; it matters whether the total number is expanding or contracting and the rate of change. Official projections in England of the future number of households are calculated using an extrapolation of past trends in household representative rates (HRPs), currently derived from the 2001 and 2011 censuses (see Chapter 9 for a wider discussion of the household projections). HRPs attempt to assess the proportion of individuals who are likely to be household heads. However, importantly, household projections are regarded

Table 4.2: Recent first-time buyers (resident for less than three years), 1995/96–2017/18

Age of household representative person	1995/96 (000s of households)	2005/06 (000s of households)	2015/16 (000s of households)	2017/18 (000s of households)
16–24	197	104	49	63
25–34	569	426	418	469
35–44	103	105	137	186
45+	53	40	50	67
All households	922	675	654	785

Source: English Housing Survey, various years

Figure 4.1: Home ownership rates, England, US and Australia (per cent), 1994–2016

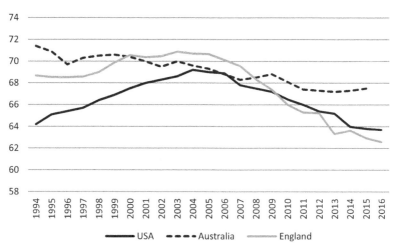

Sources: English Housing Survey; US Bureau of the Census (Housing Vacancies and Home Ownership); Australian Bureau of Statistics (Housing Occupancy and Costs Table 1.3, Catalogue No. 41300). Some years are interpolated for Australia.

as *trends* and do not explicitly allow for possible future changes in affordability, both in terms of incomes and housing costs or, indeed, any other economic variables.

As an illustration of the historical influence of affordability on household formation, Figure 4.2 sets out the household representative rates for a selection of local authorities across England, for two young age groups, 15–24 and 25–34, between 1991 and 2014. The locations in the first two parts of the figure are chosen as the three most unaffordable cities, on the basis of median house price to earnings ratios in 2014 (although we need to bear in mind the weaknesses of this indicator highlighted in Chapter 2); the fourth, Elmbridge (a wealthy local authority in the southern county of Surrey), was the most unaffordable authority in 2014. As expected, the 15–24 group has uniformly lower HRPs than the 25–34 age group, since more will still be living with parents or sharing. The declines in both groups since 1991 are striking, although some households in these age groups may compensate by moving to areas of better affordability and the decline may partly reflect increases in student debt. By contrast, the third and final part of the figure suggests that major towns in the North and Midlands did not experience the same fall for the 15–24 group – the group which showed the largest fall in the first part. The four Northern and Midlands locations are all assessed as in the top 20 most affordable authorities. Therefore, *prima facie*, fewer young individuals form independent households where housing costs are highest or incomes are weakest, although the decline in the South is not new and has been underway since at least 1991.[4]

Further information can be derived from empirical research which attempts to quantify the effects of demographic and economic factors that affect the probability that any individual will be a household head. In general demographics – age, marital status and numbers of children – have stronger impacts on household formation than economic variables.[5] For example, using Figure 4.2, in 2014 in Oxford – one of the most unaffordable cities in England – household formation differs considerably by age. Outcomes in university towns are, of course, heavily affected by student numbers but the household representative rate for 15–24-year-olds averaged 17.4 per cent, stood at 41.6 per cent for the 25–34 age group and 62.9 per cent for the 45–54 age group. Economic influences nonetheless play a role, particularly for the younger age groups, and Figure 4.3 provides an initial indicator. The graph plots household representative rates in 2014 (averaged across all household types and for the 15–24 age group separately) for English local authorities, excluding London, against the median house price to earnings ratio. The strong caveats concerning the use of price to earnings ratios as an affordability indicator again should be remembered, since changes over time are strongly related to changes in interest rates, but the indicator still provides some information across space at a particular moment in time. The correlation between the two variables is negative, but modest at −0.18 across all age groups; there is clearly considerable unexplained variation. The standard deviation of affordability is much greater than that of the HRPs across the local authorities.[6] But in the second frame, the correlation between the two variables is stronger

Figure 4.2: Household representative rates, 1991–2014

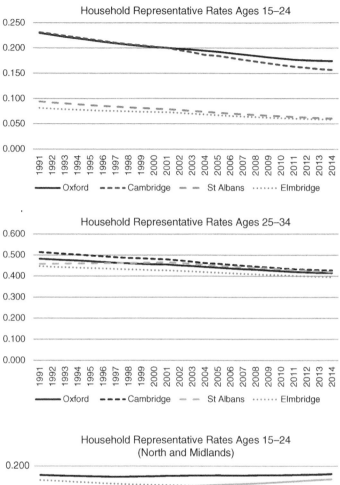

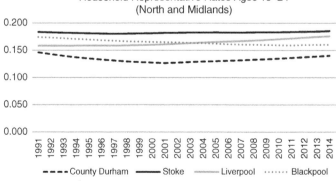

Source: Office for National Statistics

Figure 4.3: Household representative rates (vertical axis) and house price to earnings ratios (horizontal axis), local authorities, England, 2014

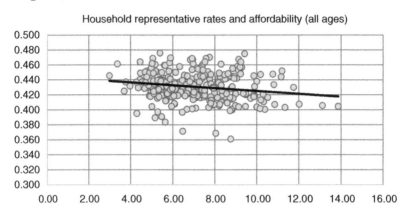

Household representative rates and affordability (all ages)

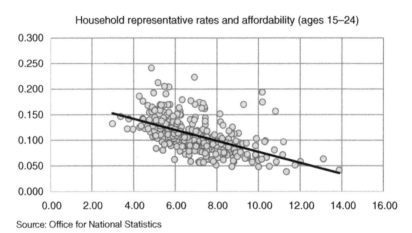

Household representative rates and affordability (ages 15–24)

Source: Office for National Statistics

for the 15–24 age group at −0.54. It appears to be the case, therefore, that the younger age groups are more heavily affected.

Home ownership choices, expectations and aspirations

According to the EHS, in 2017/18, 58 per cent of private renters and 25 per cent of social renters expected to become owners at some point in their lives, although 45 per cent then thought it would be five years or more before they were able to purchase. Expectations among social tenants are affected by the opportunity to purchase their homes through Right to Buy and of those local authority tenants expecting to become owners, approximately 60 per cent intended to buy their current home. *Prima facie*, the evidence appears to be that renting households still want to become owners and expect to delay entry into home ownership rather than give up on the hope entirely. However, it is increasingly recognized that expectations and aspirations are not the same, although the terms have often (incorrectly) been used interchangeably.[7] Furthermore, the distinction between preferences, needs and choices is often confused; aspirations can exist independently of choices which refer to an individual's actions.

Therefore, some care is needed over the use of terminology. Housing aspirations might be conceptualized as, 'referring to desires to achieve housing-related ambitions in the future, encapsulating optimistic assessments of what can be realized'.[8] Furthermore, as a long-term goal, aspirations are likely to change more slowly than expectations since the latter allow for changes in current economic conditions and, indeed as the name suggests, future conditions. It appears still to be the case that most private renters aspire to home ownership – this partly reflects, for example, the lack of security of tenure and poor quality of the private rental stock and more generally dissatisfaction with private renting. But economic conditions (including relatively low-income growth, lack of job security, and inability to raise a deposit) have led to a levelling down of expectations of achieving ownership, at least for a number of years.

Additionally, aspirations are affected by cultural issues, senses of identity and social norms. In the case of norms, aspirations are partly determined by the behaviour of peer groups;[9] if most of an individual's peer group aspire to become owners, the individual is also likely to have similar aspirations. The influence of peer groups can lead to persistence in aspirations, but it can also lead to tipping points if group norms change. It also provides a possible explanation for the high income elasticity of housing demand in the UK, found in Chapter 3. This leads to important issues for policy, to which we return in Chapter 14. Moreover, concepts of home may be tied up with questions of culture, ethnicity and identity; and ownership may be perceived as generating greater security both in terms of a buffer against crime and in terms of security of tenure. As noted, the quality of the owner occupier housing stock is also often superior to that in private renting at least at the lower end of the market.

This suggests that the demand for home ownership among young households is more complex than standard demand theory might suggest – and indeed more complex than the models employed in Chapter 3. However, there is general agreement that housing demand and tenure transition are tied up with life course events such as taking up employment, leaving home, acquiring a partner, having children and ageing. Questions of mobility are also closely related. Most moves are only short distance, possibly reflecting attachment to place as well as insecurity of tenure in the private rented sector and this has been the case since at least the 19th century.[10] According to the 2014/15 EHS, 74 per cent of movers, where the HRP was under the age of 55, relocated by under ten miles and 24 per cent moved under one mile. Of this age group, 17 per cent moved for family reasons, 11 per cent wanted a live in a better neighbourhood, 17 per cent wanted a larger property, 11 per cent moved for job-related reasons and 17 per cent wanted either to buy or live independently. More of those over the age of 55 (15 per cent) reported that they wanted to downsize. In fact, the influences on mobility are complex and include: tenure (private renters move more frequently than owners); those in professional occupations have higher rates of mobility than the unskilled; mobility falls sharply in middle age until retirement; moving rates are low for those with school-aged children or for dual income households or those facing negative equity. Furthermore, high relative house prices may discourage migration into an area, but this may be offset by expectations of future capital gains.[11]

In the presence of worsening affordability, as part of the market adjustment mechanism, we might expect households to move from high to lower priced areas and, indeed, over short distances households are mobile and the induced flows contribute to ensuring that housing costs rise at similar rates. Furthermore, partly as a result of outmigration and commuting flows, historically house prices in London and the South East have grown at similar rates, although the growth in London house prices has outstripped that in the rest of the South East since the late 1990s, but as noted in Chapter 3 London prices have eased since 2017.

As shown in Figure 4.4, net population flows between London and the rest of the country have generally been negative – outflows exceed inflows – and this is not a new event. London typically gains population from inflows by young adults but loses population from the older age groups; this contributes to the relatively young age distribution of London compared with other parts of the country. In 2017, for example, net inflows for the 20–29 age group totalled 32,200 but London lost 51,000 people in the 30–44 age group. Therefore, the attractions of London in terms of employment and cultural activities have not been fully dispelled by the higher housing costs. Furthermore, from Figure 4.4, net outflows fell sharply between 2004 and 2009, before increasing again since that time.

Figure 4.4: London net migration inflows from other regions (numbers), 2004–2017

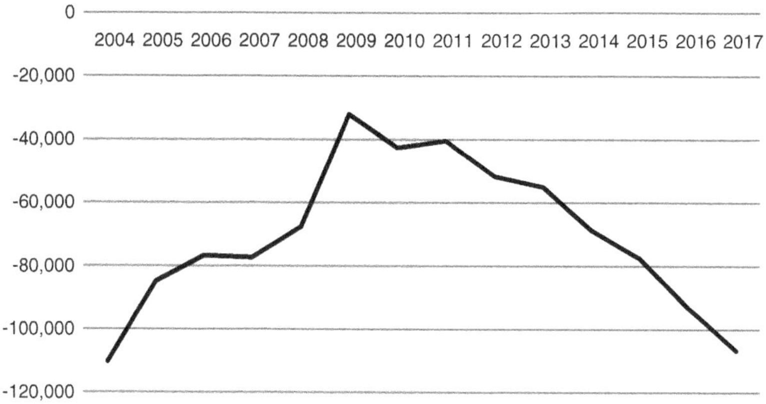

Source: Office for National Statistics

Demand by existing owners and the rise of second home ownership

We have noted that increases in housing demand arise not only from newly forming households but also from changes in demand by current owners, which may take the form of trading up to a property of higher quality or in a better location; an additional home held for investment, holiday or other purposes; or significant improvements and extensions to the current home. In contrast to first-time buyers, this can be achieved by trading on the equity in an existing home.

Consider the following example, which demonstrates the advantages of existing owners at a time of rising prices: suppose a household purchases its first home for £100,000, with a 50 per cent deposit; its annual income is £20,000. While the household lives in the property, assume all house prices rise by 20 per cent. Equity, therefore, rises from £50,000 to £70,000. If the household maintains a deposit of 50 per cent at the next move, it can purchase a home valued at £140,000. Since prices have only increased by 20 per cent, the household purchases a higher quality home, although the debt to market value ratio remains constant. It is, of course, true under this scenario that, unless the household's income rises by twice the rate of house price inflation (40 per cent), its debt to income ratio rises (and in aggregate, as Chapter 7 shows, debt to income ratios have risen rapidly) potentially making the household more vulnerable to income or interest rate shocks.[12] The point, however, is that existing owners can readily increase the quality and size of their homes by appropriate use of their equity in the current home, irrespective of the size of the household.

On the basis of a bedroom standard, households that have two or more extra bedrooms than needed for their size are deemed on official definitions to be 'under-occupying' housing (Table 4.3).[13] If these households could be persuaded to reduce consumption, then this would free up homes for other households and reduce the need for new building. On this view of the world, there is a mismatch between household size and the quantity of housing services consumed. Table 4.3 summarizes the trends in official under-occupation since the mid-1990s; whereas under-occupation has fallen in the social and private rented sectors, under-occupation has risen sharply among owners. Further analysis of the EHS indicates that a higher proportion of owners over the age of 60 are under-occupying than across all other age groups. Two-thirds of owners over the age of 60 have two or more bedrooms above the standard.

Nevertheless, bedroom standards are misleading and it cannot be concluded that affordability can be improved by downsizing older households. One view is that this group would welcome downsizing but is prevented from doing so by the absence of suitable smaller accommodation with the necessary property characteristics. In addition, alternative accommodation generally needs to be in the local area with adequate service provision. Furthermore, older households are dissuaded by the transaction costs, notably Stamp Duty Land Tax, and attachment to their current properties. These issues have recently been considered by the UK House of Commons, Communities and Local Government Select Committee.[14] In 2017/18, approximately 30 per cent of under occupiers had been in their properties for more than 30 years. An additional perspective is that older households have little incentive to move while their health remains good. Measures of

Table 4.3: Under-occupation by tenure (per cent of households), 1995/96–2017/18

Year	Owner occupiers	Private renters	Social renters	All tenures
1995/96	39.4	18.4	12.1	31.2
2000/01	42.8	16.6	12.7	34.1
2005/06	46.6	18.2	11.5	36.7
2010/11	49.3	15.5	10.0	36.9
2015/16	51.9	14.4	10.0	37.2
2017/18	53.5	14.6	9.6	38.5

Source: English Housing Survey, 2017/18

under-occupation are based on household size, but actual consumption is a market outcome reflecting family requirements, the incomes of the households and the costs of housing. In 2017/18 only approximately 10 per cent of owners over the age of 60 had any mortgage payments and, so, their only housing-related expenditures consisted of fuel and maintenance costs and Council Tax payments. Furthermore, approximately 60 per cent had incomes in the top three income quintiles and, on retirement, households are likely to spend more time in the family home, providing an added reason for wanting more space. Therefore, an unwillingness to move is a rational market response, particularly in the light of low returns on alternative financial assets, where released housing equity might be reinvested.

Although sample sizes are modest in the EHS, there is little evidence that the over-60s who do move, in fact, downsize; in 2017/18 of the over-60s who had been in their current property for two years or less, around a half were still occupying at two or more bedrooms above standard. This is not a new phenomenon, and, even in the 1970s, the normal move was to the same sized dwelling. In fact, the freeing up of properties in the older age groups arises primarily from mortality and this heavily outweighs that arising from movers under existing incentive structures.

In summary, it is unsurprising that downsizing is modest since home ownership is a market where movers respond to incentives: for most older households the current costs of ownership are low; incomes are generally adequate; the probability of moving falls with age and the young are typically more mobile; home owners are less mobile than renters across all age groups; the returns on alternative financial assets are low and it is increasingly unnecessary to move home to release equity; attachment to home is strong; transaction costs are high; and there is a shortage of suitable alternative accommodation. This all suggests that changes to incentive structures would need to be strong to overcome the inertia. Two interlinked proposals are sometimes suggested – the removal of stamp duty to encourage mobility and an enhanced form of property taxation, for example, a revision of Council Tax or an annual land value tax, designed to raise housing costs for the more expensive homes in expensive areas;[15] a version of the latter is discussed further in Chapter 13.

Some home owners (and indeed some tenants) also have second homes. In many cases these are temporary arising from moving or from inheritance, but homes held for investment, holiday or family purposes are longer-lasting and add to overall housing demand. In principle, we should expect purchases for investment purposes both to increase the level of house prices and their volatility; this is, again, because accumulated equity in existing homes can be used to finance the purchase of additional properties and this creates a form of financial accelerator.[16] Since potential first-time buyers have no accumulated equity – and generally face high deposit requirements – they are at a disadvantage relative to investment buyers. But, in fact, at the aggregate national level, it is difficult to discern any effect from the rise in the Buy to Let sector on house prices and micro data suggest that the direct competition is limited. As noted in Chapter 3, the parameters of the relationship determining house prices have been remarkably stable over time and there is only limited evidence of structural change since the 1990s.

Nevertheless, there is evidence from micro data that the demand for second homes is sensitive to income and other variables. The 2013/14 EHS provides information on the reasons for holding second homes.[17] Of the sample of 13,276 households, approximately 9 per cent had a second home; of these 90 per cent had only one or two properties. More recently, the 2018 English Landlord Survey found that half of landlords owned only one property, but the concentration of rental properties has increased over time with half of private tenancies now let by 17 per cent of landlords with five or more properties.[18] But in the EHS, those with additional homes gave the following motives:

- A property recently bought for occupation that not moved   23
  into yet
- An empty property that you plan to sell in the near future   78
- For occupation while working away from home   24
- Mainly let to others as a holiday let   34
- Mainly used by family and friends as a holiday home/   151
  weekend cottage
- Occupied by someone as their main residence   798
- Occupied by student son/daughter while at college/   13
  university
- Other   54
- Total (numbers)   1175

So, 68 per cent were 'occupied by someone as their main residence', and this might be taken as one measure of the investment market. Using the 2013/14 sample, it is possible to estimate the probability of owning at least one second home, excluding those homes which are held only for transitional purposes. The key influences turn out to be the current

Table 4.4: The probability of owning a second home, 2008/09 and 2013/14

Representative household	2008/09	2013/14
50-year-old head, living in council housing, in bottom quintile, 1 earner, 2-person household, living in South East	0.006	0.007
50-year-old head, outright owner, in top quintile, 1 earner, 2-person household, living in South East	0.270	0.349
40-year-old head, outright owner, in top quintile, 1 earner, 2-person household, living in South East	0.237	0.300
75-year-old head, outright owner, in top quintile, 1 earner, 2-person household, living in South East	0.156	0.236
50-year-old head, outright owner, in top quintile, 1 earner, 2-person household, living in North East	0.198	0.248

Source: Authors' estimates

tenure of the household, location, income and age. Unsurprisingly, those renting from the social sector had a low probability of owning an investment property; the likelihood is greatest for households living in London and the South East; the probability increases with age, but falls in the oldest groups; and those in the highest income quintiles have a much higher probability of second home ownership. The analysis can be compared with data for 2008/09 and, although there are qualitative similarities, there are also distinct differences. As examples, Table 4.4 shows the probability of second home ownership for a range of household types, varying by age, tenure, location and income. First, the probabilities are uniformly lower in 2008/09: the fact that this was during the GFC may be part of the explanation, but it also shows that the advantages of the rich (through both income and tenure) have increased over time. Whereas those at the bottom of the income distribution and living in council housing continue to have a zero probability of having an investment home, the probability for an outright owner in the top income quintile has increased from 27 per cent to 35 per cent over five years. The probability of second home ownership reaches a peak at around the age of 50.

Affordability, household formation and the tenure of young households

Most of the discussion in the previous sections concerns housing costs, but affordability also depends on income, not only in aggregate, but also through changes in its distribution. The Lorenz curve used as a

Figure 4.5: Median gross weekly earnings of full-time employees aged 22–29 relative to all employees, 1997–2017, England

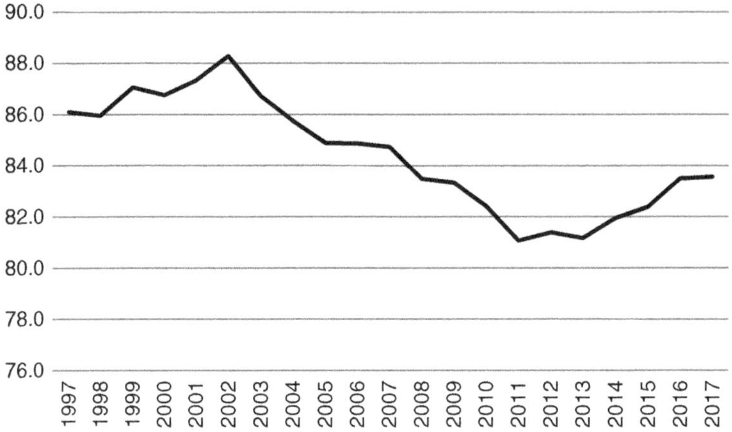

Source: Annual Survey of Hours and Earnings

measure of owner occupier affordability in Chapter 2 considered both the distributions of earnings and prices. We also saw that renters in the lower-income quintiles were more likely to face housing stress, unless they were receiving housing benefit. Therefore, changes in affordability reflect labour market as well as housing market dynamics. Figure 4.5 shows that the incomes of young full-time employees have fallen relative to employees as a whole since 1997 (the first year for which the Annual Survey of Hours and Earnings is available). By 2017, earnings of the 22–29 age group were approximately 84 per cent of the overall median. But using the earlier New Earnings Survey, there is evidence that the relative decline dates back to the early 1990s.[19] Since, from Chapter 3, the income elasticity of house prices is well in excess of one, the widening of the earnings distribution exacerbates the inability of younger age groups to achieve ownership.

The importance of income can be demonstrated using more formal modelling for both household formation and the probability of ownership from micro data, incorporating both life course demographic and economic influences. Table 4.5 sets out the probabilities that a selection of illustrative individuals living in London would have formed separate households in 2001. Although the probabilities are now a little out-of-date, the general principles still hold.[20] As the table shows, the probabilities depend very strongly on the individual's status in the previous year. If she/he had already been in a separate household (the lower half of the table), there is a high probability of remaining as a separate household, irrespective of income. By contrast, an individual

Table 4.5: The probability of household formation (London, 2001)

Representative household	Probability (%)
Not a separate household in the previous year	
Female, 25–29, single, no children, income quartile 4	27.6
Male, 20–24, single, no children, income quartile 2	9.7
Male, 30–34, single, no children, income quartile 4	24.3
Male, 30–34, partner, children, income quartile 4	60.8
Male, 30–34, partner, children, income quartile 1	50.2
A separate household in the previous year	
Female, 25–29, single, no children, income quartile 4	97.2
Male, 30–34, single, no children, income quartile 4	96.5
Male, 30–34, partner, children, income quartile 4	99.8
Male, 30–34, partner, children, income quartile 1	99.6

Source: Meen and Andrew (2008), derived from the British Household Panel Survey

previously living in the parental home or sharing was more strongly influenced by both demographics and economics: for example, comparing the third and fourth entries, having a partner and children more than doubled the probability. But entries four and five suggest that, even with a partner and children, income had a significant impact on household formation. Finally, as previously mentioned, younger age groups were less likely to form separate households.

In combination with Figures 4.2 and 4.3, the indications are, therefore, that changes in household formation, particularly among the younger age groups, form a significant element in the market adjustment process at times of poor affordability. The young are squeezed out and have to remain with their parents for longer, or share without forming separate households.

However, given the number of households, the tenure distribution is even more responsive to economic influences. Using the same data as in Table 4.5, Table 4.6 shows the probability that a household head with a given set of characteristics will be an owner occupier in the high-priced South East region. The second column indicates that households who are already owners are highly likely to maintain their status irrespective of their demographic or economic profiles. This partly reflects the fact that housing costs fall relative to income the longer the households are owners, although as discussed later, this appears to have been less evident in recent years. Older owner occupier households have low housing costs and have high levels of accumulated equity in their homes. As noted earlier, there are typically few economic reasons for older households to move out

Table 4.6: Owner occupation probabilities for those who were owners in the previous year and renters in the previous year (South East, 2003)

Representative household	Previous owner (%)	Previous renter (%)
Female household head, aged 30–34, single, no children		
Income quartile 2	93.6	2.3
Income quartile 4	96.1	4.0
Male household head, aged 35–39, partner with children		
Income quartile 2	98.2	7.8
Income quartile 4	99.1	12.0

Source: Meen and Andrew (2008), derived from the British Household Panel Survey

of ownership, or even to downsize while their health permits. But the probability that a household, who is currently a renter, becomes an owner is fairly sensitive to income. The probabilities may, at first sight, appear low, but it should be remembered that they are the probabilities of becoming an owner *in a given year*, not the probability of ever achieving ownership over the lifetime. Although not shown in the table, the probabilities for this group are also related to the relative costs of ownership and renting and, crucially, to the ability to raise a sufficient deposit as well as pay other transaction costs. Consequently, even if relative tenure costs favour ownership, an inability to raise the required deposit is expected to extend the period spent in renting, lowering the probability of ownership in any period, but not necessarily permanently lowering the ownership rate. This depends on the rate of increase in house prices relative to the rates at which households can or are willing to save.[21]

Further light can be shed by using information from the 2017/18 EHS and concentrating on the characteristics of those who have achieved ownership as first-time buyers over the previous ten years. This provides a modest sample of 953 buyers. Of those who had been in residence for fewer than three years, more than 60 per cent had previously been private renters and 30 per cent were new households. 60 per cent of first-time buyers had household incomes in the top two income quintiles (in 2017/18 rather than at the time the house was purchased). A large majority of buyers under the age of 60 had at least one member in full-time work and approximately 60 per cent of heads were in managerial or professional occupations. Seventy per cent bought semi-detached or terraced properties and 20 per cent purchased flats.

The importance of the ability to raise a deposit is also evident. In 2015/16 the mean deposit for first-time buyers was 19 per cent (the median was 16 per cent),[22] but there was a wide dispersion, including a modest number of reported 100 per cent loans and some cases where the deposit exceeded 80 per cent. However, the latter were anomalies, and typically arose from legacies.

The conventional wisdom is that mortgage repayments as a percentage of income decline with the length of residence – the servicing is front-end loaded. But, in fact, despite low interest rates, because of the weak growth in nominal earnings across the economy as a whole, the fall has been fairly modest. On average, in 2017/18 (and again there is a wide dispersion), those who became owners less than a year before were paying around 20 per cent of household gross income in mortgage repayments, but even those who had become first-time buyers between five and nine years ago were still spending only slightly less (19 per cent on average). Finally, we have tended to expect that the equity held in the home will rise over time as house prices increase, so that even first-time buyers quickly make capital gains. In fact, the GFC complicates the position. It remains the case that those who became owners after the GFC (and so usually purchased at lower prices) have on average across the country made capital gains – prices have risen since then. But there is evidence that those who purchased just before the GFC have made somewhat smaller gains. Nevertheless, given the requirement to provide high deposits, few experienced long-lasting negative equity where the size of the outstanding mortgage at the time of the survey exceeded the value of the house.

In conclusion

The UK is not alone in having experienced falling rates of home ownership, particularly among the younger age cohorts; neither is the decline limited to the most expensive areas of the country. In aggregate, the US, Australia and other countries have faced similar trends and similar discussions have taken place. If we go back to the early 1990s, one of the major policy debates was how we could reverse the long-run decline in the private rented sector and some decline in the home ownership rate among the young would have been welcomed since there were fears that high rates of home ownership discouraged labour mobility and contributed to increasing the rate of unemployment.[23] In fact, declines were already occurring at that time in Australia and Canada. But there are questions of degree: is there an optimum rate of home ownership since English ownership is now below the EU mean; and do current rates meet young household aspirations or do they represent a sub-optimal position caused by relatively weak earnings and credit market constraints? The available evidence suggests that aspirations have not changed dramatically in recent years and it is hard to believe that economic conditions are not part of the explanation. We also showed that household formation is dependent on economic conditions. One of the themes of the chapter is that the number of new households and first-time buyers are as much an outcome of market processes as drivers of demand and prices.

The reason is that prices and rents are determined more by the stocks of existing owners and renters which are much larger than the flow of new entrants. Also, housing demand reflects its role as an investment as well as a consumption good, which links it to wider macroeconomic policies, notably monetary policy, as well as to the demand for second homes for holiday, family or investment purposes. We argued that there are limited reasons for older owners to downsize since their costs are low and this impacts on the availability of housing for new entrants. Later chapters will consider further the role of housing taxation in promoting change.

Outcomes for first-time buyers are, arguably, more dependent on labour market conditions than on housing market policies and the relative decline of earnings in conjunction with job uncertainty for younger individuals is of central importance. Since house prices are highly responsive to changes in aggregate incomes, a shift in the earnings distribution away from the young has a major effect on the probability of achieving ownership; but the change in the earnings distribution is not new and represents a trend from at least the early 1990s.

This leaves plenty to be discussed in the policy chapters in the second part of the book, including the role of monetary policy – are interest rate and credit policies consistent with housing market objectives? Also, what can be achieved by fiscal reform through housing taxation? There is a danger in the view that reform is just too difficult since the market will still produce a solution, which may be considered socially undesirable. However, this is also dependent on conditions in housing supply, which is the topic for Chapter 6.

5

Rental Affordability

Introduction

Rental affordability is a rather simpler concept than that for owner occupation as, at a point in time, it relates current rent to current income.[1] In a free market, without government support, one would expect financial stress associated with housing expenditure to be directly related to the rent paid, the income of the household and to the standards of housing achieved by that household. So higher-income households could be expected to live in better quality housing, but probably to spend lower proportions of income on rents – and therefore to have higher levels of income available to purchase other goods and services than those on lower incomes. This was discussed in Chapter 2. Our interest in this chapter is therefore on the experience of lower-income households and particularly on how this is impacted by particular policy initiatives, issues which are developed further in Chapters 11 and 12.

First, we need a *definition* of what we mean by those on low incomes and whether they have a rental affordability problem. The simplest approach to determining low income is to concentrate on those in the lowest deciles, although even then it would be appropriate to take account of household structure and thus responsibilities and varying basic needs. In this context, the most policy relevant definition of low income for renters' affordability in the UK is to accept the government's implicit definition when determining housing benefit: that 'residual income' after rent paid by housing benefit should be enough to cover all other basic needs. This at least takes account of household composition. Internationally, there are two general approaches to assessing rental unaffordability: the median (or, less usually, the mean) of the ratio of housing cost over income, which takes no account of distribution but is often used across tenures; and the 'housing cost overburden rate', which measures the proportion of households or population that spend more than a set proportion of their income taking account of housing benefits (that is, net rent after benefit and income excluding benefits).[2] In Europe, that proportion is currently 40 per cent[3] but the proportion has varied over time and between countries in part because of how rent is defined (for example, with or without service and utility charges). Canada, for instance, traditionally had a 20 per cent rule, but switched to a 25 per cent rule in the 1950s and to 30 per cent in the 1980s. Current discussions often concentrate on those who are defined as severely overburdened because they are paying more than 50 per cent of their income in rent.[4] Any of these, of course, raise all the issues around affordability measures discussed in Chapter 2 as well as the need to take into account the standards of housing achieved.

What we do know is that lower-income households tend to be renters, except among the elderly, where there are large numbers of asset-rich/income-poor owner occupiers. This reflects the fact that basic housing is a necessity of life, while owning an asset can be regarded as more of a luxury good chosen by better off households, but also that there are significant constraints on entering owner occupation (see Chapter 7).

As Chapter 2 showed, problems of housing stress are not confined to renters on the lowest incomes in the UK, but, nonetheless, among those spending more than 25 per cent of their incomes on housing, households in the lowest income quintiles are much more likely to face housing stress − in terms of their ability to meet their rental payments − as compared to those in the top income quintile. But it is not the case on average that households in the bottom quintile are more likely to face stress than those in the top quintile because tenants on low incomes are typically receiving income-related support through housing benefit, which, either fully or partially, meets their rents. As a result, they generally spend less than 25 per cent of their income on housing.

The fact that in the UK, and in many other, especially Western European, countries, there are universal income-related housing allowance systems in place means that rental affordability alone is not the whole story.[5] Equally, rents are determined in different ways across the rental sector − and the rules for housing support also vary between sub-sectors and groups of households − so, who has access to the different parts is relevant to the affordability issue.

A short history of housing support for lower-income households

This position reflects the latest stage in a long history of helping poorer households to obtain adequate shelter and security, not all of which directly concentrated on affordability. Looking back over the centuries the church, charities and later some employers were all involved in providing accommodation at low or sometimes zero rents, mainly for lower-income households (although there is of course also a history of providing for high-income/wealthy households, usually as part of their remuneration package). However, the significant growth in government intervention to ensure adequate housing for all only occurred in the 19th century and was associated more with issues of public health, particularly cholera, than housing itself. *The Sanitary Conditions of the Labouring Population*,[6] sponsored by the Poor Law Commission for the central government pointed to the growth of disease in urban areas and led to the 1848 Public Health Act – although only after another cholera epidemic. The recommendations addressed how local authorities might deal with concerns around sewerage, refuse and clean water – but this could only be successful if housing conditions were improved. The first major legislation directly addressing this issue came in 1885 with *The Housing for the Working Classes Act* which introduced local authority powers to shut down unhealthy dwellings and made it illegal for landlords to let property which fell below elementary sanitary standards.

Thus, the starting rationale for intervention by local authorities first in London and then in the rest of the country was *housing quality*, something not directly even taken into account in most affordability measures. However, while increasing standards to acceptable levels, reducing negative externalities as well as potentially increasing worker productivity, were the fundamental objectives of these regulations they also inherently led to problems of affordability in addition to extreme overcrowding. Households simply could not afford the rents associated with the standards that were required. Even at the start of the 20th century, it was recognized that there was an inconsistency between the level of rent necessary to provide an adequate return on reasonable housing to landlords and what households on the lowest incomes could afford without subsidies.[7]

Rent controls

The first intervention that directly addressed affordability was the introduction of rent controls in December 1915. This was seen as a temporary wartime measure responding to the impact of worsening housing supply constraints.[8] After the war however, the controls remained in place and rents were not significantly adjusted, so the outcome was greater affordability for sitting tenants. However, it also led to declining housing standards (except with respect to overcrowding) and major problems for potential new entrants, who often had to pay illegal up-front costs to find a tenancy. Importantly it was one reason for the decline in the private rented sector from accommodating around 76 per cent of all households in 1918 to, at its minimum, perhaps around nine per cent, in the late 1980s.[9] The two other core reasons for decline were slum clearance which helped to meet quality standards but massively reduced the supply of private sector low-cost housing; and the expansion of owner occupation which was accompanied by the large-scale transfer of privately rented units into that sector. Equally, it meant that in the 1981 English House Condition Survey 63 per cent of privately rented dwellings were built before 1919.[10] Thus, private renting became the residual sector for those unable to access owner occupation or social housing and particularly for those entering the housing market for the first time.[11] This only began to change in the mid-1990s, after rent controls were abolished for almost all tenancies in 1988 and market rents became the norm for new tenancies – only mitigated by housing benefit (see later in this chapter and Chapter 12).

Increasing the supply of public and social housing

The second major form of intervention from the later part of the nineteenth century was to enable local authorities to build homes both to rent out and to sell on the market. Initially, there was no central government subsidy. The Addison Act of 1919 put in place a significant subsidy for council housing and although this was replaced by less generous schemes, including tenure neutral supply subsidies, as a result of these and local subsidies by councils, the proportion of public housing rose from 1 per cent in 1918 to 10 per cent (over a million homes) in 1939.[12] Even so, much of what was provided was in partial replacement for slum clearance – a situation which continued for more than two decades after the Second World War.

Four phases in post-1945 policy with respect to new supply can be identified in the UK, and indeed in much of Western Europe.[13] The first involved large-scale government supported construction programmes in the 1950s and 1960s to address acute housing shortages. These were provided by local authorities and, in some cases, by local housing associations. The resultant stock was allocated mainly to working households with children. How this impacted on affordability depended on the individual rental regime. In the UK, rents were set in relation to pooled historic costs taking account of local and national subsidies (see Chapter 11 for details) and rents were generally within the reach of tenants. The second stage emphasized renovation and slum clearance programmes, which were particularly prevalent in the UK between the 1950s and 1970s and were often a continuation of stalled pre-war programmes. The third comprised a transition towards a market-oriented approach to financing and a shift away from local authority provision towards new build mainly by housing associations. Government then provided targeted up-front support to associations for what became known as social rather than public housing. The fourth and current stage involves major regeneration of urban social housing within mixed tenure/use projects – a pattern which is mirrored across Europe.

This supply-based subsidy system provided sub-market rent accommodation for those allocated social housing, but it left private tenants with only diminishing support from rent control (which was dismantled starting from 1957)[14] to help with rental affordability. The result was large numbers either unable to form separate households or paying high rents in relation to their incomes. At the same time rents in the local authority sector, while not always affordable to tenants, were often inadequate to enable reasonable management and improvement.[15]

Income-related housing support

To address these affordability issues, in the early 1970s, the UK government introduced income-related subsidies, initially in the form of rent rebates for low-income social sector tenants in 1972,[16] and then as rent allowances for private and housing association tenants as well, in the following years.[17] Their introduction was a reflection, not only of the reality that overall numerical housing surpluses had been achieved so there was seen to be less need to subsidize new building, but also of a change in the ideological approach away from general supply subsidies towards means-tested demand assistance – a shift which happened well before the Thatcher government came into power in 1979. Many European countries similarly brought in income-related housing support at around the same period, with similar intentions of targeting assistance more directly at those in housing stress and reducing supply side subsidies as numerical shortages were overcome.[18]

Rent rebates and rent allowances

When rent rebates and rent allowances were introduced in the UK in the early 1970s, the basic principle was straightforward:[19] social security determined the income necessary to cover basic needs for each type of household at national level (that is, with no allowance for variations in costs across the country). It was however seen as necessary to treat housing differently because housing costs varied so greatly, both spatially and between households. A household's eligibility for a rebate or allowance covered the whole rent (and allowable service charges) if their income was equal to the basic needs allowance. Above that level, a proportion of every additional pound was withdrawn until income reached a point where it was presumed that the rent would be fully paid by the tenant. Thus, all beneficiaries were expected to receive the minimum income required for their needs. The subsidy withdrawal rate above that level was designed to ensure some incentive to find work or to work longer hours (although in practice that might be very limited, as other benefits were being withdrawn at the same time resulting in a 'tax rate' of over 90 per cent). It was assumed that people on low incomes had few housing choices, so the incentive to live in a more expensive dwelling/area did not need to be taken into account (except for limitations on the acceptable size of the dwelling in the private rented sector).[20]

Rents in the local authority sector had to be set without regard to personal circumstances and were related to cost rather than to capacity to pay. Allocations were increasingly constrained to more vulnerable households. Concerns about the incentives for private landlords to try to increase rents for private tenants in the light of greater capacity to pay were one reason why private lettings were not included in the initial legislation. However, any such impact could only be indirect as the vast majority of private and housing association tenancies were still subject to 'fair rents' set by independent rent officers, although landlord and tenant could agree such rents. This position changed however when rent regulations for new tenancies were completely removed from January 1989. But (unpublished) independent studies by consultants for government suggested that benefits would not significantly increase deregulated rents in most markets because a relatively small proportion of private tenants would be eligible for such housing assistance.

The position now has, however, become very much more complicated.[21] In the social sector it remains the case that rents are subject to regulation and households will generally receive assistance based on the actual rent charged, so basic needs are still covered by income. The exceptions relate to the withdrawal of the 'spare room subsidy';[22] the introduction of an overall welfare cap based on the principle that total welfare payments must not exceed average earnings; and the increasing importance of service charges which are not all eligible for benefits.

In the private sector, the welfare cap and service charges issues are also relevant but more importantly the situation in general is much less generous. Housing benefits are determined by the Local Housing Allowance (LHA) introduced in 2008; initially this limited rents to the 50th percentile of the distribution of rents in the Broad Rental Market Area for suitably sized accommodation, but this was then reduced to the 30th percentile.[23] Since 2016 support has become increasingly uncoupled from any defined proportion of rental property in the area by the introduction of a four-year freeze on LHA increases. Many argue that the result is an indirect rent control on lower-quality housing, but this still leaves tenants differentially facing unaffordable rents.[24] More importantly it means that increasing numbers of private tenants are having to pay significant proportions of their low wages or other welfare payments to ensure their rents are paid.[25]

Across the whole sector there are also additional constraints on benefit payments to younger single people who are eligible for assistance only towards the cost of shared accommodation, as well as exceptions and special treatment for certain groups. On the other hand, there is a system of discretionary payments to relieve housing stress paid for by central government and managed through local authorities. Most importantly housing benefit is now an element within Universal Credit which, while the housing element is based on the same rules as when it was a separate payment, requires most tenants to pay their rent directly to their landlord and has generated a range of additional complexities as well as significant rent arrears, which impact on landlords' choices of tenants.[26] Even so, the system still provides 'as of right' assistance towards housing costs to all eligible households who are able to form separate households.

Selected characteristics of benefit recipients

The EHS can be used to provide information on the characteristics of benefit recipients. In 2016/17, from the sample of renters, 45 per cent were receiving housing benefit, that is the rent and eligible service charges were either fully or partially paid.[27] Further details are provided in Table 5.1: the first part shows the proportion of benefit recipients by age group, disaggregated between the private and social sectors and the second part indicates the distribution by income quintile.

Table 5.1a: Renters receiving housing benefit, by age, 2016/17 (per cent of tenants)[1]

Age group	Private sector	Social sector
16–24	15.8	73.0
25–34	21.0	54.9
35–44	22.5	54.1
45–54	30.4	50.1
55–64	30.7	59.1
65+	44.2	71.4

Note: [1]Recipients are receiving either full or partial support. The sample excludes those with zero gross rents.

Source: English Housing Survey 2016/17

Table 5.1b: Renters receiving housing benefit, by income quintile, 2016/17 (per cent of tenants)

Income quintile	Private sector	Social sector
Quintile 1	50.0	81.9
Quintile 2	36.5	56.9
Quintile 3	17.3	35.8
Quintile 4	5.7	16.1
Quintile 5	1.2	2.9

Source: English Housing Survey 2016/17

Table 5.1a shows that a much higher percentage of tenants in the social sector receive support. This reflects the fact that, while many private tenants are very poor, the private rented sector also accommodates higher-income households, not eligible for benefits. It also reflects household composition in that approximately 70 per cent of single-parent households, who are disproportionately in the social sector, receive support and that families who rent are also more likely to be in social housing. The table suggests that the proportion in receipt of benefit rises sharply for the over-65s. Finally, Table 5.1b shows the high proportion of tenants in the lowest income quintile receiving benefits.

The figures for those receiving support give some limited indication of the minimum extent to which rents would be unaffordable given current incomes and housing circumstances – and based on current policy. In addition, there are some who do not claim benefits (although most of those who do not claim are eligible for only small amounts). More importantly, as already noted, there are now large numbers of tenants affected by additional constraints, notably the welfare cap across the sector, the withdrawal of the spare room subsidy in the social sector and most importantly the limits on LHA in the private sector.[28] All of these mean that some part of residual income is being taken up with housing costs, so households affected by any of these constraints do not have the means to buy their basic necessities. Service charges not covered by benefits may also reduce households' residual income. In addition, some at least of those whose incomes are above the level where they are eligible for benefit will be subject to housing stress – in other words the benefit system, significantly as a consequence of austerity measures, may well not be adequate to eliminate affordability problems.

What households are receiving for their rent differs very significantly between the sectors. In particular, social tenants who pay their rent traditionally had lifetime security. Now, they are more likely to have a fixed-term contract but one which will normally be automatically extended. Private tenants, on the other hand, are usually offered a six month or one-year Assured Shorthold Tenancy and are potentially subject to no-fault eviction clauses at the end of the tenancy period.[29] Equally, the types of accommodation on offer vary between sectors as does the density of occupation and the quality of maintenance and improvement. These are topics we return to in Chapter 12.

Renting, market segmentation and interactions between the tenures

There is a danger of considering the rental sectors independently of owner occupation and the wider economy more generally. At one level, the limitations that have been imposed on access to housing benefit have little to do with an assessment of need but are a result of attempts to limit overall benefits expenditure for macroeconomic purposes. The rising burden of Exchequer costs reflects, not only an increase in the number of recipients, but also a rise in the average payment, which are a consequence of the interrelationships between housing markets and labour markets. Macro policies that affect, for example, house prices, have implications for housing benefit payments, which are not necessarily adequately reflected in policy, especially given the dispersion of responsibilities across government departments. Wages and job security similarly have housing impacts which differ between tenures. The linkages between the tenures and the macroeconomy are complex and we do not have a full quantitative understanding, but it is worth setting out the basics of these interactions in this and the following section.

Two concepts are particularly important. The first concerns *segmentation* which describes the degree to which housing markets and different sectors are separated from one another or are interlinked. Again, private rental markets should not be seen in isolation from wider housing market developments notably in terms of house prices and new supply. This still applies, although to a more limited degree, to the administratively organized social sector.

In the absence of complete segmentation, a change in the price of properties at the top end of the market is likely to be associated with a related percentage change in the price of properties lower down the chain – and there are even some reverse effects. Furthermore, there is a long tradition in housing economics that improvements in the housing stock at the top end trickle down to improvements lower down. This is sometimes used as a justification for general increases in private sector housing supply (see Chapter 6). However, the evidence is that the trickle becomes ever more limited as it moves down-market as a result of growth in new entrants further up the scale and the demand response of these groups, as well as loss of supply through demolitions, conversions and long-term vacancy.

In terms of relative rents between the private and social sectors the segmentation is strong. Rents within the social sector come under a number of different subsidy frameworks but are less obviously related to market rents than it might appear – for example, even for those properties which are most directly related, via the 80 per cent of market rent rule for affordable homes, this is only a maximum. Actual rents charged for these types of tenancies vary enormously in relation to equivalent market rents. Social (or target) rents relate to the dwelling's attributes and to local labour market conditions rather than directly to market rents. The extent that relative rents between property sizes may vary is also controlled. More importantly, allocation rules mean that relative rents are rarely an element in social landlords' decisions as to whom they should grant the tenancy except in lower demand areas and tenants often have very limited choices. Finally, at the limit, in the social sector housing benefit pays the whole rent while in the private rented sector this is rarely the case.

Importantly, housing stock does not always stay in the same tenure: the Right to Buy has transferred more than two million units from social housing to home ownership – 40 per cent of which are now thought to be in the private rented sector.[30] More generally, the growth of the private rented sector, especially since the turn of the century has been achieved by moving large numbers of units from both owner occupation and social renting into private renting as well as through new supply.[31] All of these factors shift the numbers of households impacted by the different influences that determine rents and benefit payments across the rental sector.

The second concept concerns *asymmetric information*. There is a suggestion in Chapter 3 – and more evidence is needed – that long-standing private tenants pay lower rents than new tenants for comparable properties (or at least experience lower rates of increase). One possible explanation is that landlords charge lower rents to those perceived to be good tenants, but they have incomplete information. Good tenants reduce maintenance expenditures and if they remain in the property for longer periods of time, voids and inter-tenancy costs are reduced. Additionally, the costs to landlords are perceived to be higher for those on housing benefit (especially as the tenant has to make up the almost inevitable shortfall) because risks are higher. As a result, on the latest evidence, over 50 per cent of landlords acting for themselves do not wish to let to tenants on housing benefit or Universal Credit.[32] An additional complication is that almost half of all landlords still own only one property, so they have no capacity to spread such risks across a portfolio. The evidence indicates that landlords only increase rents significantly when new tenants take over the property, at which point the market dominates and individual factors are less relevant. The biggest problem with all of the evidence is that survey responses are clearly biased towards mainstream landlords who are following the rules. Equally, the evidence mainly addresses issues of risk once a tenancy has been agreed. The core issue is almost certainly who is not accepted – for instance many Buy to Let mortgages exclude letting to tenants on housing benefit or Universal Credit.

The implications of this lack of information are, first, that some landlords will not enter the market as they cannot be sure their tenants will not end up as claimants, even if they are not when they are accepted. Secondly, and far more importantly, benefit claimants may well suffer stress in finding accommodation and may have to move on more often than the average. Thirdly, they may end up paying rather more for their housing because of the perceived risks. Without benefits, of course, many would be in far worse difficulties and the size of the sector would be smaller, although rents in general are likely to be somewhat lower. However, this differential impact for low-income households with an apparently near certain form of assistance is of significant relevance to how the market works. Policy changes, such as the four-year freeze on the LHA cap, worsens that situation not least because of future uncertainties.

Rents, affordability and the wider economy

As discussed in the previous section, the rental and owner occupied sectors are not entirely independent and changes in the demand for owner occupied housing, reflected in house prices, may have implications for private rents and housing benefit. In 2017/18 housing benefit payments in Great Britain (that is excluding Northern Ireland) stood at £22.3bn, compared with £12bn in 1995/96; and, although there has been a modest decline since the peak in 2014/15, government expenditure plans show little evidence of a projected decline in these totals in the future. Again, as noted previously, total benefit payments reflect the number of recipients and the average benefit per recipient and both are related to conditions in the macroeconomy. The first reflects the probability that any household will receive benefits and depends on tenure, household income, employment, and household characteristics for example. The second takes into account household circumstances and, also, the level of rents. If rents are related to wider conditions in housing markets – notably what is occurring in the owner occupier sector – then housing markets are not fully segmented and excess demand in the owner occupier market may lead to an increase in benefit payments in rental markets. As discussed in the last section, the relationships are stronger in the private than the social sector, but higher proportions of low-income tenants are now housed in the former and so the linkages have become increasingly important.[33]

Figure 5.1 attempts to make the interactions clearer and shows how changes in the macroeconomy can modify affordability for

Figure 5.1: Selected linkages between the macroeconomy, subsidies and affordability

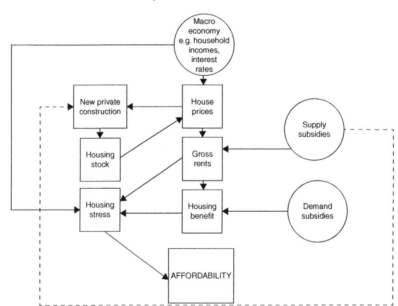

low-income households. The circle at the top of the chart indicates that among the external macroeconomic factors affecting housing are household incomes and interest rates, both of which have strong effects on house prices. The quantitative impacts of these and other variables were discussed in Chapter 3. The boxes capture key housing market variables determined within the system. Although an increase in house prices generates an increase in new construction, typically, this is insufficient to offset the rise in prices caused, for example, by an increase in incomes (see Chapter 6). The key condition was also demonstrated as relationship (3.2). If rental and ownership markets are interlinked, a rise in house prices would be expected to lead to an increase in gross market rents. Again, as shown in the last section, the impact on social rents is much less direct as there are many different rules about how rents are set and adjusted. Under current benefit rules, the rise in gross rents will be fully offset and leave net rents unaffected for all those not affected by other constraints – so the impact on housing stress and affordability is generally felt only by those paying the full rent themselves.[34]

The two circles on the right-hand side summarize the policy regime, in terms of supply or demand interventions. Their role is to 'break' the link between the macroeconomy and low-income housing affordability. A tightening of the rules – for example access limitations for younger households, removal of the spare bedroom subsidy, or limiting the LHA to below the 30th percentile of local market rents – has the intention of cutting payments and therefore worsens affordability. Similarly, changes to the tax and regulatory regimes for owner occupation, for private landlords and developers/landowners all impact on rental supply and rents and therefore affordability.

If the relationship between the macroeconomy and affordability for low-income households is to be quantified, there are a number of steps to be evaluated, some of which have already been explored in earlier chapters:

(i) the relationship between macroeconomic variables and house prices;
(ii) the relationship between house prices and gross market rents;
(iii) the probability that a household with given demographic/ economic characteristics is eligible for benefits;
(iv) for those households eligible for benefits, the amount to be received per week and therefore the net rent paid;
(v) the relationship between net rents, incomes, stress and affordability;

(vi) the sensitivity of affordability to changes in the policy regime; this final element is probably the least understood as it depends on all of the earlier elements.

In particular, Chapter 3 has already discussed extensively the relationship between the *macroeconomy and house prices*, demonstrating that both incomes and the cost of capital have major impacts. Moreover, long-run changes in the ratio of house prices to incomes are strongly driven by the relative growth rates of incomes and housing supply. General increases in private construction improve affordability and reduce benefit payments, but as Chapter 6 demonstrates these will rarely be of sufficient magnitude fully to offset the problem or make a significant difference.

If rental markets operated independently of owner occupation markets, the relationship between *house prices and gross rents* would not be important for either subsidy or affordability purposes. We have argued that at least a degree of segmentation exists, but nonetheless, Chapter 3 finds some relationship between the two variables. But this is not the only way that macroeconomic factors affect tenants. In addition to any indirect link through house prices, tenants are affected directly through changes in their incomes. If incomes do not rise in line with rents, then private tenants may well find themselves in financial stress, whether or not they are eligible for benefits. This can result in slower household formation, increases in concealed households as well as worsening levels of poverty. At the limit, there may be an increased possibility of homelessness with its associated costs for the household, the local authority and the Exchequer.

Furthermore, it is important to note that macro policy also impacts on the tenure mix and therefore, in this context, on the total supply of privately rented housing. For example, tax changes for Buy to Let landlords, as well as mortgage regulation – notably the stress tests now in operation – can significantly affect the available supply at any given rent level – and therefore, given demand, the rents obtainable.

As already noted, *the probability that any household will receive benefits* depends on the level of household income but is also affected by household characteristics such as age and household size and the source of the rented property. The key determinants of the *amount of housing benefit received* are the gross rent paid and the level of household income as well as the sector in which the household lives. Chapter 2 has already explored the relationship between *net rents, incomes, affordability and stress* and the key results were shown as Tables 2.1 and 2.2. To summarize, households are more likely to experience stress if they spend more than 25 per cent of their income on housing costs and are in the lowest income quintiles. However, Figure 2.1 and Table 5.1b indicate that those in the lowest quintiles are more likely to receive housing benefit, which improves affordability and reduces, although not always removes, housing stress. Table 2.2 provided one example of the sensitivity of affordability to the policy regime. In the absence of benefit, housing stress would rise sharply for the lower-income groups. This is of course the reason for the policy.

In conclusion

This chapter has focused on the determinants of rental affordability in a world where many different policy approaches have been used to try to ensure that low-income households are able to access what government and the wider society regard as adequate housing. The starting point must be rents and incomes and in particular that, once rent is paid, there is enough left over to buy the necessities of life. This in turn brings in issues of household composition, age and vulnerability and indeed the way that government policy impacts on the costs of other necessities, for example whether education is provided free of charge. Historically, government intervention was mainly in the form of regulation, which often left poorer households worse off. This led to an increasing emphasis on government subsidies to provide a supply of adequate-standard housing that could be let at sub-market rents. In the private rented sector, it was also a major reason for introducing rent controls which enabled those able to find such accommodation to pay but also negatively impacted on the quality of housing available and access difficulties for new entrants.

Since the 1970s, however, the main government interventions have concerned income-related housing assistance which is more readily targeted at those in need and, in principle, can ensure that all households who are able to find rented accommodation have sufficient income to obtain both adequate housing and buy other necessities. In practice, the implementation of wider government policies has significantly eroded that safety net. We return to the practicalities of both supply and demand side policies in later chapters.

But perhaps the most important message from this chapter is that housing affordability cannot be siloed from the affordability of other goods and services, including necessities. Equally, rents and the availability of rental housing are determined not only by observed demand and supply for rental properties. They are also affected by the factors (including macroeconomic policies) that impact on demand and supply of housing in other tenures, as well as the comparative profitability and value of housing as compared to other uses of resources. The system is thus integrated, although policy often takes little notice of these interactions.

6

What Determines the Number of New Homes Built?

Introduction

Consider two alternative interpretations of conditions in Britain. The first argues that there must be a housing shortage because house prices have consistently risen faster than other prices – real house prices have increased by approximately 3.5 per cent per annum since the early 1970s. The solution, therefore, is to build more homes led primarily by the private sector. This will help not only those on higher incomes, but the benefits will also trickle down to those on lower incomes and in this case the need for additional social housing is reduced. Our problems, therefore, arise from the inability to construct more homes. Under this view, the main constraint has arisen from the nature of the land use planning system, which is excessively restrictive (and is discussed in detail in Chapters 9 and 10), although additional constraints have occurred from shortages of skilled labour and finance. Furthermore, the concentration of the residential construction industry into a small number of large builders, which dominate the market, has reduced competition. Arguably, this has, in turn, weakened the incentives to innovate in an industry that has long suffered from low productivity compared with, for example, manufacturing industry. Moreover, the objectives of builders have not necessarily been to meet demand as quickly as possible for fear of disturbing the market. Instead, builders would prefer to bring forward new properties gradually in line with the ability of the market to absorb the increase.

The second view emphasizes the role of housing as an investment as well as a form of shelter.[1] Chapter 3 discussed the relationship between the two, including that between market rents and house prices. However, since the expansion of the Buy to Let market in the late 1990s, market rents appear to have increased more slowly than house prices and, indeed, have risen at a similar rate to overall inflation. There are multiple reasons for the differences between rent and house price growth rates discussed in earlier chapters, but one view is that the near constancy of real market rents suggests that there is no absolute shortage in the number of dwellings to meet the number of households (although we showed in Chapter 4 that the number of households is itself affected by housing market conditions). Rather, house prices are being driven mainly by investment demand, particularly since the returns on financial assets have been low. The demand for second homes, for example, was discussed in Chapter 4. The problem, therefore, is primarily one of distribution. The first view is the main focus of the current chapter, whereas Chapter 7 is more concerned with the second.

Industrial structure and productivity

At first sight, the discussion seems simple and straightforward. Housebuilding is characterised by the existence of a large number of relatively small firms. They also use production techniques that are labour-intensive and change relatively slowly. They also are 'flexible' in order to be able to adapt to potentially large variations in output. Generally, as a result, scale economies are low, which helps both to make entry and exit from the industry relatively easy and to explain the small average firm size. Housing supply, consequently, seems to fit neatly into the standard economics lexicon as a competitive industry.[2]

However, Michael Ball goes on to demonstrate that the industry is not that simple and the structure varies internationally. Table 6.1 shows that, at least in terms of firm size, measured by employment, residential building is still dominated by large numbers of small operatives. Eighty per cent of firms had three or fewer operatives in 2016, although most of these will rarely complete a new property, concentrating primarily on extensions and improvements and acting as sub-contractors in the new build sector. Furthermore, construction (rather than just housebuilding) is a low productivity industry measured in terms of output per hour: between 1994 and 2017, productivity grew by only 0.7 per cent per annum compared with 2.2 per cent in manufacturing, 1.6 per cent in production industries more widely and 1.2 per cent in services.

Narrowing the analysis to house builders, the National House Building Council (NHBC) register shows the decline in the number of small or medium-sized enterprises (SMEs) since the 1980s, a fall which accelerated during the GFC, leading to an increasingly heavy concentration of production. At their peak in 1988 there were 12,215 SME builders (constructing between 1 and 100 units per annum), but this had fallen to under 3,000 by 2013 after the GFC. Although in 2008 the Office for Fair Trading found no evidence of uncompetitive practices, the decline in the number of SMEs has attracted concern and there are a number of contributory factors to the fall. These include take overs and mergers by larger companies in part to extend access to land across a greater range of sites. As will be discussed, builders are concerned with absorption capacities and this is less of an issue where they are constructing modest numbers of homes across a large number of locations. Small firms have also been affected by retirements of older workers and owners and a failure to replace them sufficiently by younger operatives. Moreover, at a time of wider bank credit shortages during the GFC, SMEs suffered disproportionately, although most large developers were also forced to restructure. Finally, SMEs have been affected by the tendency of local authority plans to target larger sites, more suitable for the volume builders and are more heavily constrained by planning regulations and delays.[3]

Long-run trends in housing construction

Figure 6.1 shows the total number of new housing completions since 1856. Excluding the war years when building came to a halt, two characteristics stand out; first, there was a step change in output after the First World War, which coincided with the introduction of significant building subsidies for the first time for both the public and private sectors (noted in Chapter 5). Secondly, there has been no increase in the trend since that time. The strong expansion after the Second World War partly reflected slum clearance programmes originally introduced in the 1930s but primarily taking place between the 1950s and 1970s, so that net additions to the housing stock – that is, excluding demolitions – were noticeably smaller than gross completions. The absence of a positive trend is unusual in economic time series – usually variables such as GDP, consumers' expenditure or investment grow over time – but the absence of a trend in housing completions is not confined to Britain; the US and Australia, for example, show similar patterns.[4] Nevertheless, some care in interpretation is needed; the figures refer to the *number* of dwellings and, so, do not allow for

Table 6.1: Size distribution of firms (by employment) where the main trade is residential building, 2016, Great Britain

Size of firm (by number employed)	Main trade residential buildings
0 (sole proprietors)	3,356
1	15,798
2–3	10,694
4–7	4,053
8–13	1,391
14–24	728
25–34	251
35–59	294
60–79	88
80–114	82
115–299	121
300–599	33
600–1,199	17
1,200+	14
All firms	**36,920**

Source: Office for National Statistics

improvements in quality or in the quantity of housing services that each dwelling can provide. Importantly, nor do they include the large amount of extension work that is carried out each year to the existing dwelling stock.

Figure 6.1 also shows that completions have been below trend since the 1980s but, from Figure 6.2, the decline has been confined to the social sector where the fall in local authority construction has not been fully offset by an increase in provision by housing associations. This graph lies behind the common assertion that construction is at its lowest level since the Second World War; in fact, *private* construction has been highly volatile, but has experienced no long-run change.

Explaining the trends in private construction

Considerable attention has been paid in the literature to one key parameter – the price elasticity of housing supply – which shows the sensitivity of house building to changes in house prices. The reason for its importance is that basic housing models show that the greater is the responsiveness of construction to house prices, the more likely it is that an increase in demand will generate a rise in new homes rather than adding to price pressures.[5] But even relatively simple questions such as the price elasticity produce a wide range of estimates in empirical studies, both within countries and internationally, and this is clearly not helpful for policy. Low elasticities imply an upward trend in real

Figure 6.1: Total housing completions, England and Wales (000s), 1856–2018

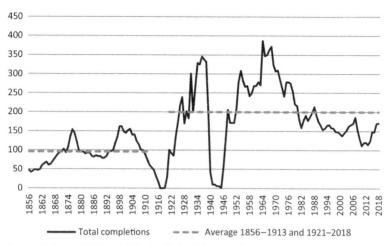

Source: Holmans (2005) and Office for National Statistics for later years

Figure 6.2: Housing completions, private and social sectors, Great Britain (numbers), 1946–2018

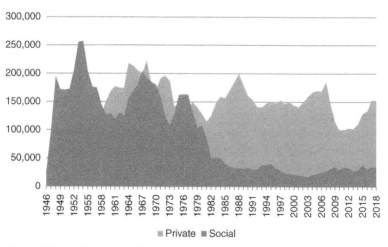

Source: Office for National Statistics

house prices, whereas very high elasticities suggest little change in real prices. Furthermore, price bubbles are less likely to occur when the price elasticity of supply is high.[6]

In fact, the results differ according to the indicator of house building chosen; there are a number of measures that can be used to describe housing construction – housing starts, completions, net additions to the housing stock and investment are the most commonly chosen and the time-series trends are not the same.[7] The time-series properties affect the estimated price elasticity of supply and those construction indicators that have no trend are more likely to show low price elasticities.

It is also the case that English government housing targets are now set in terms of net additions, which is a wider definition than completions, and considerably larger in size, although this was less so when social housing and slum clearance was at its height. In 2017/18 in England, 222,000 net additions took place; of these new buildings were the largest component (195,000), but net additions also include demolitions, which are now modest (8,100), conversions (such as changes of houses into flats, 4,500) and changes of use (particularly from offices, which occurred under permitted development rights and, therefore, did not require full planning permission, 29,700[8]). Clearly, the wider definition makes it easier to reach the government's target of 300,000 units per annum by the mid-2020s.

Nevertheless most (but by no means all[9]) empirical work has concentrated on the factors that influence the level of housing starts on the grounds that the decision to begin construction is the indicator most under the control of the builder. Quarterly private housing starts in thousands are shown in the first frame of Figure 6.3 and relative to the volume of housing transactions – the number of sales of all properties – in the second frame. In both cases, starts exhibit significant seasonality (building is affected by the weather), which contributes to the volatility within each year. In the first frame, the recessions in the early 1990s and following the GFC are particularly evident. But these are less clear cut in the second frame which standardizes on the overall level of market sales; since transactions also fell sharply in these downturns, the ratio showed less change.

Therefore, the first point to make is that there is a strong correlation between the level of new housing construction and overall activity in the housing market.[10] One explanation is that builders prefer to 'drip feed' new properties onto the market according to current market conditions, in order to avoid flooding the market and potentially driving down prices. A further explanation is that transactions provide a forward indicator of the future state of the market, given the inherent

Figure 6.3: Private housing starts and starts/transactions, Great Britain

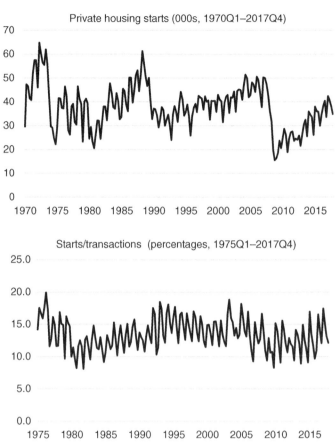

Source: Office for National Statistics

difficulties in predicting house prices, and therefore profitability. To see why this is the case, it is helpful to consider construction, transactions and house prices together; all three variables, in fact, are sensitive to whether conditions of excess demand or supply exist in the housing market (that is, whether there is disequilibrium in the market), but they do not all change at the same time. In a downturn, sellers are, typically, reluctant to reduce the prices of their houses and, so, the length of time that the property is on the market is likely to rise and, therefore, by definition transactions fall; thus, the first variable to be affected is the number of property transactions. But since transactions are a forward indicator of future price falls, the level of housing starts, then, begins to decline. Only later do 'sticky' prices start to fall. In summary, the

Figure 6.4: Real house prices (2015=100 and annual percentage change), 1969Q1–2017Q4, UK

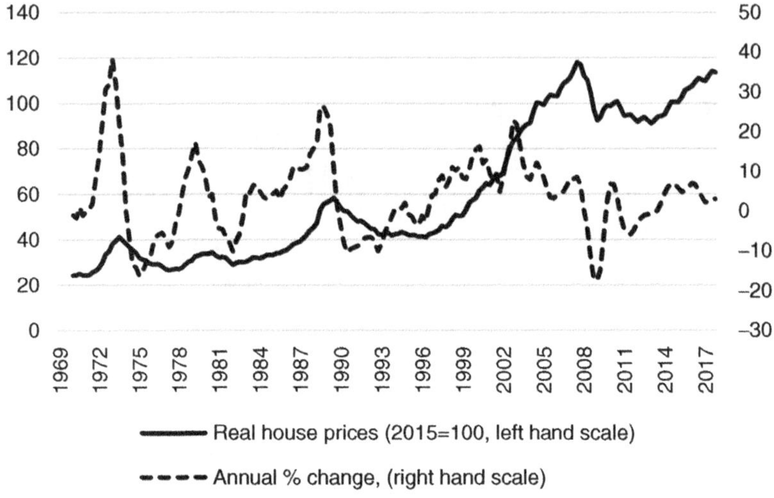

Real house prices (2015=100, left hand scale)

Annual % change, (right hand scale)

Source: Office for National Statistics

evidence suggests that the chain of action is, first, transactions, then construction and, finally, prices.

In its most basic form, housing construction is determined by profitability although, as demonstrated below, other variables also play an important role. As a key element in profitability, we might expect the *level* of house prices (and construction costs) to have a strong effect on housing starts. But, in fact, it is not the *level* of house prices that has the greatest influence, but the *rate of growth*, where the latter reflects the change in the former (the two are shown in Figure 6.4). Empirically, there are two reasons why this occurs. First, from the previous arguments, construction expands when there is excess demand in the market and excess demand is associated with a stronger growth rate of prices. Therefore, price growth measures the extent of market disequilibrium. The second reason is more technical; in Figure 6.4 the level of real prices has a trend – as already noted, the price level increases by approximately 3.5 per cent per annum, but the growth rate does not. But a variable, such as housing starts, which has no trend (Figure 6.3) can only be explained by variables that also have no trend,[11] and the growth rate of house prices is a good example. In fact, in Britain, the US and Australia, it is the case that the growth rate in prices has the strongest effect on construction.[12]

Internationally, the cost of finance is also widely found to affect the level of construction since the industry relies heavily on borrowing and

Britain has been no exception. But data shortages make it difficult to test the importance of the availability of credit in the UK in addition to its cost, although the former is generally believed to have affected builders – particularly small builders – during the GFC.[13] However, the factors discussed previously do not fully account for the fall in construction during the GFC and, typically, the errors from equations using these variables are large – in the order of 10 per cent even within the sample estimation period. Given the volatility this is unsurprising, but there are clearly additional factors that affect construction. These include the impact of the weather on house building,[14] impact fees (in the US),[15] crowding out,[16] and land use and topography.[17] Skilled labour shortages are also widely believed to impose constraints, although these have attracted less academic research.[18] But it is the impact of planning controls which has been most widely discussed in both Britain and the US.[19]

Planning and housing construction

Policy related to land use planning is discussed in detail in Chapters 9 and 10 but, additionally, there are analytical issues that arise here. Much of housing policy since the 2004 Barker Review of Housing Supply has attempted to develop ways to increase the responsiveness of land release to market signals and, therefore, increase construction. Three issues have attracted particular attention: the relationship between planning and the responsiveness of construction to price signals (again captured through the price elasticity of supply); the relationship between planning, construction and the level (and volatility) of house prices; and the relationship between planning, market risk and required profit margins on developments.

Testing the impact of planning on changes in aggregate measures of housing construction is not straightforward and, indeed, most of the literature does not adopt this approach. This is because national planning indicators do not possess sufficient variation over time – changes to planning legislation take place infrequently. However, an exception occurred with the introduction of the plan-led system in the 1990 Town and Country Planning Act, which attracted widespread criticism from builders and academics. Table 6.2 shows the responsiveness of housing starts before and after 1990 to the factors discussed earlier. For comparison, the second column shows the results from a published study over a slightly different time period.[20] In a similar manner to Table 3.1 in Chapter 3, each value shows an elasticity; therefore, the first entry shows that in the study covering the period 1973Q2–2007Q4, a 1 per cent increase in market disequilibrium – measured by the difference between housing demand and supply – would be expected to increase

Table 6.2: The long-run responsiveness of private housing starts to market indicators

Market indicator	1973 Q2–2007 Q4	1973Q4–1989Q4	1990Q1–2017Q3
Market disequilibrium*	0.448	**0.998**	**0.301**
Transactions*	0.481	0.430	0.515
House prices/construction costs*	0.157	**0.272**	**0.109**
Interest rates**	-0.024	-0.030	-0.030

Notes: * elasticity; **semi-elasticity

Source: Ball et al (2010) for the second column and authors' estimates for the remaining columns

the number of housing starts by 0.45 per cent. The only difference in interpretation arises with respect to the interest rate variable, which implies that a 1 percentage *point* increase in market interest rates would reduce starts by 2.4 per cent.

The key comparison arises from the last two columns. This shows that the responses to the degree of market disequilibrium and the ratio of house prices to construction costs (shown in bold) were approximately three times larger prior to the legislation than afterwards. The legislative change does appear to have had an important impact on construction – reducing the responsiveness to market signals – although the responsiveness to borrowing costs or housing transactions changed much less. Simulations using the construction equations in Table 6.2 and the house price equations in Table 3.1 indicate that the legislative change may have reduced starts by approximately 10 per cent to 20 per cent per annum.

Rather than concentrating on legislative changes over time, many studies in the literature exploit the fact that the strength of planning controls varies internationally or across areas within countries.[21] A widespread finding is that the price elasticity of supply is low in the UK by most international standards[22] and it is inferred that this is attributable to the restrictiveness of the planning system. Across English local authorities, as the theory implies, house prices are more responsive to changes in earnings in those areas that face strong planning controls.[23] As noted previously, in response to demand changes, the effect on prices will be greater where the price elasticity of supply is weak. However, some care is needed with international comparisons since the methodologies and the choice of construction variable vary considerably.[24]

In Chapter 3, Table 3.3, we saw that there was a strong correlation between house prices (rather than construction) and the strength of US state planning regulations and the evidence is striking.[25] Similarly, although England is subject to a nationwide planning framework, there are large variations in the attitudes towards housing development between local authorities with controls typically being stronger in the south of the country where the demand for housing is highest and Conservative authorities more in evidence.[26] Local spatial studies that directly include measures of regulation are, perhaps, more convincing than those that infer the strength of controls from the estimated price responses.[27] For example, low local supply responses can arise from the constraints arising from historical land use patterns rather than regulation,[28] but those that include planning indicators typically support the view that planning restricts the amount of development.

Expectations and uncertainty introduce a further strand to the literature. For example, builders have to form expectations of future prices because of the length of time it takes to plan and build properties, although we showed that current transactions can act as a forward indicator. Particularly, when future conditions are uncertain – including the probability of obtaining planning permission – there is an incentive to delay construction during times of price volatility.[29] Furthermore, uncertainty may give rise to what are known as backward-bending supply curves, where a rise in current prices actually reduces the level of construction. This is because, even if prices are currently rising and it is profitable to build, it may still be better to delay construction if prices are expected to rise further, because in effect building today gives up a valuable future option. A consequence of the level of uncertainty is that builders require high profit margins, frequently cited as 20 per cent.[30]

Increasing housebuilding and the effect on affordability

Relationship (3.2) in Chapter 3 summarized the impact of housing supply on changes in affordability. This depends in the long run on the relative growth rates of income and the housing stock. In this section we explore this further, including the extent to which expansion of supply can realistically be expected to improve affordability.

At one level it appears obvious that, if affordability is worsening, then there must be a housing shortage and, so, increasing housing supply would mitigate the decline. Particularly since the publication of the Barker Review of Housing Supply,[31] land use planning has been the focus of attention, although the debate has been going on for much longer than this. The 2019 reforms to the National Planning Policy Framework set out in Planning Practice Guidance include a formula by which all local authorities are required to incorporate affordability indicators, based on median house price to earnings ratios, into local needs assessments. More radical proposals have argued that presumption in favour of land development should be triggered when land prices exceed a threshold, unless a public interest can be demonstrated.[32]

The Barker Review provided estimates of the increase in housing supply that would be necessary to reduce the rate of growth of real house prices to European average levels. The headline figures suggested a doubling of output would be necessary from the levels at the time. This would not be just a temporary change but would have to be a permanent shift on a scale that had rarely been observed historically. From Figure 6.3, since the late 1960s, private starts have exhibited considerable volatility but no permanent upward shift. These conclusions were later broadly confirmed in more detailed empirical analysis.[33] To stress the point, in order to have a significant effect on affordability – however it is measured – increases in supply have to be long-lasting and large. But this does not imply that generating increases in supply are unimportant. It simply emphasizes the scale of the problem and the policy changes that would be needed. Most reports that advocate supply increases as the solution fail to provide quantitative estimates of the necessary changes or to consider adequately the feasibility of these changes. As a guide, estimates published in 2011 indicated that a 50 per cent increase in the number of housing starts in England for ten years compared with current levels might improve affordability, measured by the price to earnings ratio, by about one percentage point.[34] But even increases of this magnitude could not bring price to earnings ratios – the measure required in the National Planning Policy Framework – back to the levels experienced, for example, in 2000. In that year the median house price to earnings ratio in England stood at 4.2 compared with 8.0 in 2018. As discussed in Chapter 2, this reflects the weaknesses of the price to earnings ratio as an affordability indicator, because the rise between the years has occurred from the capitalization of low interest rates into prices – an issue to which we return in the next chapter. This also suggests that it is not possible to bring back this affordability indicator to the equilibrium level implied by the National Planning Policy Framework (4.0) by increases in supply alone, because the current value reflects interest rates as well as supply shortages.

Social housing and crowding out

There is now a wider recognition that the trickle-down benefits from a general expansion in market housing are insufficient[35] to improve conditions significantly for low-income households. Indeed, the problems are not confined only to those on lower incomes, and it is hard to reach any other conclusion than that an expansion of social or affordable housing needs to play a role. Resistance to an expansion is not now primarily ideological but arises from concerns with methods of public finance and the possibility that an expansion might crowd out private housing since the sectors compete for resources.[36] Figure 6.2 shows housing completions since the Second World War split between the private sector and housing associations/local authorities; as noted previously, since the ending of private building controls in the 1950s, private completions have exhibited no trend, although considerable volatility. However, there has been a major decline in local authority construction since the 1970s, not fully compensated by a rise in housing association building. These changes are well known, but slightly misrepresent the levels of affordable housing since the private sector values shown in this figure include some homes built under Section 106 agreements and other initiatives (see Chapter 10 for further discussion).

Although purely market-based solutions are unlikely to provide adequately for those in the lower part of the income distribution, one objection to an expansion in social housing arises from possible crowding out. The crowding out of private construction by social housing may arise from two sources; 'old style' occurs from competition for resources (both for land and other factors such as skilled labour and finance) between the two sectors, particularly at times of full employment. This is less likely to occur at times of excess industry capacity and social housing can be used counter-cyclically since it is less constrained by market pressures. But this is not to say that crowding out can never occur and there is international evidence to support this.[37] The second source arises from the requirement to provide social housing under Section 106 agreements which may, under some circumstances, reduce the output of private developments.[38]

In conclusion

The Introduction put forward alternative views concerning the causes of price rises and the implications for possible supply shortages. The first – which has become the conventional (and widely accepted) wisdom – is discussed in this chapter; the rise in real house prices reflects a shortage of homes and the land use planning system plays a significant role. The rise in real prices took place mainly after the Second World War when controls were strengthened. The arrival of the plan-led system in 1990 reduced the opportunities for individual action by builders and there is evidence from econometric work that housebuilding became less sensitive to market indicators after that time. These legislative changes are discussed further in Chapters 9 and 10. A key indicator is the huge difference between the agricultural price of land and the price of land in similar locations with planning permission.[39] Further evidence, as discussed in Chapter 3, comes from the international literature which suggests that those areas and countries that have more stringent planning controls exhibit stronger price trends and volatility.

We showed that increases in housing supply can improve affordability, but changes need to be large and sustained to produce a significant effect. They cannot reduce price to earnings ratios back to the levels in, say, 2000 but this reflects the problems of using this indicator as a measure of affordability. Furthermore, supply expansion is only one part of the package needed and a general expansion in private supply does not necessarily filter down to those on low incomes. More comprehensive approaches also include measures aimed at the demand side of the market and these begin to be discussed in the next chapter.

7

Housing Demand, Financial Markets and Taxation

Introduction

Housing is an investment in addition to providing services as a place to live. However, both depend heavily on the cost and availability of mortgage finance. This chapter is, therefore, firstly concerned with the growth in mortgage finance, monetary policies more generally and their effects on housing demand. In the UK, the mortgage stock as a percentage of household disposable income is now more than three times higher than it was at the start of the 1970s when the market was heavily regulated. Other countries have also experienced sharp increases as a consequence of liberalization of national mortgage and more general finance markets, the expansion in international finance and the wider securitization of mortgages. Yet, some groups – notably aspiring first-time buyers even with unimpaired credit histories – struggle to obtain mortgages or at least are required to provide deposits beyond their means. Therefore, there appears to be an anomaly or at least a distributional problem. One increasingly important reason arises from the use of housing as an investment at times of low yields on financial assets and as a hedge against inflation. Chapter 4 showed how rising volumes of mortgage credit allow existing owners and other investors to purchase additional homes without increasing their debt relative to the market value of their property portfolios.

In principle, the increased availability of mortgages may generate changes in real house prices and, under some conditions, may squeeze out potential first-time buyers from the market. Therefore, are rising prices primarily occurring from credit-fuelled investment? Furthermore, macro stabilization policies disproportionately affect first-time buyers because current owners are less affected by controls on loan to income or loan to value ratios. These problems require us to look closely at the relationship between house prices and monetary policy, a topic also explored in Chapter 8. This is an area of the literature which has expanded rapidly in recent years. In the UK, the relationship between house prices and debt is complicated by the Buy to Let market and, in the US, by the sub-prime market and the increase in lending to non-conventional borrowers. In other words, the nature of the market and its customers has changed as the more conventional market in loans has become satiated.

Housing demand is also influenced by fiscal as well as monetary policy and the effects of taxation and subsidies for owners provide the second topic for the chapter. Although still controversial, subsidies are sometimes justified on the grounds of the externalities to which ownership gives rise, for example the promotion of greater employment stability, better citizens and neighbourhoods,[1] or as a contribution to improving equality and reducing the costs to government for older households. But the danger of subsidies is that they are often capitalized into house prices rather than aiding affordability for aspiring owners, even in the longer term. The idea that there may be too much investment in homes due to subsidies is not new and dates back to a literature from the 1970s, but has been recently resurrected in both academic and policy circles; this argues that tax subsidies to housing have led to over-investment to the detriment of investment in 'more productive' industries such as manufacturing. We saw in Chapter 6 that productivity in construction is low compared with manufacturing and, indeed, most other industrial sectors. Therefore, arguments about a possible over supply of housing are not just about monetary policy, but also fiscal policy.

Trends in mortgage indebtedness

As noted in the last section, growth in mortgages has been an international phenomenon and the UK has not been alone. But internationally, mortgage markets developed historically along different paths and still exhibit varying structures today.[2] The US system of secondary mortgage markets arose originally in the early years of the twentieth century, although the collapse of property prices in the Great Depression led to its reconfiguration in the 1930s. The existence of a secondary market in securitized mortgage debt, in principle, increases the liquidity of the mortgage system and reduces mortgage rates to households, through the spreading of risk. These virtues are particularly relevant in the US federal system but have also been put forward to support the case for other countries adopting the US model.[3] Although perhaps less transparent than the retail funding model, securitized markets were seen as an efficient mortgage market structure, reducing the likelihood of credit shortages, since countries with savings surpluses can, in effect, provide funding for those with savings shortages.

By contrast, in the UK, building societies which dominated the market until the early 1980s were originally developed as mutual organizations to promote home ownership among members and relied heavily on a retail funding model. Within continental Europe, Denmark introduced a bond system in 1797 which is still current and is often called the best housing finance system in the world.[4] Germany also introduced a covered bond system in the eighteenth century. A central difference from mortgage-backed securities is that the institutions that package the mortgage loans into covered bonds keep the loans on their books. More rural economies have traditionally relied heavily on family support or informal networks to provide housing finance, so that official institutional borrowing still often plays a smaller role. Furthermore, internationally, there appears to be little relationship between mortgage debt and home ownership rates, recognizing that the aims of a well-functioning mortgage system are wider than simply promoting ownership.

Figure 7.1 shows the change in mortgage debt as a percentage of GDP before the GFC and in 2017 for a selection of European countries and the US and Australia. They are ordered by the debt ratio in 2017. With notable exceptions, most countries either did not experience a fall in debt during the GFC or indebtedness had recovered by 2017. The prominent exceptions are Ireland and the US where debt fell sharply (and to a lesser extent the UK, Spain and Portugal). But it was not the case that those countries that were highly indebted before the GFC experienced the largest falls; for instance, both the Netherlands and Denmark have maintained particularly high debt ratios.

The experiences of three countries are considered in more detail – the US, UK and Australia where home ownership rates are broadly similar (and Chapter 4 showed that rates had fallen in each case in recent years). The US and the UK were heavily affected by the GFC, but Australia emerged relatively unscathed. Figure 7.2 shows that debt levels in the US and UK are similar, despite the fact that, historically, their finance systems developed differently. But the UK liberalization of mortgage markets led to an expansion in bank mortgage lending and to the use of wholesale funding which became important for a short time in the early 1980s and then again from the 1990s. Australia

Figure 7.1: Ratio of outstanding residential loans to GDP (per cent)

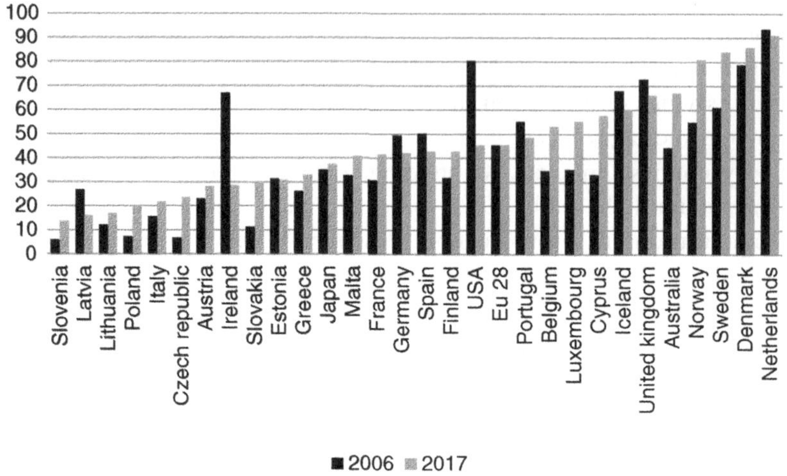

■ 2006 ▨ 2017

Source: European Mortgage Federation

originally followed the UK retail model, but the mortgage-backed securities market took off on a large scale from 1997.

The figure shows the stock of housing mortgage debt relative to household disposable income, rather than GDP since most mortgage debt is held by the household sector. Although the available data start later in the case of Australia (from 1990), the ratios show strong upward trends in all cases. For the UK, four distinct phases are evident, corresponding to institutional mortgage market developments. In the first phase, up to the early 1980s, the ratio is low, reflecting the dominance of building societies, which provided approximately 80 per cent of the mortgage stock; the existence of the building societies' interest rate cartel; the society-specific government regulations; and the entirely retail deposit-based funding model. At the time, mortgage availability was often insufficient to meet mortgage demand and rationing was common, using restrictions on the proportion of the purchase price that could be financed by a mortgage (the loan to value ratio) and the size of the loan relative to the household's income (the loan to income ratio). Additionally, the potential borrower was often required to save with the lender for a period before becoming eligible for a loan and the lender might favour couples over single persons. An important point for the later analysis is that the constraints were *imposed* by the lender, partly because of insufficient funds to meet demand but also because of the culture of the building society system. They were not *chosen* by the household who may well have preferred to take out

Figure 7.2: Mortgage debt as a percentage of household disposable income, UK, US and Australia, 1969–2017

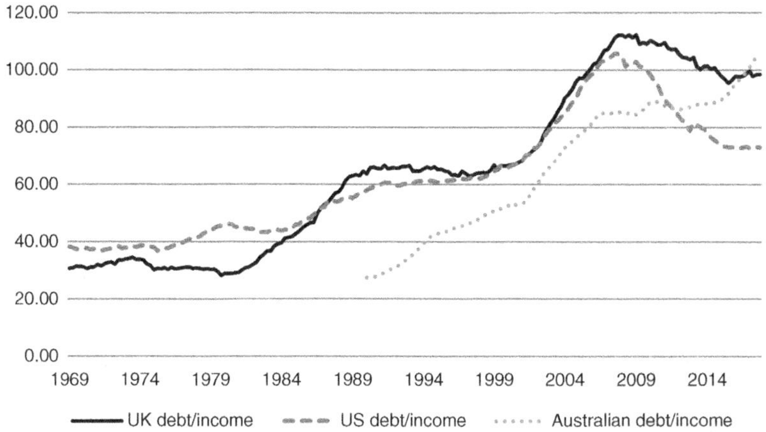

Sources: UK – Bank of England and ONS; US – Federal Reserve Board and Bureau of Economic Analysis; Australia – Reserve Bank of Australia

a larger mortgage. Therefore, the demand for housing – and house price increases – were constrained by the availability of finance; we expect, therefore, to observe a *causal* relationship where changes in house prices are affected by indicators such as the loan to value and loan to income ratios, since they represent an easing or tightening of credit conditions.

This was to change in the second phase which continued until the early 1990s and Figure 7.2 shows the growth of lending as the market was liberalized. Debt rose sharply over this period with households adjusting their portfolios to more unconstrained positions. Again, and importantly for the later analysis, as a reasonable approximation, mortgage shortages were not generally a feature of the market for conventional borrowers. In contrast to the earlier period, as long as borrowers could satisfy minimum conditions in terms of credit worthiness, typically they could *choose* their desired loan to value and loan to income ratios, although still required to provide a modest (by today's standards) deposit; this implies that, for conventional borrowers and homes, housing demand (and house prices) were less affected by variations in credit availability. As noted in Chapter 3, we still expect to observe a *correlation* between changes in house prices and changes in mortgages, but there is no *causality* or the causality may be the other way round – the change in the demand for mortgage debt is determined by changes in house prices. In fact, the house price models in Table 3.1

take this into account and exclude indicators of credit availability in unconstrained periods.[5]

However, the *cost* of finance remains important and, in fact, the demand for housing and house prices become more sensitive to changes in mortgage interest rates because demand is less constrained by the availability of finance. This is discussed further in Chapter 8. Finally, notice from Figure 7.2 that the aggregate debt to income ratio in the US also rose over the whole period, but the discrete change that occurred in the UK around 1980 did not take place in the US because there were no similar changes to the structure of financial services around this time. This does not necessarily mean there were no mortgage shortages in the US, for example, in poorer or lower quality neighbourhoods, but it does suggest that applying the same model in different institutional conditions needs to be treated with caution.

The third phase, from the early to mid-1990s, was a period of economic recession in the UK but the long-term nature of mortgage contracts ensured that debt did not fall significantly. Households could only reduce debt by: (1) selling their properties, but both transactions volumes and prices fell during the period, (2) early repayment of principal, which was difficult for many households during a recession or (3) by mortgage default. Although default rates reached record levels in the period, under the UK system, households still remain liable for debt in contrast to some US states.

In the fourth phase, the subsequent boom in mortgage lending is apparent until the 2008 GFC in all three countries but subsequently the changes differed. Although the debt to income ratio fell in both the US and the UK – the first time this had occurred over the sample period – the decline was much sharper in the US, reflecting the greater impact of the sub-prime market and the much larger increase in default rates. Defaults in the UK were very small as compared to those experienced in the early 1990s. By contrast, the increase in debt continued unabated in Australia. Indeed, by 2017, the Australian ratio appears to have overtaken the other two countries.

Lending controls and the distributional consequences

Even with a modest decline in the UK debt *stock* to income ratio – the ratio still remains well above that at the start of the century – net mortgage advances expressed relative to the level of house prices (see Figure 7.3) have never recovered after the GFC. In fact, real net advances appear to remain below the level of the pre-liberalization period of the 1970s (although this conclusion needs to be treated with

Figure 7.3: Net mortgage advances divided by the house price index (£m, at 2015 house prices), 1970–2017, UK

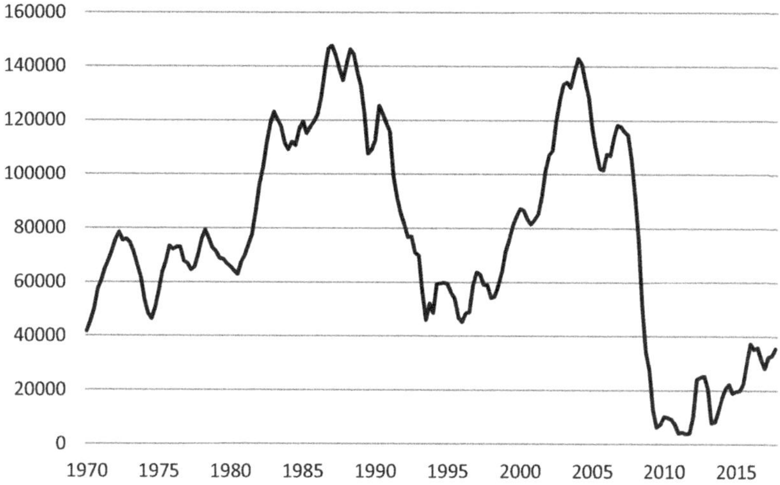

Note: Net advances are derived as the difference between the mortgage stock in any quarter and the stock in the same quarter of the previous year.

Sources: Bank of England and Office for National Statistics

some caution because of changes in definition over time). This suggests a possible return to the era of mortgage shortages and, indeed, this is incorporated into the measure of the user cost of capital in Chapter 3.

As discussed earlier, one indicator of shortage is the percentage deposit that purchasers are required to provide (which is equal to a hundred minus the loan to value ratio). Typically, deposits do not provide a constraint for current owners moving upmarket because they are able to reinvest the equity in their existing property but the deposit requirements for first-time buyers are more onerous (averaging approximately 20 per cent of the purchase price in 2019). There is, however, some evidence that the deposits partly reflect choice – even for first-time buyers – because of risk aversion and the use of the Bank of Mum and Dad to support borrowing.[6] However, the aggregate indicator hides important underlying changes. Those households most at risk of default have generally been those taking out high-value loans in proportion to incomes or the value of the property, those where household income is volatile or those where evidence of income is not provided when the loan is taken out. Since 2014 the Financial Policy Committee (FPC) of the Bank of England has had powers of Direction which currently limit the number of mortgages at loan to income ratios exceeding 4.5 to 15 per cent of new mortgage lending. New borrowers are also required to undertake stress tests to ensure that they can adequately respond to significant increases in interest rates.

Additionally, the FPC has powers over the proportion of loans exceeding loan to value limits, but these have yet to be used.[7] Importantly, the Directions are not intended directly to constrain current lending but are an insurance against future fluctuations in the housing and macroeconomic environments. Indeed, since the introduction of the controls, high-value lending has remained well below the permissible levels and the historical norm and controls appear to have had only a modest impact on lending, given the tightening of lenders' own underwriting standards. In 2007, before the GFC, the proportion of regulated residential loans for which households were not required to provide evidence on their incomes[8] exceeded 20 per cent of the total. The share had already started to fall by 2009 and in 2017 the proportion was close to zero. Furthermore, in 2007, approximately 4 per cent of loans both exceeded 95 per cent of the purchase price and 3.5 times the income of single borrowers (2.75 times the incomes of joint borrowers), but these loans had almost disappeared by 2009 and have never recovered.[9]

Arguably, the cost of macro stability has been weaker access to credit for first-time buyers and the thrust of direct housing policy has been to mitigate the deposit constraints (the main scheme, Help to Buy, is discussed in Chapter 13). For those who can achieve ownership themselves, or have family support, the costs, in terms of mortgage repayments, are not exceptional by historical standards, but access is constrained by the inability to raise sufficient finance.

The Buy to Let market

The expansion of the UK Buy to Let market has come under increasing scrutiny from government and the Bank of England, particularly because of concerns with macro stability, which has led to the introduction of lending controls and stress tests for Buy to Let landlords. Figure 7.4 shows the growth in the share of gross mortgage advances going to Buy to Let investors since 2007 and adds loans to first-time buyers for comparison. Although the share fell sharply during the GFC, it steadily recovered until early 2016, when it approached the first-time buyer share. However, investor loans peaked with a spike in the first quarter of 2016, after the announcement in November 2015 of the addition, in April 2016, of a three percentage point stamp duty rate surcharge for these and for second home

Figure 7.4: Mortgage advances to Buy to Let investors and first-time buyers (per cent shares of the total), 2007–2017, UK

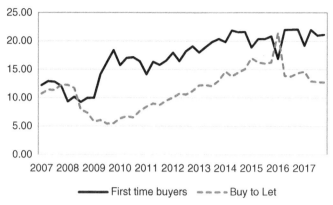

Sources: Bank of England/FCA MLAR Statistics

purchasers. The peak also took place before the introduction of phased restrictions on the tax deductibility of mortgage interest payments for Buy to Let investors. The fall in advances (and the recovery in the first-time buyer share) is evident in Figure 7.4. Nevertheless, the *stock* of loans to Buy to Let investors has not fallen, suggesting that, although further expansion might have been discouraged, those already in the market are not necessarily attempting to seek other investments.

Is it the case that the expansion in Buy to Let mortgages has had detrimental effects on potential first-time buyers since we might expect them to be competing for similar properties and even mortgages given the decline in the overall supply of funds shown in Figure 7.3?[10] If there is evidence that Buy to Let mortgages have increased house prices – bearing in mind we suggested earlier that increases in conventional lending since deregulation do not necessarily raise prices – then aspiring first-time buyers face additional hurdles.

The problem arises from the fact that first-time buyers and existing owners are not operating on a level playing field; in particular, existing owners can use the accumulated equity in their current homes to outbid first-time buyers for additional properties. We showed in Chapter 2 that existing owners generally do not face deposit constraints (and many can afford to purchase homes at most points in the house price distribution except the most expensive), whereas constraints are pervasive for potential first-time buyers, even for those on median incomes. Existing owners can be thought of as housing market 'insiders' whereas aspiring first-time buyers are 'outsiders'.

In principle, the ability to increase demand on the basis of accumulated equity might influence house prices. Existing owners, in effect, face a lower price. Remembering the definition of the user cost of capital, which represents the annual cost of owner occupier services, the absence of borrowing constraints for current owners implies that the user cost is lower than for potential first-time buyers. It can be shown formally[11] that the higher deposit percentages that existing owners are able to put down on buying property to let out raise the responsiveness of house prices to changes in household incomes. As income grows over time, this leads to a greater proportionate increase in house prices (for a given housing supply). In turn, this allows existing owners to put down an even bigger deposit on their next (or additional) purchase and the user cost is even lower. However, this induced increase in demand[12] raises prices yet further. The effect is mitigated if housing supply is able to respond strongly to the increase in prices – from Chapter 6 if the price elasticity of supply is high. But overall, as outsiders, potential first-time buyers suffer from four disadvantages compared with existing owners. First, they may face an increase in prices, arising from the actions of existing owners. Secondly, if the aggregate income elasticity of housing demand is greater than the price elasticity, they are likely to suffer from worsening affordability into the future in the absence of strong increases in housing supply (see Chapter 3). Thirdly, in the presence of deposit requirements, they face a higher user cost of capital than current owners. Fourthly, as shown in Chapter 4, younger households, who are more likely to be first-time buyers, have experienced weaker growth in earnings.

In fact, at the aggregate level, as noted in Chapters 3 and 4, surprisingly there is rather little evidence that the expansion in the Buy to Let market has had a major impact on house prices. From Table 3.1 the long-run responsiveness of house prices to a change in income and other key variables has been similar before and after the mid-1990s, whereas an increase would have been expected in the later period. If this is the case, then the effects of the Buy to Let market appear to have been distributional rather than producing major effects on house prices. Alternatively, aggregate house price equations may be too blunt a tool to pick up what are fairly subtle changes that have taken place in one segment of the market over a number of years since the 1990s. But this does not imply that the investment market is unimportant (and we discuss its implications for macro stability in the next chapter) – the investment aspects of housing are much wider than just Buy to Let.

Housing taxation and subsidies: an over–investment in housing?

In addition to the stance of monetary policy, distortions in house prices relative to rents can be caused by the fiscal system; subsidies may be capitalized into prices, whereas taxes such as stamp duty can, also, influence the level of transactions. Both affect housing demand relative to a neutral system and may give the impression that demand is high compared with the available stock. But rather than increasing supply the more appropriate response may be to remove the distortions. In terms of the models of Chapter 3, subsidies reduce the user cost of capital and, therefore, raise prices. At different times, home owners have benefitted from combinations of mortgage interest tax relief, an absence of tax on imputed rents, capital gains tax concessions on primary residences and lately support under the various Help to Buy initiatives (see Chapter 13 for more details). Support is not confined to the UK and most developed countries provide help in different forms.

In fact, all tenures receive some form of support, but current subsidies are not tenure neutral, nor inter-generationally neutral, nor neutral across asset classes. However, we need to be clearer what is meant by neutrality; one definition can be found in the 2011 Mirrlees Review, where it defined 'a neutral tax system – one that taxes similar activities similarly – avoids giving people encouragement to shift from high- to low-taxed activities in a way that is economically costly'.[13] Consequently, if owner occupied housing is seen as an investment in a similar way as equities then tax advantages might lead to a distortion of resources away from investment in the economy's productive capacity. Nevertheless, non-neutrality may still be desirable, for example, if there are positive externalities arising from housing or particular tenures.

However, most economists are highly critical of the current housing tax system.[14] Stamp Duty Land Tax is widely believed to reduce mobility and to be a contributory factor in an unwillingness of older households to downsize;[15] Council Tax is seen as regressive because of the limited number of tax bands and arguments have been put forward for its replacement with either a tax that is proportional to property values or a land value tax. In the former case, the tax has the potential to dampen house price cycles.[16]

Concern with questions of non-neutrality are not new and arose as a research issue in the 1970s,[17] in part because, in the presence of subsidies, real house prices are not independent of the rate of inflation. Since UK consumer price inflation peaked at more than 20 per cent in 1975 and remained in double digits until 1981, the interest was unsurprising. In fact, most research was conducted in the US, where inflation also rose sharply, but the conclusions were also largely applicable to the UK because, at that time, taxation of owner occupied housing was broadly comparable. The subsequent decline in inflation meant that the issue became less immediately pressing, but concern with the distortions introduced by housing tax subsidies has never entirely gone away.

The early US studies were both partial – examining the effect of subsidies on the owner occupied market alone – or more general covering tenure decisions and the differential returns to owner occupied housing as opposed to non-residential investment where tax provisions differed. The implication was that, at times of high inflation, the relative return to housing rises, leading to a reduction in stock market prices and to a misallocation of the capital stock between housing and other uses. A further distinction is between short and long-run studies, the difference being that, in the former, the stock of residential dwellings is held constant so that subsidies are reflected primarily in price changes. In a long-run framework, the price effect is weaker as housing supply begins to increase. From the last chapter, the effect depends strongly on the price elasticity of housing supply. However, there are a number of factors that may mitigate the distortions from the subsidy. These include uncertainty, so that households do not utilize fully the reduction in the user cost; the existence of credit market restrictions that prevent households from taking advantage of a lower user cost; and the effects of transaction costs (including stamp duty, although this introduces further distortions). Although research has concentrated on financial transaction costs, arguably non-financial costs, such as attachment to place are even more important. Nevertheless, more recent research in the current low inflation environment and even without allowing for housing subsidies[18] still suggests that housing investment crowds out financial investment in models where the riskiness of both housing and financial assets is taken into account.

Concern with transaction costs has been a theme for international research[19] and there is considerable evidence that transaction taxes and costs more generally have been rising and affect both prices and mobility.[20] However, any consequential detrimental effects on labour markets are less clear cut. It does appear to be true that residential mobility is weaker in those countries where transaction costs are higher[21] – households are locked in by the cost– but at least in the UK case the adverse effects on mobility appear to be limited to short distance moves (which are the majority), rather than longer distance, job-related moves.[22] Finally, although their position has been modified by recent significant tax changes, first-time buyers have been more likely to be affected by stamp duty than existing home owners because households in the first group are closer to their borrowing limits, whereas current owners can use accumulated equity from their properties to cover transaction costs.

In conclusion

This chapter has been concerned with the effects of monetary and fiscal policy on housing demand and house prices. The former is related to a theme from Chapter 5 that housing cannot be divorced from wider developments in the macroeconomy; from Chapter 3, house prices are sensitive to both the level of interest rates and (under some conditions[23]) the availability of finance, but housing is only one factor taken into account in the setting of monetary policy instruments. Furthermore, the level of interest rates necessary for reducing volatility in housing markets is not necessarily the same as that required for meeting broader inflation targets and this is discussed further in the next chapter. The current chapter also shows the strong growth in mortgage lending in both the UK and internationally until the GFC but stresses the distributional consequences of restrictions in mortgage finance that have taken place since then, which fall more heavily on aspiring first-time buyers.

We also discuss some of the effects of fiscal policy and, particularly, tax subsidies to owner occupation; subsidies have been widely criticized because the benefits may not fall on the community at which they are aimed – often first-time buyers – but if they are capitalized into house prices, primarily provide additional capital gains to existing owners. Furthermore, it has been argued that subsidies lead to over-investment in housing at the expense of so-called productive investment, for example, in manufacturing industry.

In this and the previous chapter, two important views have been put forward with implications for housing policy. Chapter 6 concentrates on the extent to which there is an absolute shortage of homes as a result of the planning system and the structure of the building industry. This chapter discusses the extent to which housing shortages are primarily distributional arising from monetary and fiscal policy. In fact, few would doubt that there is an issue of housing distribution: low returns on financial assets, the expansion of mortgage credit, the rise in the Buy to Let market and the investment market more generally, and the impact of tax distortions, have contributed to the rise in house prices, although the relationships are more complex than sometimes supposed. But this is not sufficient to conclude that there is no shortage of homes or to overturn the direction of policy of the last 20 years or more and to reduce the emphasis on housing supply improvements, particularly at the lower priced end of the market. Nonetheless, there is still a strong argument that more attention needs to be paid to the demand side of the market as well.

Housing, Affordability and the Macroeconomy

Introduction

The last chapter emphasized that changes in affordability are not independent of the macroeconomy. Indeed, it can be argued that general monetary and fiscal policies are more important influences than policies explicitly aimed at the housing market. But it is also the case that developments in housing markets affect the macroeconomy – the interactions are, therefore, bidirectional – and this has to be taken into account in macro stabilization policies. An expanding literature demonstrates the ways in which housing and housing finance contribute to the generation of macroeconomic cycles. The importance of debt deflation was first recognized in the 1930s, but more recent work formalizes the role of household mortgage credit which, as we showed in the last chapter, has grown rapidly since the liberalization of mortgage markets in many countries. This strand of research became particularly important in the light of the GFC, although work had begun well before this date. Research also indicates that a rise in the household debt to income ratio may subsequently lead to lower growth in GDP.[1]

Credit cycles are, by no means, the only way in which housing affects the macroeconomy, although they have received most attention recently and are the primary focus of this chapter. In addition, housing and housing taxation affect labour mobility and, so, can influence national productivity, regional economic performance and local disparities. In summary, this chapter includes both analytical and policy elements and so bridges the divide between the two parts of the book. It shows why housing has become more integrated into general macroeconomic policy, which adds further constraints on the setting of independent housing objectives. For example, the need for macro stabilization led to the controls on lending discussed in the last chapter.

In the UK, initial research on housing and the macroeconomy took place in the late 1980s and concentrated on the relationship between housing and consumers' expenditure and this was subsequently extended to other countries. In addition, a considerable amount of theoretical and empirical research began to be conducted into the transmission mechanisms through which housing markets could affect consumption. Initially, research concentrated on housing as a form of wealth, but has subsequently been refined and the role of housing as a means of providing collateral in imperfect capital markets has been stressed. Furthermore, more emphasis is now placed on housing as part of a general equilibrium framework, stressing induced effects across the economy as a whole, rather than the partial framework which only considers a subset of markets. The impact of the liberalization of international capital markets and the financialization of housing, with housing increasingly becoming fully integrated with the wider financial system and adding to systemic risk, has been widely recognized.[2] There is evidence that those countries that have undergone the greatest degree of liberalization – including in mortgage markets – have experienced a higher degree of volatility. US research on debt default, which had always been a strand of the literature, became particularly relevant after the GFC. More generally, this leads to further consideration of the impact of housing market risk.

Housing and household consumption expenditure

In most developed economies, housing investment comprises a modest percentage of GDP – typically less than 5 per cent – although its volatility means that it exerts a disproportionate effect on macroeconomic cycles. Taking account of related industries, such as the provision of real estate services, boosts its impact but nevertheless, traditionally, housing received limited attention from macroeconomists. But this began to change as a result of four events; first, in the UK in the late 1980s[3] consumers' expenditure began to rise faster than standard models in use at the time had anticipated, with real household consumption growing at more than 7 per cent in 1988. Since household consumption exceeds 60 per cent of GDP in the UK – with similar proportions in other countries – any unanticipated rise in consumers' expenditure has implications for policy. Since real house prices were also rising sharply at the time, the associated rise in real wealth was put forward as a possible causal explanation. Therefore, housing became important, not because of its size, but because of the induced indirect effects on other parts of the economy. Secondly, in 2003, structural housing market differences between the UK and the rest of Europe were cited as one of the reasons why the UK did not join the Economic and Monetary Union. Thirdly, in the early years of this century, the strength of US house prices and housing markets generally were factors supporting the growth in the US economy and, therefore, led to an expansion in US research in the field. Finally, the fall-out from the GFC, where housing was seen as a trigger, if not the underlying cause, fundamentally changed the way in which housing was seen in terms of macro stabilization.

There is little doubt that changes in house prices and household expenditure are positively correlated, but the question is whether there is causality and if so the nature of the transmission mechanism. There are three main possibilities. First, consumption increases are caused by rises in housing wealth in a similar manner to changes in financial wealth;[4] secondly, there is no causal influence, but both prices and household consumption are related to an additional common factor;[5] thirdly, housing acts as collateral for loans to be used for consumption purposes.[6] In fact, it is difficult to distinguish between the hypotheses from time-series data alone. In terms of the first hypothesis, a problem is that an increase in house prices raises the wealth of current owners, but worsens the position of renters and those who hope to become future home owners. Therefore, it is not necessarily the case that aggregate consumption would be expected to rise.[7] These distributional issues are more readily examined from micro data: since the young and renters did not benefit from the rise in house prices, then the consumption of older owners would be expected to rise disproportionately. UK findings were not entirely consistent, although there was some supporting evidence.[8] But it appears to have been the case that the strength of the relationship between consumption and house prices in the UK has weakened over time.[9] These results are, arguably, more consistent with the second view that both consumption and house prices were driven by a third indicator, notably a rise in income expectations.

The UK was not alone in finding a relationship between household expenditure and house prices, although the strength of the possible wealth effect varies considerably internationally and, in some cases, housing wealth appears to exert a stronger influence than financial wealth.[10] Given its illiquidity, this is surprising, although one argument is that house prices are less volatile than stock market prices and, so, changes in housing wealth are more likely to be permanent. There is, perhaps, a view that any relationship between housing and consumption adds to macroeconomic volatility, but it should be remembered that, under some conditions, housing may play a supporting role. For example, as noted, in the US, strong house prices aided a weakening economy in the early years of this century.

Housing as collateral

Even if housing is not a form of aggregate wealth, it may still provide collateral for loans. An increase in individual housing wealth raises credit worthiness and, therefore, reduces the risk premiums that households are charged.[11] Additionally, there is evidence that housing provides collateral for business start-ups.[12] It is the case that, in both the UK and the US, there is a positive relationship between the growth in consumers' expenditure and housing equity withdrawal. At times of rising house prices, households borrow more than is necessary to finance the purchase of properties. Most of the withdrawal appears to be spent on consumer goods rather than the acquisition of additional financial assets. Of course, this could still be consistent with a wealth effect, but the US evidence suggests that the channel is not identical across different types of households. Households with relatively low credit scores are more likely to borrow against an increase in home equity, but there is little effect for those with high credit scores.[13] Those with low scores are more likely to face borrowing constraints and are in greater need of housing as collateral.

Whereas most of the early research on the relationship between consumption and house prices took place in isolation from possible wider linkages to other parts of the economy, this began to change with research that concentrated specifically on the role of housing as collateral and debt. Models adopted a more general framework in order to illustrate the importance of credit cycles for the economy as a whole,[14] operating through what are known as financial accelerators. The importance of debt deflation and firm and household balance sheets in helping to model business cycles has a long history dating back to the work of Irving Fisher, published in 1933 as an explanation of the Great Depression, but more recently interest has revived.[15] Modern insights provide a possible transmission mechanism between housing and the macroeconomy.[16] If, for example, the economy receives a positive shock to income, consumers' expenditure and both house prices and general prices are expected to rise. This rise in asset prices raises the borrowing capacity of debtors as their net worth increases, allowing them to spend even more, whereas the rise in general prices reduces the real value of outstanding debt, which is typically denominated in nominal terms. These mechanisms act as an amplifier to the initial demand shock. Under this view of the world a positive correlation is observed between consumption and house prices, but the transmission process is different from a pure wealth effect. An alternative, but related, story emphasizes the role of supply – rather than demand – credit shocks, which have the ability to generate macroeconomic cycles; this is discussed further later.

These models suggest that those countries that have undergone the highest degree of financial liberalization are more likely to experience strong macroeconomic fluctuations. International comparisons also indicate that high levels of household debt relative to income are associated with lower rates of GDP growth in later time periods.[17] As noted in Chapter 7, where there are few controls on borrowing, the responsiveness of housing markets to changes in interest rates becomes stronger, because lending controls do not act as a buffer. In these countries, loan to income and loan to value ratios tend to be higher and there is empirical evidence that greater macroeconomic and house price volatility are associated with these higher ratios[18] – although volatility may be mitigated where the price elasticity of housing supply is high. As will be discussed further, this provides one reason why controls on lending have been introduced in a number of countries and why some have argued,[19] that the strength of house price growth is primarily attributable to an excess supply of funds, rather than to a shortage of homes (but remembering from the last chapter that, in the UK, real net mortgage advances have fallen sharply in recent years).

Mortgage default

Given the importance of mortgages in bank balance sheets, it is unsurprising that central banks pay close attention to the outstanding stock of household debt, of which mortgages comprise the largest component. Risk in the housing market has major implications for wider macro stability. There is little doubt that increases in house prices generate an increase in the demand for mortgages and the last section indicated that a significant proportion of the additional credit is spent on consumer goods. Consequently, regulatory authorities are concerned with house price growth and its volatility. Furthermore, it has long been recognized that mortgage default is more likely to occur where borrowers are over-extended; recent US research shows that households with low credit scores who extracted equity before the GFC were more likely to experience default subsequently.[20]

However, it is helpful to start with events prior to the GFC. Figure 8.1 shows the home ownership rate in the US between 1980 and 2019, taking a longer perspective than Figure 4.1 (and expressing the data on a quarterly basis). The sharp rises in the rate during the 1990s and the first years of the 21st century are clearly evident, with the rate peaking at more than 69 per cent early in 2005 before falling to 63 per cent in 2016. Figure 7.2 had shown a similar pattern for the mortgage debt to income ratio, although it should be remembered that by no means all the increase in debt was spent on housing. Nor was the increase in consumption necessarily at the time of the increase in debt. The expansion in ownership in the 1990s was particularly noticeable for those with relatively low incomes, with government initiatives introduced to encourage lenders to meet the needs of entire communities rather than just those higher up the income scale. Minority households made up almost half of the increase in the number of home owners between 1995 and 2005.[21] The drive to extend ownership arose partly from the perceived externalities associated with ownership – in particular by increasing personal stakes in local neighbourhoods, problems of crime or poor education might be expected to decline.

Extending owner occupation to lower-income households potentially generates higher lender risk through default. But, at least in the US case, default is not the only type of risk as cash flows to

Figure 8.1: US home ownership rates, 1980–2019 (per cent, seasonally adjusted)

Source: US Bureau of the Census (Housing Vacancies and Home Ownership)

lenders depend not only on the extent of default but also on the extent to which borrowers prepay their mortgages. An issue for US research was to identify the factors that trigger this option and, therefore, much of the early US literature was set in the context of option pricing of securitized mortgages, allowing for the possibility of default and prepayment. The approach is not fully transferable to the UK because prepayment risk arises primarily from the fact that the majority of US mortgages are at fixed interest rates, providing an incentive to prepay if interest rates fall. But, nevertheless, there are lessons about the factors that affect default risk.

A fall in property values leads to a rise in default risk. As the value of the outstanding mortgage loan rises relative to the value of the property, the household's equity falls and the incentive to default rises. In this case, default is a choice made by the household rather than a necessity and, arguably, this is less applicable to the UK where lenders may still chase outstanding debts above the sale value of the property. In the US, the extent to which this takes place varies by state and, in some, loans are non-recourse. In the US, it has been argued that a good predictor of default is the current ratio of the loan to property market value[22] and the variable appears in most default models, although pure option pricing models typically predict a greater incidence of default than actually occurs. Furthermore, any relationship may be non-linear, triggered only when the ratio rises above a critical value.[23]

In its purest form, the option pricing approach suggests only a limited role for the factors that might be expected to be important *a priori* in explaining default. In practice, empirical default models take into account factors such as income, solvency, individual characteristics, unemployment, family break up and location. In other words, default is related to household crises rather than an optimizing choice that occurs when the outstanding loan exceeds the value of the property. Crises provide trigger events which are a combination of both economic and lifestyle changes. Additionally, there is not a perfect analogy between housing markets and the financial markets to which option pricing is typically applied. Related problems arose when we discussed the relationship between house prices and rents in Chapter 3. Furthermore, in the presence of transaction costs, even in an option pricing framework, there is no necessary reason why the household should default immediately, since defaulting now gives up the option to default at a later date – the delay may arise from uncertainty over future house price rises. If prices are expected to recover there is little reason to default now.

As noted previously, we might expect lending to low-income households to be riskier and the issue became particularly important in the US after the extension of lending to this group from the 1990s. But, at least prior to the GFC, the US evidence on whether low-income households faced a higher default probability appears mixed.[24] There is, however, strong evidence that the increase in US default rates in the 2005 to 2007 period was heavily concentrated in the local areas where the expansion in sub-prime lending was strongest between 2002 and 2005.[25] This expansion took place even though relative income growth in these areas declined; therefore, the growth in lending could not be explained by income growth. A more plausible explanation was in terms of an expansion in the supply of mortgage credit by lenders, associated with the securitization of sub-prime mortgages. Sub-prime mortgages rose much more rapidly than prime mortgages in this period.

Household debt and credit cycles: their applicability to the UK

Previous sections highlighted the increasing attention that has been paid to the role of housing as a form of collateral, particularly for those more likely to face borrowing constraints, perhaps because of poor credit histories or low incomes. We also noted that, internationally, there is evidence that the rise in aggregate debt to income ratios is associated with subsequent lower GDP growth. From Figure 7.2, we saw that in the UK there had been two major periods of mortgage expansion – with the liberalization of mortgage markets in the early 1980s and from the mid-1990s until the collapse with the GFC. Although we hinted at the possible transmission mechanisms earlier, more needs to be added if the approach is to be applied directly to the UK.

The international rise in household debt can be ascribed to two possible causes. First, it may be a response to an increase in the *demand* for mortgage debt. This might occur from a rise in expectations of future income growth – households would like to consume more now in expectation of the increase in future income. However, at least in the US, this does not appear to be the most likely explanation.[26] Under the 'demand' view, we might have expected to see an accompanying rise in interest rates for mortgages, whereas the reverse occurred in the pre-GFC period. Instead, this is more consistent with a supply-based expansion in mortgage debt. Again, in the UK, this occurred with the relaxation of controls in the early 1980s but, in the US, it has been argued that the increases resulted from flawed expectations on the part of lenders, who underestimated the probability of future mortgage default. In competing for market share, lenders underestimated the downside risks during booms which made them more willing to relax lending criteria and to make further loans available at cheaper rates (enhanced by foreign international capital inflows), including to sub-prime borrowers.[27] The increase in lending generated, under this view, a rise in house prices, adding to loan collateral (the nature of the risks and their relationship to house prices is considered in more detail in the next section). Although this may provide an explanation of the rise in household debt, in itself, it does not provide an explanation of the subsequent lower GDP growth. There are a number of possibilities: there may have been a reversal of lender sentiment or there may have been external negative influences on economic growth that were amplified by the reintroduction of tighter lending controls. Furthermore, if there are nominal rigidities in the economy – for example on the adjustment of wages to weaker economic conditions – unemployment is likely to rise.

Internationally, housing markets have different institutional structures and the primarily US evidence is indicative but cannot necessarily be applied without modification to the UK. The UK did not have a sub-prime crisis on the same scale and default (or possession) rates peaked in 1991 at approximately 0.75 per cent of the outstanding mortgage stock. Although defaults rose during the GFC, they never came anywhere near the 1991 value and have subsequently fallen to even lower levels. This is commonly associated with much lower nominal interest rates than in 1991 and a greater degree of lender forbearance (in part at the behest of government following the experience in the early 1990s). Furthermore, the association between higher levels of mortgage lending and higher house prices is an important part of the story outlined for the US. There is little doubt that a rise in house prices leads to a rise in household indebtedness – whether it results from the demand or supply sides – but once we dig a little deeper, whether a rise in mortgage debt causes a rise in house prices is more controversial, although widely accepted in the international literature.[28] The question is examined further in Appendix 8.1.

We indicated in Chapter 3 that the coefficients representing the responsiveness of house prices to the main variables did not change significantly after the expansion in mortgage debt in the mid-1990s. Furthermore, after the liberalization of mortgage markets in the early 1980s, there was no need to include explicit lending variables in models of house prices. This was because conventional (prime) borrowers no longer faced serious mortgage shortages – in most cases, they could choose the size of the required mortgage. If an expansion in mortgage supply was to affect housing demand and, therefore, house prices, it had to be because lending was targeted at new markets, either households who faced greater risks or Buy to Let investors. But we found limited evidence that this expansion had had a major impact on house prices.

This does not necessarily lead to a rejection of the conclusions of the credit cycle model in the UK, but the story needs to be modified slightly. The key change was the liberalization of mortgage markets in the early 1980s. This raised the responsiveness of house prices to changes in nominal and real interest rates, which was particularly important in a variable mortgage rate system. For similar reasons, the reduction in interest rates in the GFC had only a limited effect on prices because it was accompanied by a reduction in the availability of mortgages. At first sight, this might seem surprising. Table 3.1 showed some, but only modest variations in the responsiveness of prices to interest rates, through the cost of capital. The coefficient was approximately −0.05, implying that a one percentage point reduction in interest rates would increase house prices by 5 per cent. But in order to reconcile the constancy of the coefficient with a statement that the responsiveness of house prices to a change in interest rates has increased, we need to look more closely at the user cost definition on which more detail is provided in Appendix 8.1. In fact, the result that house prices are more sensitive to changes in interest rates (and other policy variables) in a liberalized mortgage environment has been known since at least the late 1980s.[29] The main point is that a relaxation of mortgage controls reduces the user cost – formally any credit constraints reflect a shadow price. In some cases, the removal of the constraint was accompanied by a rise in interest rates, which in total left the user cost broadly unchanged.

Therefore, the low level of nominal interest rates operating in a liberalized mortgage market (and *nominal* interest rates as well as real rates are important, because of front-end loading) was a key factor, along with the strength of the economy, in explaining price growth from the mid-1990s until the crash. Front-end loading implies that a fall in nominal interest rates, even if matched by a change in the inflation rate, so that real interest rates are unchanged, shifts the burden of the mortgage away from the early years of the loan. As shown in Figure 3.1, the cost of capital fell for significant parts of the post-1996 period adding to the price boom. Moreover, the effect of low interest rates on prices was greater than it would have been if a similar fall in interest rates had taken place in, say, the 1970s when mortgage shortages still occurred. To emphasize the point, at least in the UK, it was not the contemporaneous increase in mortgage advances that caused the strong rise in house prices from the second half of the 1990s, but the greater responsiveness of prices to low mortgage interest rates that occurred in a deregulated financial environment. Under these conditions, moreover, it becomes more likely that the level of interest rates required for stability in house prices is inconsistent with the level required for more general macro stability.

In itself, this does not explain the subsequent fall in house prices and mortgages, although in the last chapter we discussed the tightening of borrowing criteria imposed by the lenders themselves and arising from central bank stress tests. This generated a reduction in the supply of credit rather than demand which, as shown in the last chapter, had important distributional consequences, particularly for aspiring first-time buyers. But in order to understand aggregate changes and the implications for the macroeconomy, a more detailed discussion of the nature of housing market risk is required, an issue we first raised in Chapter 3.

On the nature of housing risk

In Chapter 3, based on relationship (3.2), we discussed the question of what factors prevented affordability from worsening without limit. The relationship suggested that if real incomes rose faster than the housing stock, then affordability would continue to deteriorate, but this could not be the whole story because, historically, house prices relative to incomes have shown only limited evidence of a long-run trend. Furthermore, the issue has not been raised as important in those parts of the academic literature where house prices are determined by the present discounted value of a rental stream. Can the two approaches be reconciled? In (3.2) affordability worsens more quickly if the income elasticity of housing demand is greater than the price elasticity. But, particularly in the US literature,[30] the price elasticity of demand is often found to be higher than or similar to the income elasticity, so the problem becomes less severe. But this raises the question of the 'true' values of the elasticities. Suppose we re-estimate the UK price equations in Table 3.1 but exclude the housing stock variable. In this case the income elasticity of house prices falls from 2.46 to 1.2. In other words, house prices rise at a similar rate to incomes in the long run,[31] but this is achieved by introducing a misspecification – increases in housing supply have no effect on house prices.[32] This would certainly be a controversial view and is neither consistent with the theoretical discounting model nor the findings of Chapter 6. Therefore, the model still lacks a factor that ensures that affordability does not continue to worsen in the long run. Housing risk is part of the explanation.

We noted earlier, in a US context, that the pre-GFC expansion in mortgage supply was consistent with a misperception of downside risk and an under-estimation of default probabilities. However, measures of housing risk can be incorporated through a modification to the user cost definition.[33] This turns out to be important in helping to explain how housing cycles are transmitted to the economy more generally. In models where investors can choose between investing in housing, risky financial assets (such as the stock market) or safe assets (such as bank or building society deposits), the premium that households require to invest in housing depends on three factors: first, the extent to which investors are risk averse; secondly, the correlation between the returns on housing and risky financial assets and the respective variances of the returns. But the third element is particularly important here: as absolute holdings of housing wealth rise through changes in house prices, housing risk increases, if accompanied by an increase in the volatility in house prices (see Appendix 8.1 for the formal details). Therefore, there is an in-built mechanism for market downturn as holdings of housing wealth rise, triggered by external events. These might come from abroad, such as the GFC or internally, for example, related to labour market developments. The risk premium, therefore, varies over time – it is not a simple mark-up over the risk-free rate – and if the market is expanding rapidly then the risk premium and the user cost both rise. These cyclical variations in the user cost generate cycles in both house prices and the economy more widely. They also prevent affordability from deteriorating without bound.

Additional influences on housing and macro stability: animal spirits

Although considerable research has been devoted to the role of credit cycles, they are by no means the only mechanism generating house price and macro volatility. There are a number of additional explanations, which are not mutually exclusive. First, construction lags and transaction costs are inherent to housing. Both the time required to build new properties and search costs exacerbate housing volatility, because of the failure of markets to adjust quickly and smoothly to changes in economic conditions.

Furthermore, an important strand of the literature concentrates on the role of expectations, herd behaviour and animal spirits in housing markets:[34]

> ... the recent enormous bubble in the prices of homes in
> the early twenty-first century are driven by the same animal
> spirits that we have seen at work elsewhere in the economy.
> And most of the now familiar elements of animal spirits –
> confidence, corruption, money illusion and storytelling –
> play a central role in real estate markets as well.[35]

Some of these ideas have been incorporated in what are known as
Agent Based Models (ABMs). Most conventional models of the
macroeconomy rely on the idea of representative agents: the optimizing
behaviour of a representative household can be aggregated to describe
the behaviour of the economy as a whole. This includes the idea that all
agents hold the same expectations about the future. By contrast ABMs
assume that agents are heterogeneous and hold different expectations
of the future. Heterogeneous expectations typically lead to a higher
degree of volatility than homogeneous expectations. This was originally
shown in the context of stock markets[36] but the principles are equally
applicable to housing.

In ABMs expectations are typically derived from simple rules or
heuristics (see Chapter 2), but they may additionally come from
copying the behaviour of peers. This leads to the formation of networks
and herd behaviour. The concept of allelomimesis, the tendency of
an individual to imitate the actions of neighbours, is also relevant.
This, in turn, leads to model properties consistent with those of
complex systems, which imply that housing markets may undergo
phase transitions with highly non-linear outcomes. Under some
circumstances, large external shocks may have little effect on housing
outcomes, but, on other (possibly unpredictable) occasions, change
may be major. An analogy to events in the animal world is sometimes
made, for example, the murmurations of starlings, where actions follow
the behaviour of nearest neighbours.

Complex systems are those with a very large number of interacting
parts where the behaviour of the system as a whole cannot be
understood simply from a consideration of the constituent elements.
Consequently, modelling housing market behaviour using complexity
is fundamentally different from traditional neo-classical econometric
models in which all agents are homogeneous and random errors are
considered a nuisance. By contrast, the properties of agent-based
computation models, are dependent on stochastic distributions,
stressing the heterogeneity between agents. Agents interact with one
another, and aggregate outcomes result from the interactions. Multiple

equilibria are the norm; the equilibria may be unstable; and the system may remain out of equilibrium for very long periods of time.

In conclusion

The chapter has concentrated primarily on the influences of housing on the demand side of the economy, particularly through consumers' expenditure and this reflects much of the recent literature and policy concerns. Despite initial scepticism, there is now general agreement that the linkages are quantitatively important and are based on firm theoretical foundations. But, additionally, housing can affect the supply side of the economy, for example productivity (see Chapter 14), and, since housing is inherently spatial, contributes to long-standing disparities in regional and urban economic growth rates.[37] We discussed, in Chapter 3, the variation in house prices that occurs across the English regions and within countries internationally and these differences can prevent the free movement of labour from areas of high unemployment to low unemployment, although recognizing that most moves are short distance. High house prices may also lead to higher wage settlements.[38]

It is not, however, sufficient simply to highlight regional differences in house prices or other housing indicators, since these may be a *result* of differences in regional growth rather than a *cause*. Just as in the analysis of the demand side, in order to establish that housing has an independent causal effect, structural characteristics of regional and urban housing markets have to be identified that have permanent effects on economic performance. The transmission mechanisms, therefore, have to be highlighted. A number of possibilities are prime candidates – (i) transaction costs, which are interpreted here to include lock-in through history, property rights, information issues associated with search costs, and attachment to place; (ii) regionally varying policy constraints of which land use controls are one example, but spatially varying property taxes are another and, indeed, national fiscal and monetary policies may have spatially varying effects; (iii) the relationship between housing and endogenous growth or decline. These possibilities are likely to have their strongest effects by influencing the human and physical capital stocks in each area and, through this, affect each area's long-run growth rate. The quality of housing can affect the resident labour force through its influence on health, education and labour productivity, as well as through migration. Furthermore, there is evidence that the distribution of housing tenures within cities locks in the local skills base. For example, over the 20th century, the construction of large public housing estates was often on the sites of former slum clearance programmes.[39] With the increasing concentration of social housing on low wage groups, local areas exhibit persistence in social structures.

Furthermore, housing may affect the physical capital stock of industrial and commercial companies, through crowding out and the possibility that tax subsidies to housing lead to a market distortion and to under-investment in so-called productive capital (see Chapter 7). Residential structures may also be spatially locked in more than commercial structures, partly because property rights are more dispersed. Finally, even in response to very large shocks, there is evidence that the structure of most cities does not fundamentally change. This has been demonstrated by examining the effects of wars and natural disasters on city population distributions. In many cases, the distributions appear to revert to their pre-war positions, possibly because the natural advantages and agglomeration economies in these areas outweigh the short-term losses.[40]

9

Planning and the Assessment of Housing Need and Demand

Introduction

In this second part of the book we turn to more detailed analysis of the policies that governments have introduced to make the housing system more effective. We start by looking at how the land use planning system has developed and how housing needs are estimated to determine required land supply. This is seen as a core reason why supply is so unresponsive to demand and price in Britain. In Chapter 10, we then move on to look in more detail at the impact of the system on stakeholder behaviour and the impact of particular planning policies on housing delivery.

In this chapter we first clarify how the land use planning system has evolved over the last 75 years, and how it has framed and continues to frame the residential development environment. In particular we examine the emphasis English governments have put on matching new housing supply to household formation – something that we have already argued goes against the economic analysis which implied that household formation is endogenous to the system. Importantly, required supply is almost always based on estimates of housing need, even though the majority of the dwellings will be provided in the market sector.

Most developed countries make some estimate of the numbers of homes that they need to accommodate their populations; some go further and estimate how these numbers will change in the future and what particular needs should be fulfilled. Historically, these estimates have been very simple and entirely based on demographics – maybe just an assumption that requirements will rise in line with population (or adult population) or perhaps building in an assumption about projected household size.

Governments in some developed countries (notably in North Western Europe where housing has tended to be seen as part of the social contract and indeed the welfare state) have become increasingly interested in obtaining a more nuanced picture of future requirements. There are two main reasons: first, in most such countries post-war numerical shortfalls, which were very large indeed, have been eradicated – that is, the number of households has come to exceed the number of dwellings. Future needs have therefore become more directly associated with the projected growth in household numbers together with concerns around minimum standards and the exclusion of certain groups from access to adequate affordable housing. Secondly, pressures on government budgets have increased, leading to a desire to reduce traditional levels of housing support, given that the vast majority of households/voters are reasonably well-housed. The emphasis therefore moved towards estimating the numbers of households and the characteristics of those in need of subsidized housing.

Most of these estimates of housing requirements are government led. For instance, the current French Housing Strategy calls for 80,000 homes for younger households over the next five years and 40,000 dwellings per annum for very low-income households.[1] However, estimates may sometimes come more from political parties at election time, as was the case when the CDU in Germany pointed to a requirement of 1.5 million units to be built over the period 2017–2021, a target which was then taken up after the election by the coalition government.[2] These estimates tend to concentrate on overall numbers, while pointing to particular groups of households who will need additional assistance. In some countries independent organizations may also provide estimates of future needs to support their arguments in favour of policy change and higher government investment.[3]

In more market-oriented countries (such as the USA) there is often no national assessment of the numbers of dwellings required. This is mainly because it is argued that the market will provide but it is also because housing responsibilities generally lie at regional or local level and so requirements tend to be addressed, if at all, when zoning systems are updated. These assessments rarely include detailed quantitative measures but rather are part of the negotiation between landowners, developers and authorities about land release and infrastructure provision. What is instead quite regularly reported is how household formation has varied over time and the extent to which new construction has kept pace or exceeded those figures.[4]

Australia is an interesting example of a more sophisticated approach. In 2008 the then Labour government set up a National Housing Supply

Council. One of its key activities was to provide household projections as an element in estimating future housing demand. This was then balanced against evidence on supply to estimate the demand/supply balance and its likely impact on affordability.[5] However, the Council was disbanded in 2013 and, since then, estimates of housing requirements have mainly concentrated on the need for affordable housing and have been made as part of academic research projects with apparently little impact on government policy.[6]

Regulatory controls over the supply of land for housing

To our knowledge, the UK is the only country that has, starting in the 1970s,[7] developed a system for addressing housing requirements under which central government provides detailed estimates of household projections by household type at both national and local level. These then form the basis for local housing needs assessments, for which the local authority must identify the land to enable requirements to be met over a specified period.[8] The core rationale for this unique position lies in the attributes of our land use planning system, notably the need for a legal framework for determining individual planning permissions and to ensure adequate land is made available to meet requirements, together with the national government's central role in providing subsidy to support the provision of social and affordable housing.

To understand how this position has emerged we need to look at how the land use planning system developed with respect to ensuring the supply of housing land and why this has become such a problematic policy area. In some ways the starting point is the interwar period when the planning system was very fragmented and was regarded as unable to deal effectively with the rapid expansion of private sector housing. This expansion was seen as having generated urban sprawl and problems around the provision of infrastructure and housing standards.[9] In response to these and other issues the government set up the Barlow Commission in 1938 which reported in 1940 and called for a comprehensive planning response to the distribution of population and its needs.

The core of the 1947 Town and Country Planning Act which followed was a mechanism to control the change of use of land by requiring that all proposals for development be subject to individual planning permission. The more detailed objectives were better to plan the growth of urban areas; to ensure the more efficient use of infrastructure; to limit urban sprawl; and to enable central areas to be regenerated as demands changed.[10] However, the overarching objective was for the state to take control of the 'Commanding Heights of the Economy' including importantly the use – and value – of land.[11] The post-war Labour government did this not by nationalizing land itself – as has occurred in many other countries – but by nationalizing development rights. In addition, they addressed the question of the distributional impacts of this approach through complementary legislation, by which increases in land values were to be taxed in full. Local authorities were also given strong compulsory purchase powers to buy land at existing use value to be used for housing and other strategic purposes.

Once established by the 1947 Town and Country Planning Act, the idea that government should have fundamental and detailed control over the allocation of land uses became accepted wisdom.[12] Equally, it was generally accepted that one of the most important objectives of the Act was to ensure that there would be land made available to provide adequate housing for all households, with a particular emphasis on housing for those not able to afford market prices.[13]

Achieving these objectives was the responsibility of local authorities – they were not only in charge of granting planning permission for housing but were the only providers of public housing. They also had the power to purchase land compulsorily for the purpose of providing that housing. Many local authorities also owned large amounts of land in their own areas on which they could give themselves planning permission to build public housing. In addition, legislation was put in place to enable New Town Corporations to be set up.[14] These Corporations had the power to purchase land at near existing use value (especially as there was rarely any other use envisaged); borrow to provide the necessary infrastructure to support the new population; and take the uplift in land values to pay off the debt.

The challenge: post-war housing conditions

The new system depended on there being local authorities that were prepared to take these housing responsibilities seriously and to ensure land was made available to meet needs. It also depended on central government and local government providing subsidy to ensure that public housing was affordable to those for whom it was intended. Local authorities were expected to put in place land use plans that identified where development might be appropriate to achieve the numbers of dwellings thought to be required. In practice the processes were complicated, slow and subject to local political pressures, which were often anti-development. Moreover, there was no significant attempt to ensure that there was consistency between national, regional and local estimates of requirements and how they might be achieved. And even when the land was identified, local authorities generally only had negative powers over the private sector (that is, they could refuse planning permission) so their main mechanism for ensuring housing requirements were met depended on their own preparedness and capacity to provide public housing.

In a post-war era, when around two million households were sharing and there was an estimated need for 750,000 additional homes, there was an acceptance that there must be a massive programme of new housebuilding across the whole country. Despite completions rising from around 200,000 per annum in the early 1950s to over 300,000 per annum in the early 1960s, the backlog of need remained high. Even in 1965, when the government was putting forward plans for the following five years (as part of the National Plan), the Cabinet identified:

> needs existing now (i) about 1 million to replace unfit houses already identified as slums; (ii) up to 2 million more to replace old houses not yet slums but not worth improving; (iii) about 700,000 to overcome shortages and provide a margin for mobility; (iv) 30,000 a year to replace the losses caused by demolition – road widening and other forms of redevelopment; and (v) 150,000 a year to keep up with new households being formed in the rising population.[15]

It was in this context that a housing programme was put in place as part of the National Plan.[16] This looked to build half a million units per annum in the UK by 1970 (noting that this was modest as compared to requirements in most of the rest of Europe). The maximum number of completions actually achieved was in 1968 at 425,000 dwellings across the whole of the UK. Thereafter, housing numbers fell fairly consistently. In part, this was a result of much reduced public housing output arising from three main pressures: first, local authorities began to be concerned about whether there were continuing local needs; secondly, because the costs borne by the ratepayers were rising as public sector rents (based on historic costs) were inadequate to keep up with the costs of delivering adequate housing, particularly repair and maintenance expenditure; and thirdly, because of changes in national policy which reduced subsidies and ultimately constrained local authorities' capacity to develop.

With fewer numbers being directly provided by local authorities, there was more pressure on ensuring that adequate quantities of land were made available so that private developers could fill the gap. Equally, with less emphasis on slum clearance, additional housing needed additional land rather than simply reusing cleared sites. Importantly, there was discussion about whether the public sector had been crowding out private development and thus whether the private sector was in a position to step up output levels to achieve identified requirements.[17] Policy emphasis however was almost entirely on the provision of land, where they had continuing powers, rather than on housing delivery, where powers were increasingly being depleted.

Planning and its impact on land supply

It was not really until the 1970s and 1980s that concerns began to grow about whether the planning system was acting as a constraint on housing development, rather than as a facilitator. There was an important debate between planners and economists[18] where it was argued, on the one hand, that targets were being met or even exceeded so the system was working well and, on the other, that house prices were being pushed up and housing mix modified in ways that damaged consumer interests. At the same time the government employed the consultants Coopers and Lybrand to look in detail at whether identified land was actually suitable for development and likely to come forward.[19] The consultants concluded that the system was generating significant constraints on land coming forward that could not be justified on planning grounds.

The government's response, in the Planning and Compensation Act 1991, remained in line with traditional planning thinking putting in place additional obligations. The Act formally required that each local planning authority prepare a Local Plan with the objective that this would more directly guide development control and identify the necessary land for development. However, a number of evaluations[20] provided detailed evidence of the impact of planning on land supply for housing which suggested that the plan-led system silted up the process of identifying land for housing and tightened the constraints on land supply (discussed in Chapter 6). More qualitative analysis at regional and local levels suggested that its main impact was to add another stage to the process of identifying land.[21]

The latest attempts to address the issue are to be found in the National Planning Policy Framework (NPPF) introduced in 2012 and updated in 2018 and 2019. This requires all planning authorities to have an up-to-date adopted Local Plan in place. This must include a supply of specific deliverable sites sufficient to provide five years' worth of housing against a housing requirement set out in adopted strategic policies, or against a local housing need figure where appropriate, in accordance with paragraph 73 of the NPPF.[22] If there is no such adopted plan developers may bring forward land by appeal with a presumption in favour of sustainable development. The latest initiative is to introduce a housing delivery test which is now an element in the NPPF which can lead to sanctions being imposed on local authorities if delivery is running significantly behind identified targets.[23]

Underlying these developments is an increasingly frenzied attempt to force local authorities to meet land supply and housing targets in the context of what is perceived to be a national housing crisis.[24] More fundamentally, it reflects a continued belief in the benefits of an administrative-led system as a means of ensuring housing provision. The problem is that, not only does it require a vast amount of time and energy to put these plans in place and to keep them updated, but it also tends to generate an antagonistic relationship between government at all levels on the one hand and developers and landowners on the other. Most importantly, it contains no direct mechanism by which government can ensure the delivery of that housing supply in the absence of large-scale subsidies.[25]

The growing importance of household projections

The approach

A core element in the government's approach to planning for the future was to put in place an evidence-based method for estimating projected housing demand and need. This was made possible by the publication of official household projection estimates in 1969, which took account of different headship rates for different types of household. In 1970, Alan Holmans, then a senior analyst at the Department of the Environment (the government department responsible for housing at the time), published the first attempt to forecast effective housing demand and need for England, based mainly on these household projections. The outputs included estimates of both private housing requirements and the numbers of dwellings which would be needed to be provided at sub-market rents.[26]

In the Housing Policy Review published in 1977,[27] Holmans set out a far more detailed model including both demographic and behavioural factors such as price and income elasticities of demand (see Chapter 3 for a discussion of the importance of these elasticities). This was to be used as the evidence base for both the numbers of dwellings for which land must be made available and the amount of subsidy which government would need to provide to ensure identified needs were met. At that point however it was only calibrated to provide national numbers in England. Local authorities still had control of measuring their own housing demands and needs and determining the land requirement to be identified to meet these needs.

Thereafter, Holmans published regular updates of his housing demand and need estimates based on household projections produced by the Department of the Environment, together with measures of affordability, to estimate the proportion needing subsidy. Initially, these were developed from within the Department and then from the University of Cambridge. Importantly the measures of housing demand and need included estimates of the unmet backlog based on government determined housing standards.[28]

A range of other methods and estimates were also developed outside government,[29] but always with fundamentally the same structure of estimating demographically based change and including requirements which could not be delivered by the market. Government's role increasingly became that of providing the necessary data for the Department's own household projections rather than estimating housing demand and need. It is only in 2019 that government has taken back control as part of the new NPPF approach to centralizing the estimation of local housing requirements.

Household projections to 2014

Throughout the early decades, most updates of household projections showed previous estimates to have underestimated actual household numbers,[30] in part because of underestimates in terms of increased longevity but more because higher incomes enabled higher household formation. But since the turn of the century, and especially since the financial crisis, the numbers of households actually forming have tended to be increasingly below the earlier projected figures. The main reasons given for this is that worsening affordability, the slowdown in economic growth and earnings, and a range of policy changes, including student loans and welfare changes, have all made it more difficult for households to form (see Chapter 4). As the values of determining variables change so do the outcomes in terms of households formed – and these outcomes in turn modify projections. In other words, projections can only be estimates of what might happen in the future, if the future environment is like the past.

The 2014 population–based projections published in 2016[31] suggested that the number of households in England would increase from 22.7 million in 2014 to 28.0 million in 2039. This implies that 25 years on, there would be not far short of one additional household for every four that existed in 2014. Within this total, some 43 per cent were projected to live in London and the South East (compared to just over 30 per cent in 2014) and some 65 per cent in the South (compared to not much over 50 per cent in 2014). As in Figure 9.1, the result of this is that for instance the number of households in London was projected to grow by more than one-third over a quarter of a century. Going down to local authority level the figures become even more spatially skewed, reflecting past capacity and preparedness to build in different locations, often themselves significantly determined by local planning decisions.

On the basis of these figures, household growth would on average run at 214,000 per annum. Allowing for vacancies and second homes these projections implied a housing requirement of well over 220,000 per annum at the national level and around 55,000 dwellings per annum in London – remembering that these numbers exclude both replacement and any attempt to address the backlog of housing need.

Further household projection estimates were made in 2018 but by the Office for National Statistics (ONS) which had taken over responsibility.[32] These generated much lower overall projections of

Figure 9.1: Household projections (2014 based, percentage increases) England, 2014–2039

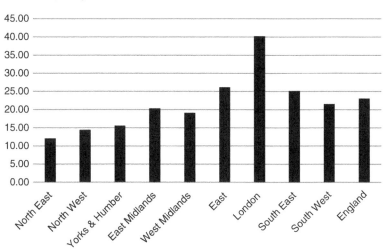

Source: Department of Communities and Local Government

national household numbers at around 159,000 per annum through to 2045. These were based on the latest data available which were particularly influenced by the impact of the financial crisis.[33] In response to considerable concerns about these very different figures, the ONS published a blog clarifying why these new figures should not be taken to imply that government target housing numbers should be reduced.[34] The Ministry then went out to consultation suggesting that the earlier 2014-based projections should continue to be used in local planning until a further review of the methodology and data is undertaken. The majority of those who responded said that to use out-of-date information was inappropriate, especially as the 2014-based estimates themselves did not take full account of relevant evidence from the 2011 Census – but the decision has not been changed.[35] As a result, central government estimates of local housing requirements will continue to apply the 2014-based projections at least until 2022. This has important implications not just for overall target numbers but also for the size mix of the homes to be built, as the main driver of increased household numbers is the growth in single (particularly elderly) adult households resulting in increasing emphasis on smaller units.

Household projections: a critique

Given that household projections lie at the core of government-sponsored estimates of housing requirements, it is important to understand how they are measured and how robust these estimates are. Projections are just what they say they are. In other words, they are not what anyone actually expects to happen, but rather what might happen if past trends were carried forward. One important issue is that, while the estimates of demographic change take account of the evidence over the previous 30 years, data availability means that other drivers may be measured over a much shorter period. For instance, international migration has generally been measured over five or so years. Importantly past economic trends are implicitly included, so the projections made in 2008 after a period of economic growth suggested very many more households would form into the future as compared to those made in 2012, which in part reflected the impact of the financial crisis and were very much lower. The 2014-based projections showed some increase but still fell well below those made in the early years of the century.

Household projections have become increasingly important at local level as authorities have been required to develop Local Plans using estimates of housing need based crucially on local household projections as a basis for their land supply decisions. However, at the local level, these household projections are even less robust, particularly because they depend on estimates of inter-area migration based on ONS population flows, which in turn depend on a range of quite poor data sources. Moreover, household projections are not the only drivers of housing requirements. In their needs assessment the local authority must take account of how the existing stock is being used and what levels of replacement might be necessary as well as housing type and affordable housing requirements. Most importantly, to determine the five-year land supply, development densities must be estimated. Densities are measured in many different ways, and actual densities are often quite different from estimated levels.[36] Finally, the viability of development on these sites is now to be assessed at the plan level, which clearly depends on local economic circumstances, particularly in terms of what land will come forward and when (see Chapter 10 for more detailed discussion).

Economists continue to argue that Objectively Assessed Need (a term introduced in the 2012 NPPF defining how a local authority should calculate requirements in their Local Plan) is simply unfit for purpose. This is not only because of all the uncertainties listed previously, but because demand pressure would be better measured by evidence about house prices and rents together with incomes, employment and other aspects of the local economy. They also note that administrative areas are not the right spatial measure for estimating either demand or need but that these should be based on local HMAs. The system has addressed these issues in part through general requirements that affordability be taken into account and that authorities have a duty to cooperate with their neighbours. But these requirements have been specified in very general terms and interpreted differently between authorities, resulting in a lack of coherence across Local Plans. In particular, the fact that each local authority is legally responsible for determining need and ensuring the five-year land supply in its own area means there is little incentive to cooperate. This is because, if an authority takes on the job of meeting demands for its neighbours, these needs become self-reinforcing as the number of households increases in line with the decision to build more and thus increases the next requirement based on past trends. All these factors taken together imply that measurement is more an art than a science that generates a robust measure. In addition, the numbers will always be subject to shorter-term variations in economic conditions and behavioural change.

The core problem is that effective implementation of the NPPF requires a measure which looks longer term (because planners have to plan for decades ahead) and which can stand up to appeals within the existing legal framework. Unless quite massive reforms were to be implemented, there remains a need for legally based rules which can be easily implemented and which can help ensure compliance in local authority areas where there is resistance to development. What we have actually seen over the last decades is a system where in practice there is a great deal of local freedom. This has generated very different ways of interpreting need together with a mechanism for linking that need to the legally mandated five-year land supply on which the required dwellings are expected to be built based entirely on household projections. The result is a system which is inherently adversarial and repetitious, in that many of the arguments are endlessly repeated both at Local Plan making stage and then with respect to each individual planning permission.

A new approach: centrally determined local housing needs assessments

The current approach introduced in the 2018 NPPF, and modified in 2019, is one in which all local authorities must use the same government-specified standard method to estimate minimum housing needs. It is made up of two main elements: the local household projections (as previously noted, for the moment to be based on 2014 estimates) and an adjustment based on a clearly defined local measure of affordability, using the local house price to earnings ratio. Given that this will result in very large increases in local housing needs assessments in some areas, a cap has been introduced to limit the speed of change as compared to current estimates.

At the time of its introduction the Ministry estimated that, if the model were applied as specified, their proposed approach would generate a figure for England of 266,000 units per annum – at the higher end of most estimates of national requirements. Within this total, London would need to provide 72,000 units per annum, more than twice current levels of output.

The major objectives of this new approach are simplification and consistency. But what it also does is to make household projections even more central to the process of estimating need. In addition, affordability is introduced so that it modifies this estimate (rather than as in earlier iterations as a separate element). So, if the projections are wrong then the adjustments are also wrong.

Even so, the idea of simplification could be seen as an improvement, although there are three obvious causes of concern:

- that what is being suggested is 'one wrong model rather than hundreds' – which may not matter in principle if it is no more wrong than the current average;
- politically, it may look too much like a return to the old 'predict and provide' model where central government was seen as taking away any local power over what are formally, and legally, local responsibilities; and
- the calculations of need may not be robust enough to ensure that local authorities are prepared to accept the estimates when developing their Local Plans.

On the face of it, including affordability in the estimate of housing requirements appears to be a positive move. Using affordability rather than a backlog of housing need has a benefit to government in that it no longer has to provide a direct assessment of how many homes require subsidy if identified needs are to be met. Rather it simply implies that house prices and affordability measures reflect the extent of housing market pressures and therefore indicate the need for more homes – and that worse affordability ratios (however mis-measured as we have set out in Chapter 2) mean a greater shortage in market terms. While this approach can be argued to be more in line with economic thinking, it begs at least three questions: why this particular formula has been chosen; how needs which are not reflected in the market are to be included; and where the funding is to come from to turn this into effective demand.

In the context of the chosen formula, it is informative to look at the estimates of housing demand and need in the Greater London Authority's New London Plan – which has been subject to examination in 2019, but under the old rules that required a measure of housing need based on household projections and the backlog of unmet need.[37] The Plan's estimated figure is roughly 10 per cent below that which would have been required under the new affordability rules. Importantly, however, the Enquiry Panel has called for the required numbers to be reduced on the basis that it has not been possible to identify capacity – an issue which may not be confined to London.

Although, formally, authorities have the right to say that their local area is different and should therefore be assessed in a different way, the government's emphasis is on the official estimates as THE right number. Yet, the formula as currently specified results in some very large changes in requirements – both up and down – even with caps and other adjustments in place. Some authorities will find it hard to accept the scale or indeed the trajectory of change. The politics of what will be seen as a top down imposition on a local issue will be a major problem and could result in large numbers of authorities challenging the imposed numbers. On the other hand, some lawyers may argue that the numbers themselves hardly matter – it is the process that has to be implemented. But, if there is too much objection, on whatever grounds, the result may be to slow rather than simplify the process.

It is difficult not to conclude that the criticisms made about the approach after its formal introduction in the 1990 Town and Country Planning Act still apply in full: that what looks like a technical relationship between the numbers of households and the numbers of dwellings based on well-founded trends is really determined more by policy considerations than by analysis.[38]

Does it matter? The implications of a centralized, administrative approach to land supply

The previous discussion may appear to reflect a highly esoteric exercise in government intervention which many find it difficult to take seriously. However, it has had, and continues to have, very real impacts on how land supply and land prices are determined, and thus on how many new homes are provided and ultimately the cost and affordability of housing across the country.

The core of the problem lies in the fact that the land use planning system was developed in a period when the state saw it as both possible and desirable to substitute administrative allocation for market methods, on the principle that this would increase social welfare and ensure a more equitable distribution of resources. Initially, the responsibilities were concentrated in local authorities (although the related taxation system was wholly national) with considerable powers lying with elected representatives, which inherently brought local politics into the equation. The result was that planning decisions were based more on what established, usually well-housed, households wanted than on the demands and needs of newcomers. The outcome in many areas has been too little land being made available to meet identified needs (let alone what the market might want).

Central government addressed this issue by introducing Local Plans and a requirement to provide a five-year land supply to meet identified needs. When this did not solve the problem, local authorities were penalized for not updating their Plans so that the five-year land supply was in place and now by introducing both the centralized approach to estimating housing need and a housing delivery test with further penalties if the homes are not built.[39] This does, at least in principle, stop local politics entering the process until the actual planning permission comes forward, but equally it loses sight of any local insights. Furthermore, it also leaves the administrative system even further away from what the market can/will deliver.

Only one positive incentive to local authorities – the New Homes Bonus – is currently in place to make higher levels of output more attractive to local authorities. This was introduced in 2011 in the form of a grant paid by central government to local councils for increasing the number of homes and their use. The New Homes Bonus is paid each year for six years; it is based on the amount of extra Council Tax revenue raised from new build homes, conversions and long-term empty homes brought back into use. There is also an extra payment for providing affordable homes. Authorities have freedom to spend the money as they like in consultation with their communities. The Bonus has made a considerable difference to some local authorities' free money, but it has proved extremely difficult to assess its direct effect on housing supply. This reinforces the view that the Bonus has generated a large deadweight loss arising from the fact that, above a threshold level, the money is paid whether or not the dwelling would anyway have been developed.[40]

A more fundamental issue is whether this type of administrative approach can make any real sense in a policy and economic environment quite different from that envisaged when it was first introduced in the 1940s. Then it was perhaps reasonable to use an approach based on quantities rather than anything to do with prices. We now live in a mixed economy where not only the market housing but also much of the social and affordable housing provision depends upon how the market operates. Therefore, requiring a given number of dwellings to be built, and penalizing the authority if they are not, does not ensure that there will be an appetite or capacity to build them. Yet, it remains the case that the current system provides a legal framework which it is much easier to modify in its own terms (as governments since 1947 have done) than to introduce fundamental change.

Importantly, a core aim of the framework was to overcome market failure and ensure decisions improved social welfare rather than simply responding to market pressures. A big issue in this context is that how such planning decisions are made is at best opaque, so it is difficult to identify the potential social benefits. Economists, on the other hand, argue that differences in market prices before and after permission provide clear evidence that the planning system is over-restrictive, sometimes massively so and that quantitative measures of the costs of negative externalities and other market imperfections would almost certainly not generate anything like existing levels of restriction in high demand areas.[41]

Planners, however, see using prices in this way as simply reinforcing the imperfections of the system while the objective of planning is to change the outcomes. More immediately they argue that if the system becomes more flexible the capacity to meet broader urban objectives, such as effective regeneration and limiting urban sprawl, may be undermined as the market looks to bring forward additional land. More broadly, they note that planning aims to address not just the allocation of residential land, but also the overall mix of land uses and thus local economic performance. This in itself raises much more fundamental questions of regional balance and the lack of national policy around the location of economic opportunity. Yet the reality is that allocating land on the basis of local household projections simply reinforces existing trends.

Alternative approaches to identifying local land supply for housing and housing need

As we noted at the beginning of this chapter, while many countries provide estimates of how much housing is required to meet future needs (although never at the same level of detail) there is no comparable system which operates at national and local level to set the housing land requirements to achieve specific numbers of units – importantly without the capacity actually to make these numbers happen.

So, what happens elsewhere? A study of some 24 countries showed that most countries use zoning systems to allocate land to urban uses. Most also have a regional layer of government with the strategic responsibility to provide the framework for urban containment and growth boundaries.[42] These authorities generally put in place plans which identify metropolitan urban limits and then enable local authorities to develop zoning arrangements which identify land within these limits for different purposes. They often also set acceptable densities and dwelling types within residential zones. Developers may then build compliant developments without further intervention. While this has the benefit of making all the decisions at a particular time rather than for each development, more detailed analysis shows very considerable variation in the extent of built-in flexibility. Indeed, in some zonal systems, the study found that the extent of constraint was similar to that observed in England. What emerged from the evidence was the importance of authorities taking a positive approach to monitoring land supply and ensuring that land could come forward for development. Often, local authorities also took a proactive role in land assembly and the provision of infrastructure as well as economic growth potential.

What also emerges from the international literature is that setting metropolitan urban limits, however forward looking, does affect even un-serviced land prices. A wide range of analyzes in the US[43] all show very considerable increases in urban land prices, even when the constraints are not currently binding. However, the literature also accepts that some of these price increases are not simply the result of constraint but also of the positive impact of effective planning and infrastructure provision on urban land values.[44]

These results can be replicated in other market-oriented countries. For instance, detailed analysis of the Auckland Metropolitan Urban Limit[45] – which has traditionally been set to ensure that there was adequate developable land for up to 20 years of urban growth – indicates considerable upward pressure on residential land prices within the urban area. This impact is found to be uneven, with a much larger effect on land at the lower end of the land price distribution, suggesting that the impact on housing affordability is most pronounced for poorer households.

The implications to be drawn from these studies is that there are always trade-offs to be made between allowing unfettered development and the containment of such development to allow more efficient infrastructure and development. Zoning systems do not inherently produce better answers. However, they do provide a framework for strategic decisions. The system in England lacks that strategic level outside London. Even with respect to London, there are very few mechanisms for mitigating the effect of set administrative boundaries because of the lack of effective planning relationships with the wider South East and a presumption that the capital should 'consume its own smoke'. Authorities outside London have very different objectives and powers and the Greater London boundaries have remained almost unchanged since 1963.

In conclusion

This chapter has stressed the uniqueness of the English land use planning system in terms of bringing land forward for development and the extent to which we are continuing to use an administrative approach to ensure land is available for development in a market-led economy, where there is now very limited preparedness by government directly to provide housing for those unable to afford market prices. So, what have the costs of the system been?

Most obviously, the total supply of land for housing has been restricted, helping to increase the cost of that land in the face of demand-determined house prices. Secondly, land supply is relatively unresponsive to increases in prices, most notably because the basis of allocation lies in demographic rather than economic changes. Thirdly, the allocation between local authorities is based on past decisions about land allocation as much as it is about demand.

Second round effects of these constraints include modifications to the mix of dwelling types actually built, increasing planning densities and reducing the range of dwellings identified as required within Local Plans. There also appear to be negative impacts on housing quality, even though higher quality/higher cost construction could have been offset by lower land prices. More generally, higher house prices mean that greater proportions of households are unable to afford adequate market housing and so have put further pressure on the need for subsidized housing.

A further issue has been the impact on the structure of the house building industry. The antagonistic nature of the relationship between market players and local planners has negatively impacted on local decisions and particularly on the costs of obtaining planning permission. This, in turn, has made it more difficult for smaller builders to maintain a flow of development and has helped to lead to a limited number of large firms dominating the market (see Chapters 6 and 10).

The most obvious shortcomings of the system are therefore that: (i) while local authorities can be required to identify land to satisfy a five-year development programme in line with estimated needs, there is no mechanism by which that housing can be required to come forward. This is mainly in the hands of market actors in a market where imperfect competition dominates; and (ii) the way in which estimated needs are calculated takes very little account of either the economic or indeed the social drivers of demand, while the emphasis on providing subsidy to ensure certain accepted standards are met has become a much lower priority than in the past. The result is an increasing problem of affordability.

While it is easy to set out the problems associated with the current system, it is much harder to see how the system can be changed. Moreover, the evidence from other countries suggests that alternative approaches are not exempt from similar problems. Fundamental insider/outsider issues are undoubtedly present in zoning and master planning systems, and to some extent reflect the attitudes of people as incomes grow as much as anything to do with planning mechanisms.

Finally, all levels of government have invested so much in the current system, which is deeply embedded in our legal framework, that it is difficult to imagine shifting to a rules-based zoning approach. Nor is there any political commitment to a strategic revolution as opposed simply to greater centralization. As is often the case in the UK, incremental, piecemeal change is more likely to be acceptable and can potentially enable some improvement in outcomes. Some of these possibilities are discussed in the next chapter in the context of the new housing market. The core contribution that economists can make is to work with planners and other stakeholders to ensure robust, consistent evidence-based decisions aimed at maximizing social rather than private values.

Raising the Level of Private Housing Construction

Introduction

Since the 1970s, commentators have been worried about housing supply shortages in England when land availability was first raised in policy documents.[1] As noted in Chapter 6, concerns about why housing supply in England is so unresponsive came to a head when the Treasury sponsored the Barker Review in the early 2000s. The report stressed the lack of economic indicators used by local authorities when determining land supply through the planning system but also noted many other factors adversely affecting new supply.[2] Barker suggested that more than 200,000 dwellings per annum would be necessary to accommodate the growth in household numbers and to limit house price increases in line with affordability across Europe. Since then there have been many different numbers suggested, mainly in the 200,000–250,000 range but both the House of Lords Economic Affairs Committee and the Chancellor have pointed to the need for 300,000 per annum if affordability is to be significantly improved.[3]

What is clear is that private sector *completions* in England have rarely exceeded 150,000 per annum since the early 1970s. Indeed, in the last 45 years, they only went above 150,000 in the three years from 1987 to 1989, then to be followed by a major macroeconomic and housing market crisis. In the early 2000s there was a similar pattern, but levels of output only achieved more than 150,000 in 2007 before the financial crisis and the deep recession in the housing market, from which we have not yet fully recovered. In 2018, private completions were only 134,500 and on the basis of already falling starts may well peak in 2019.[4] These figures point to two main issues: levels of output are not very responsive on the upswing but respond more rapidly to sudden reductions in demand.

Over the years there has been a vast amount of discussion around the relative importance of different barriers to increasing delivery of new build homes.[5] The main blame is directed at the planning system as a whole and the way that it restricts rather than supports new supply. But, from Chapter 9, what has to be remembered is that at least in part the post-war policy was put in place to overcome market failures in how land was being developed, to support positive externalities within urban areas and to ensure adequate numbers of affordable homes. What has changed are the institutional arrangements to meet these objectives.[6]

Moreover, there are clearly other important constraints on ensuring adequate housing supply, including: a range of specific planning policies; behavioural responses to the system, including the incentives facing local authorities and developers, particularly in the context of large sites, which mitigate against speedy delivery; the structure of the housebuilding industry, notably the business model among larger speculative builders; the skills base and productivity in the industry; and the extent to which demand (as opposed to need) is actually there to maintain the steadily increasing output levels that national government is looking for.[7]

In this chapter, it is unavoidable that we discuss these barriers as well as how policy has attempted to address them and how successful these policies have been – starting with what is seen as the main culprit, the land use planning system – extending the discussion in Chapters 6 and 9.

Land use planning: inherently negative?

In what is often seen as the golden age of housing delivery in the 1930s, there were very few restrictions on where and how development could take place. The result was large scale new building at low densities, supported both by an expanding mortgage market and by government subsidies to all types of tenure. The absence of planning regulations resulted in piecemeal development across the country leading to growing concern about the quality of the British townscape, the efficient provision of infrastructure and indeed housing standards. So, even before the war, there were moves towards introducing a more comprehensive national planning framework (reflected in the Barlow Commission on Geographical Distribution of the Industrial Population, which reported in 1940).[8]

As noted in Chapter 9, the starting point for the modern system of planning was the nationalization of development rights in the 1947 Town and Country Planning Act. This put in place a system which required individual planning permissions for all changes of use, to be determined within a national framework. This approach has survived almost intact for over 70 years and remains the basis on which the NPPF was implemented in 2012 and revised in 2018 and 2019.

Economists stress traditional market failure reasons for land use regulation. Figure 10.1 provides a simplified picture of how planning might be valuable even though planning by definition constrains the uses of land. One rationale is that market-based development would generate negative locational externalities such as congestion and costs to neighbouring activities as well as urban sprawl. Addressing these negative externalities both shifts and steepens the supply curve, increasing land prices to take account of these costs. However, good planning, that takes account of locational synergies, would increase the demand for land at all prices and thus lead to more land being made available. In this diagram the good offsets the bad and both prices AND land supply increase.

Figure 10.1: Good and bad planning outcomes

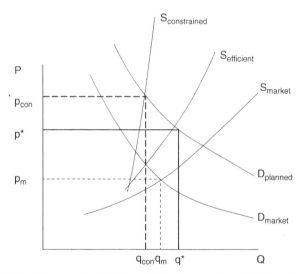

Note: S$_{market}$, D$_{market}$, P$_m$ and q$_m$ = Market supply, demand and resultant market price and quantity
D$_{planned}$ = Demand under good planning; S$_{efficient}$ = supply based on social costs; p* and q* = resultant optimal price and quantity
S$_{constrained}$, P$_{con}$ and q$_{con}$ = constrained supply and resultant constrained price and quantity.

Source: Crook et al (2016, page 30)

However, planning may also constrain land supply more than would be implied by robust measurements of social costs and benefits (as proposed by Barker[9]) by making supply less responsive than would be desirable and so both increases prices and reduces supply. This is shown by the constrained supply curve in the diagram. If this is the case, it restricts the range of uses, limits adjustments and reduces productivity. It is this picture which is often thought to be the reality especially in high demand areas – and, even in lower demand areas, there may be significant costs because the mix of uses allowed does not reflect demand.

A system based on individual planning permission, while, in principle, highly democratic and responsive to changing circumstances, in practice tends to generate uncertainties, costs and delays. The British system is very much at one extreme of the spectrum of planning regimes with a full zoning system (where land uses are identified and anything that meets the specified criteria can be developed without further intervention) at the other (see Chapter 9). Traditionally, planners in the UK have seen their job as both providing certainty and adding value to the area. In that process, they have wished to facilitate building to meet housing need defined in planning terms. However, each decision involves weighing a range of partial evidence, so it is hardly surprising that developers and economists often see the process as inconsistent and inefficient. This adversarial environment is made worse by the fact that planning tools used alone are almost all negative – stopping things happening rather than enabling change.

Specific planning policies

Green Belt

The specific land use policy that receives the most attention and generates perhaps the most division in England is the Green Belt. Its aim was to limit urban sprawl and provide open space for the urban population. It was first formally introduced in London in the 1930s but did not become national policy until 1955. Currently there are some 1.6 million hectares of Green Belt in England, around 12 per cent of the land area, compared to 1.4 million (10.6 per cent) of urban land. Furthermore, the extent of Green Belt land was significantly increased in the 1970s when issues around land supply were already causing concern (although often it involved simply a change in designation from one form of constraint to another).

London's Green Belt accounts for not far short of one-third of the total area of Green Belt in the country. Importantly, 22 per cent of the area within the Greater London administrative boundary is Green Belt and, since much of the Outer Metropolitan Area is also Green Belt, it is extremely hard to increase housing output, even when the land is definitely not green. Although there is a system in place by which local authorities can review their Green Belt designations, changes are always a matter of political debate. At the moment both national government and the London Mayor have policies in place which aim to preserve the Green Belt almost untouched.[10]

There are four main issues around Green Belt which directly affect both levels of output and affordability. First, and most obviously, it constrains the total amount of land that can be made available for housing purposes and so increases the prices of land that does come forward. The expectation of its continuation also impacts on the house prices in the existing stock. Secondly, it is extremely difficult to modify the designations when new infrastructure − such as London's Crossrail − comes into play so that many of the increased benefits of accessibility can be lost because the housing cannot be built. Thirdly, it puts up commuting costs as people who live further out, because of the restrictions, have to travel through the Green Belt in order to get to their jobs in the centre. This in turn impacts on household budgets as well as productivity and employment. Finally, it generates significant environmental costs mainly because of the increased need for transportation, but also because of lower density development outside the Green Belt.

Many economists and indeed many planners find the logic of keeping the Green Belt sacrosanct particularly difficult because it goes against the rational cost − benefit approach to land use. The NPPF allows for Green Belt Reviews but the concerns that 'it will be the thin end of the wedge' if land is released are strong.[11] There are a wide range of proposals aimed at realizing the benefits of large scale infrastructure provision − for instance, by releasing greenbelt land close to transport links and taxing the development gains to support housing and other productive development.[12]

Brownfield first and other specific planning policy constraints

While the Green Belt receives most of the attention, there are a whole range of other national policies which are also important in constraining available land. Perhaps the most important is the brownfield first policy which was first introduced in 1998 and was included in the NPPF in somewhat modified form.[13] The policy was rationalized on the basis that it supported regeneration and reduced the needs for additional infrastructure on greenfield land, the costs of which were not always directly borne by developers.

However, there are also additional costs from brownfield development which builders do take into account. Building costs are often higher because of accessibility and decontamination problems; the types of housing built may be higher cost and less desirable from the consumer point of view. But, equally, there are clearly negative externalities when land is left empty or derelict. Even so, the policy must lead to increased house prices both on greenfield sites, as supply is constrained, and on brownfield sites because of higher costs. Again, therefore, the policy negatively impacts affordability. However, there is little evidence on the extent of these costs, with most of the discussion being based on a general acceptance of the policy – concentrating on how many homes could be built on brownfield land – with no mention of costs and, latterly, on the introduction of brownfield registers as a means of increasing brownfield use.[14] Other relevant regulatory controls relate for instance to conservation areas; Special Areas of Conservation (protecting habitats); Sites of Special Scientific Interest; and many other designations.

Overall, therefore, England is seen as having a very tight regulatory framework. The literature on land use regulation and metropolitan urban boundaries, while stressing the many benefits associated with limiting sprawl and reusing land, also makes it clear that even relatively light constraints impact on land and house prices by limiting development. As already noted, one relevant measure of these costs is the difference in the price of land with planning permission for housing as compared to existing use value, which is very large indeed at the margins of many urban areas.

Local authority, developer and land owner incentives

Local authorities

What is particularly concerning about the English system is the effects on stakeholder incentives which can lead to non-optimal outcomes. Planning is a political process with decisions made by elected representatives. In this context, the incentives that local authorities have are mainly to keep their existing voters happy, rather than to help outsiders who might potentially be the main beneficiaries of decisions to build. It is rational for local voters to be 'nimbies' if the results of development worsen their immediate environment and reduce their access to services. Consequently, the incentive for authorities is to choose lower value, less accessible sites, even if they have lower potential than high profile, high-value sites which impact more on local households. Equally, it is easier to go for brownfield sites which are not close to established residential areas (something which has clearly been occurring based on the evidence of where dwellings have been built in the last decades).[15] Furthermore, it is politically much easier to identify a small number of large sites rather than a larger number of smaller sites which will impact on more local voters.

Moreover, the planning process requires considerable skills and other resources to ensure that it is carried out in a timely manner and in a way that can be defended and enforced effectively. Particular elements, such as whether the five-year land supply is in place and whether specific planning obligations adversely impact on viability, inherently generate costly and often sub-optimal outcomes. All of these are aspects of administrative failure even if the underlying objective is to offset market failure.

Developers

While developers and local authorities may often appear to be at odds, developer incentives can reinforce local authority behaviour. It is easier, at least for large developers, to work on a small number of large sites than on many smaller ones.[16] Equally, it is easier to work with a subset of local authorities and to build relationships and trust as well as local knowledge. In turn, this means that they will not necessarily go against local authority decisions, so policies such as those introduced under the NPPF which threaten local authorities that do not have an up to date Local Plan in place may not have the teeth that national government expects.

Developers may also share with local authorities an incentive to increase densities in order to reduce the amount of land that has to be identified for development. This might be desirable if higher densities helped to increase supply but the evidence from a study of densities within London shows that enabling higher densities has not resulted in more housing being built; instead it has simply meant that less land has been used.[17] The fact that new entrants have not come into the market place suggests that there are strong entry barriers that limit market response.

Land owners

Underlying these relationships is the core question of whether the land identified in the Local Plan will come forward for development and whether other, what are known as windfall sites, will also become available. The simplest economic models would suggest that as planning permission generates higher land values for the landowner, there would be large numbers of such owners who would want to bring their land forward. But land is also an asset with a near infinite lifespan with both costs of bringing it into a particular use and costs of transferring it into another use. Values into the future are uncertain and different actors in the market can take very different views about what they may be – especially given the extent to which the value of a given plot of land can be affected by the provision of infrastructure, locational externalities, general economic growth and, indeed, changes in government policy. There may therefore be a whole range of reasons why particular landowners may wish to hold land off the market because they think opportunities in the future will be better (see Chapter 6 for a discussion of the effects on supply elasticities). Indeed, in certain circumstances, almost all landowners may choose to wait, as happened after the Second World War when the Labour government introduced a 100 per cent tax on any increases in value over existing use value.[18] Since the consensus was that this would change if a Conservative government came into power almost everyone chose to wait.[19] And they were, of course, proved correct.

Under the current framework, each local planning authority must ensure that land put into the plan as part of the five-year land supply is likely to come forward for development, but the actual request for planning permission normally comes from the landowner or developer. Other land may also be brought into the system, but the process is aimed at securing a stable flow of land in line with requirements and thus generate a constrained environment, both in terms of the total and of land attributes.

There are two particularly important and interrelated issues which currently impact on how much land actually comes forward for development: the ownership of that land and the impact of planning obligations and levies on the net land price achieved. First, private land owners may have very different motives for their decisions: some, such as major estates and indeed Oxbridge colleges, tend to have time horizons that may stretch into centuries, and to have their own ideas about how to build and maintain thriving communities; others have small family holdings which they wish to maintain in current use; still others – and perhaps the majority – are looking to make the best return possible, although with different time horizons. But a considerable proportion of land that can potentially come forward for development or redevelopment is owned by the public sector; by local authorities with their own local understanding of opportunities, but also often with a commitment to increase the supply of social and affordable housing; by central government, notably the Ministry of Defence; by National Health Trusts; and many other agencies. All of these are subject to the Treasury requirement to achieve the 'highest and best use' value on land that they sell and many have a pressing need to raise revenues from land sales to support their mainstream objectives.[20]

The other relevant issue is that planning obligations codified under Section 106 of the 1990 Town and Country Planning Act enable local authorities to negotiate with the developer a proportion of affordable housing on residential sites (in line with their Local Plan) as well as contributions to local infrastructure to 'make the development acceptable in planning terms'. Equally, since 2012, local authorities can put in place a Community Infrastructure Levy on all net development, which goes towards providing local authority-wide infrastructure.[21] Both of these reduce the value of the land to the owner and therefore change the incentives to make that land available, as would any attempt to bring in additional forms of land value taxation which are currently much under discussion.[22]

The structure of the housebuilding industry

As noted in Chapter 6, the structure of the housebuilding industry has changed very significantly over the last few decades, and notably since the financial crisis. A small number of large developers build the vast majority of the homes, almost all of whom were heavily restructured after the financial crisis, when a number of mergers also occurred.[23]

The numbers and proportion of smaller builders have also fallen consistently: in 1988 12,000 SME builders built some 40 per cent of homes; now around 2,500 build 12 per cent of the output. In part this is because around one-third of SMEs went out of business immediately after the financial crisis. But it is also because many such builders have simply retired and have not been replaced. A core reason given by stakeholders for the lack of replacement is that there are significant barriers to entry in terms of access to land purchase, the rising costs of obtaining planning permission, and the small builders' dependence on borrowed finance.[24] Another more positive reason is that there is a great deal of renovation work to be had, which is reasonably profitable and avoids at least some of these issues.[25]

Of particular importance in determining output levels is the business model for the speculative house builder. The vast majority of private sector building is only sold when it is near completion or has actually been completed, so the builder not only has to provide all the development finance but also has to take account of the considerable volatility in demand, which is strongly affected by macroeconomic instability. Because of the oligopolistic nature of the industry, it is possible for builders to drip feed the market by closely relating construction activity to sales in order to keep up local house prices and ensure that they are able to maintain their own prices as they build out the site (see Chapter 6 for empirical evidence). Absorption rates are therefore often seen to dominate delivery especially on large sites, although, in some cases, they may be improved by including a wider range of dwelling types and increasing the number of outlets – but the fundamentals remain the same.

The Letwin Independent review of build-out which reported to the Chancellor at the time of the Autumn budget in 2018[26] argued for an extension of this diversification approach to include not just more builders per site but also more types and tenures of housing using different methods of financing. He argued that to speed up development it was important to widen demand and to include providers with different business models – to include for example custom build; developing Build to Rent properties for institutional investors under contract; expanding the proportion of affordable housing as this is also based on contracts with social landlords; as well as increasing the range of other attributes such as dwelling size.

Very large builders and very large sites

The discussion around the behaviour of large builders is often closely linked to the issue of very large sites and, particularly, the regeneration of such sites on contaminated urban land, for example decommissioned gas works. The process of development, from initial thoughts about what might work on the site, through the planning permission process, to actual development can take decades; has to be maintained through a number of economic cycles; and involves not only a great deal of risk but also large scale up-front finance. By definition, such development also needs additional infrastructure – notably transport, water and sewerage which has to be delivered at the appropriate times to meet site requirements – as well as first-class project management. In the private sector, only very large builders are able to undertake this scale of development and, even then, they will often sub-contract significant elements to other providers.

The biggest concern around very large sites is whether they can deliver the numbers the government is looking for effectively. Evidence from London showed that between 2004 and 2011 half of all planning permissions were on very large sites, but only 5 per cent of the actual output over the same period was on these sites.[27] Partly, this is about built form – blocks of flats make for lumpy delivery – but it is far more about overcoming constraints on the one hand and managing demand on the other.

New models for speeding up development

In this context there have been two new developments since the financial crisis: first, the growing importance of pre-sales and, second, the increasing involvement of housing associations who do not just deliver affordable homes but also take an increasing role in providing market housing to generate profits. These enable cross subsidy to support their core activity of providing sub-market homes, mainly to poorer households.

Major developers, notably those based in London, began to use off-plan pre-sales, mainly as a means of reducing risks when the market went into recession after the financial crisis. The main markets for these products were in Asia and the Middle East and included not just luxury apartments in the best parts of London but mainstream flats suitable for the Buy to Let market across the whole of the capital and beyond. This type of development has been much criticized for modifying the style of new building, making it less suitable for local households because of the belief that the properties were being kept vacant, and most straightforwardly because locals could not compete since mortgages could only be arranged near the completion date. Detailed studies for the Greater London Authority by The London School for Economics (LSE) and the University of York suggested, however, that the demand had led to some net additional housing being delivered and that relatively few properties have been kept vacant, with around 80 per cent being let to locals in the private rented sector.[28]

Since the financial crisis the government has encouraged housing associations to take a much larger role in the mainstream new build market, bringing in additional finance from the wholesale market and spreading the risks associated with specific developments.[29] There has been little discussion, and no formal analysis, of the extent to which this approach has increased the levels of new build, especially as they are usually built by the lead private developer and show in the data as privately provided. However, one would expect there to have been some increase in total output because of reduced risk and increased finance.[30]

Historically very large developments, notably new towns, were organized through development corporations whose sole purpose was to plan and deliver not just the housing but also the infrastructure and services. In their heyday they were mainly developed on greenfield land which could be purchased at close to existing use value. Rising values associated with increased opportunities provided the funding for maintaining development and over time they moved into profit. One of Letwin's recommendations was that local authorities should be required to set up development corporations for all very large sites that come forward in the future with a somewhat similar structure to earlier examples. Of course, the big difference is that many would be on brownfield land with their inherently greater complexities and few would be on land with limited other profitable uses.

Medium and smaller sites

Particularly outside London and the biggest conurbations the majority of sites are likely to be less challenging, even though most will still be on brownfield land. Many larger builders concentrate on these types of site (from say 20–500 units) where absorption rates are easier and timescales more reasonable. It is probably in this segment that there is a shortage of new entrants and expanding firms (including local firms) that could increase the numbers of sites under construction at any one time. And it is probably here that the costs of oligopoly are highest.

The main constraints on entry/expansion seem to be generic – land availability, including the issue that large developers have options on many sites; the timescale, costs and uncertainties around planning permission; the need for debt financing which is difficult to obtain until permission is granted; the capacity to maintain throughput in a volatile housing market environment; labour market constraints; and the availability of relevant entrepreneurial skills and equity. Taken together these constraints appear to result in rapidly lost capacity during downturns in the market and very slow expansion during upturns.

A core issue here is, again, the land made available through local planning authorities' five-year land supplies which, as already noted, tend to concentrate more on larger sites. Another issue is simply that the five-year land supply is itself a constraint, even though additional windfall sites may come forward. Much of the discussion in the public domain is about there being far too many uncompleted planning permissions but a number of commentators have suggested that given how the overall system works, there are actually far too few outstanding planning permissions if delivery is to get anywhere near government targets.[31]

Skills shortages

There has been continuing concern about whether there are the skills available to enable rapid expansion of private sector output and indeed output overall.[32] This was another topic that was looked into in detail in the Letwin Review. He suggested that most skills were not specific to the housing construction sector and that the main immediate issue was around the shortage of bricklayers (made worse by some local authorities requiring brick cladding on many buildings where it is not really required). However, he also argued, as have others before him, that there were more fundamental issues into the longer term. These include whether EU workers will have ready access to the UK; the ageing of the construction workforce; on-site working conditions; and poor productivity.

One aspect of government policy here has concentrated on trying to develop apprenticeships using a levy from the industry. But far more fundamental is the potential for introducing modern construction methods, including not just modularization and off-site manufacturing but also a whole range of new techniques, including much greater use of computerization, which can open up the skills base to wider segments of the workforce, notably women.[33] This is a topic which has reappeared certainly every decade since the Second World War but, as yet, has not been taken up to any significant degree. The potential benefits are clear in terms of speed of delivery, far higher quality including little or no 'snagging,' a different set of skills and a system which can better address the move in the market towards flats and large-scale developments.[34] However, past attempts have failed because of demand volatility; inflexibilities of many kinds including local authority regulations; the capacity to transport the units from the location where they are manufactured to the site; on-site costs; and concerns about consumer attitudes. Perhaps most importantly the construction process is, in many cases, a relatively limited part of the overall development timeframe. Even so, in this current cycle, there are signs of greater acceptance and Homes England (the government's development sponsor) is beginning to take a role in increasing opportunities.

Learning from other countries

The UK model of housebuilding is very different from that found in much of Europe – and indeed in countries such as Australia and New Zealand. A core reason for this difference is local authority involvement in infrastructure provision as well as planning.[35] Another is that, in many countries, self – or more correctly custom – build is the norm for low-density single family homes. In this model the customer is involved from the start and may provide the land. The customer then makes regular payments until completion, reducing the need for loan finance. More generally smaller builders working in local markets are the norm, except in the context of larger urban developments.[36] Finally, modern methods of construction are more embedded in construction across Europe than in the UK.[37]

Avoiding the individual permission system?

Permitted development

One of the biggest policy changes that government has introduced to increase private sector output has been a range of permitted development rights to enable the change of use of existing office buildings, together with certain retail units and now some light industrial units, into housing without the need for individual planning permission. The main thinking behind this approach was that there were large numbers of vacant offices which could readily be modified to provide additional housing rapidly and at relatively low cost. These rights were initially intended to run until 2017 but were quickly made permanent.[38] Initially the effect was expected to be quite small but in the first three years, when the housing market was mainly booming, permitted development of offices added some 40,000 units to the housing stock in England, with about a third of this number being in London. Numbers however peaked in 2016/17 and are now running at around 12,000 per annum.

The policy has been subject to considerable criticism for three main reasons: first, the size of units and their quality are often seen to be very poor; secondly, permitted development is not subject to Section 106 requirements or to the Community Infrastructure Levy if the floorspace is not significantly increased and, so, there is no contribution towards the additional services and infrastructure required as a result of the development; and, thirdly, in some areas permitted development is increasing office rents especially for smaller units.[39]

What is unclear is whether there is a continuing supply of suitable office properties or whether the peak in conversions was already reached in the second operational year of the policy. This seems unlikely to remain the case, especially if we see more retail to residential conversions over the coming years as the retail sector readjusts to changing shopping habits.[40] Government is also looking to include the addition of storeys to existing blocks of flats into the policy.

Planning in principle

A rather different approach, introduced in 2017, was to enable (indeed encourage) local planning authorities to identify sites on which they would give Planning in Principle. This would specify what could be built on that site and so reduce the costs and increase the speed by which formal permission would be granted. This is one move towards introducing some of the benefits of a zoning system and so reducing elements of planning risk. This initiative has been seen as most suitable for smaller sites and as a means of helping smaller builders who require planning permission before they can raise debt finance. However, the policy is not intended to be limited to smaller sites. Were it to be seen to be working well, it could readily be extended to larger sites, where development possibilities are reasonably clear cut. However, at the present time, it suffers from two major disadvantages: first, it moves the costs of deciding what might be the most suitable form of development on each site from the developer to the local authority where resources are generally strained; secondly, until there is operational experience it is unlikely that finance will be readily forthcoming because it still suffers from the possibility that final permission will be delayed or even turned down.[41]

The impact of other policy initiatives on private development

Taxation policy

The most direct forms of 'taxation' on private development are at the local level through the cost of planning obligations under Section 106 and the Community Infrastructure Levy in authorities where it has been introduced.[42] Here, the issue can be seen as one of trade-offs between the positive benefits of infrastructure provision to the developments as compared to the direct costs of these contributions to the developer and landowner. These taxes are technically levied on the developer and must also maintain the viability of the development. In a reasonably transparent environment, they will be paid mainly by the landowner, especially on larger sites where there is an option arrangement in place.[43] To the extent that these costs impact on landowners' preparedness to bring land forward they also affect the capacity to supply housing. An important issue is therefore whether they are regarded as predictable. In this context, the Greater London Authority's threshold approach, by which developers of privately owned land must offer at least 30 per cent affordable housing on residential sites, is a way to drive down land prices and to persuade people that the policy will remain in place into the longer term and so reduce negative impacts on supply.[44] However, there are many other uncertainties associated with policy which impact directly on developer profitability and risk and so make for reduced preparedness to build. Currently government policy is to move away from Section 106 except on the larger sites and to put more emphasis on the Community Infrastructure Levy with the objective of increasing certainty and reducing the costs of negotiation. However, the levy itself is not certain as rates can change many times over the period of development and because the lists of infrastructure which will be built provide no certainty of timing or indeed actual provision. This can negatively impact on proposed developments.[45]

Chapter 7 considered the effects of housing taxation on housing demand (Chapter 13 returns to the topic), but property taxes aimed at demand also indirectly affect housing supply through induced changes in house prices. While housing taxation has generally favoured owner occupation and housing consumption (through, for instance, the fact that the principal private home is exempt from capital gains tax in an environment of rising prices), changes in housing taxation policy over the last two decades have, in the main, reduced incentives to add to the housing stock. In particular, over a more than 30-year period from 1968 to 2000, owner occupier mortgage tax relief was restricted and finally removed. Both in terms of house prices and demand, the impact must have to some extent been negative, and therefore put some downward pressure on new output rates.

Historically, rental housing has been treated as an investment good for tax purposes although as a perpetual asset, unlike in most other European countries.[46] From the mid-1990s, when Buy to Let mortgages became readily available the benefits of mortgage tax relief (which continued in the private rental sector until recently) became of increasing importance to individual investors. Moreover, there has been evidence that growing proportions of new build housing has been purchased by landlords, increasing output at least to a limited extent.

However, as discussed in Chapter 7, in the last few years government has become increasingly concerned that owner occupiers have been disadvantaged and so has cut back both on mortgage tax relief and on the costs that can be set against income. Figure 7.4 showed some evidence of a slowdown in activity in this sector with consequent impact on developers' incentives to build.[47]

By contrast, following the Montague Report on private renting,[48] government has incentivized investment in the Build to Rent sector, which comprises purpose-built rental housing financed and owned by institutional investment. This has so far added about 30,000 units to the stock with a considerably larger number in the pipeline. About half of completions so far have been in London. Most of these units can be expected to be additional housing except to the extent that there are shortages in construction capacity.[49]

Direct support for private housing development

The UK is fairly unusual in that there have been relatively few policies that provide direct support to private building since the interwar period when government gave tenure neutral subsidies to all new build.[50] When support has been provided, as after the financial crisis in 2009, it has been directed at increasing the supply of affordable housing through direct subsidies and the capacity of the sector to buy up unsold private dwellings.

Such policies, of course, had as one objective to help maintain the housebuilding industry in difficult times. But it was not until after the financial crisis that, through a number of partial equity models, culminating in the introduction of Help to Buy in 2013, government introduced policies wholly directed at the private sector. These were seen as short-term measures aimed at increasing demand for new build owner occupied housing and thus incentivizing developers to increase output more rapidly. However, the scheme was extended in 2017 and now runs, with significant modifications, until 2022. We discuss the demand side of this policy in Chapter 13. Here we note that, in terms of incentivizing supply, the policy helped to stop further declines in output[51] by stabilizing and expanding demand; throughput was significantly increased with new build additionality measured at around 15 per cent of total output; that there were few signs of pressure on housing and land prices, although it affected the types of dwelling built; but that it was easiest for large housebuilders to make use of the policy and to increase profitability – strengthening the oligopolistic nature of the industry.

In conclusion

Most of the emphasis in terms of increasing private construction remains on streamlining process and increasing transparency as set out in the 2017 White Paper.[52] Despite increasing central government intervention, for example in the context of housing delivery tests, land use planning thus remains a policy based on local administrative decisions around land supply and related issues such as densities and dwelling mix to help ensure that housing need, now identified by central government, is met. Equally the system technically remains a very democratic one in which locals can have their say through council decisions.

The result however is one of continuing tension between central government aiming to achieve their own goals and local government attempting to satisfy their communities. Market factors mainly enter the equation through whether and when the land actually comes forward for development and the extent that demand of all types is there to enable that development to take place and the speed of that development.

Yet many of the problems of delivery which we observe are more to do with the economic environment in which the new housing market operates than with the actors involved in that process. In policy terms they are also more to do with other Departments of State than the English Ministry of Housing, Communities and Local Government.[53] Fundamentally, policies introduced to ensure macroeconomic stability – notably quantitative easing and interest rate decisions – have increased asset prices, including house prices; mortgage and other financial market regulations have made it more difficult to fund development and demand for that development; and expectations are changed not only by Brexit, but also more broadly by low economic growth and job security. All these impact on behaviour. Improving the responsiveness of the planning system and especially, as now, potentially penalizing local authorities for non-delivery of administratively determined targets, cannot solve the long-term problem of slow supply adjustment.

11

Subsidizing the Supply of Rental Housing

Introduction

In the long history of attempting to ensure housing affordability in Britain, the most constant theme has been that of supporting the provision of housing to be let at sub-market rents and allocated administratively. This has mainly been addressed by supply subsidies to local authorities and social sector organizations. There has been only very limited use of direct subsidies to other providers.[1] In this chapter, we therefore concentrate on understanding the nature of these subsidies and how they have impacted on the supply of affordable housing and the rents charged for these properties. We also compare the development of our policy approaches to those in other countries, notably in Europe where in many cases there has been a long history of government involvement.

The policy objectives of social housing provision appear simple: to ensure that everyone is adequately housed, and that housing does not limit the capacity to obtain the other necessities of life, or to take advantage of life's opportunities. Social housing can help to achieve these goals by increasing the total available stock; allocating it to those in need; providing rent and/or income subsidies to those still unable to afford adequate accommodation; and by effective management and support, including enabling access to jobs, services and a safe and secure environment.

Economists tend to argue more in their own terms, that the provision of affordable housing can address issues of market failure in the supply of both new building and the existing stock; but that it may also take account of housing as a 'merit' good (where society values the good more than individuals);[2] or most importantly that through administrative allocation it can help meet distributional objectives.

Many commentators in the past assumed that once minimum physical standards were achieved the task would be complete. The reality has proved to be very different as aspirations, standards and social objectives have expanded and the increased capacity to implement different forms of intervention has opened up other opportunities. Here we stress how these factors have modified the role of social housing over time.

The case for social provision is disputed,[3] but is generally based on three strands of reasoning:

- In the face of supply shortages, government-sponsored housing is the easiest way of increasing supply rapidly, especially where government controls at least some land and infrastructure provision and has risk-free access to finance.
- The social housing provided can be allocated in line with government priorities and identified housing needs. It can also enable more appropriate management standards unconstrained by profit motives.
- At the political level it is often seen as more acceptable than subsidizing private suppliers to deliver additional housing or introducing demand side subsidies that may simply increase prices. Equally, social housing investment can support macroeconomic objectives by reducing housing market volatility and may be a factor in voting behaviour.

In looking at how the role of social housing has developed, it is important to recognize that, historically, supply subsidies were the only means to deliver assistance, as the mechanisms did not exist to support income-related subsidies.[4] Thus, it was only in the 1970s and 1980s when data improved and computerization started to be put in place that housing allowances began to be introduced across a range of countries (see Chapter 5).

Defining subsidy

Economists will normally define subsidy as being the difference between what someone pays for a good – in the case of rental housing, the rent and associated charges – and the market price of the resources that go into the product. Governments, however, tend to define subsidy in terms of the financial instruments and the contributions that they make towards provision, including in more sophisticated systems the opportunity costs of resources, such as land, that may be provided in kind. Thus, it is usually the case that what is measured in official statistics is the financing cost rather than the economic subsidy.[5]

In order to understand the overall picture of subsidies and their impact it is necessary to understand how rents are determined – which is often itself closely related to financing choices. In turn, these rents and the availability of finance help to determine the total amount of subsidized housing provided.

In the main, supply subsidies are seen as coming from government, both national and local, in the form of grants and revenue support. In the housing context, they may include subsidies in kind, most notably when land is provided sometimes without even a transaction being noted, let alone a price being charged. More generally, subsidy can come from a whole range of sources not just from government. Charitable organizations and employers have often played some role in social provision across countries and over centuries. Equally because housing is an asset, it may be that earlier generations of housing and its occupants help to pay for later supply, as their rents rise above the direct costs of provision. Other actors – notably landowners – transfer their land and sometimes other resources at below market price as a result of compulsory purchase or planning obligations. In addition, cash and other contributions may come from developers, particularly in the form of support to new building and regeneration, further reducing direct costs.

Direct payments to social landlords can be either in the form of revenue subsidies (that is, annual payments) or capital grants from central and local government. But subsidies also include reductions in interest rates and other costs of production, notably land, as well as access to public sector borrowing at below market interest rates. Government guarantees also reduce the costs of finance.

The effect of these direct and indirect subsidies to production and the maintenance and improvement of the stock is to reduce the costs that have to be covered by borrowing and rents. The resultant difference between actual rents for the properties and the rent these properties would attract on the private market measures the extent to which households benefit from the subsidies that have been made available.[6] Income-related subsidies to tenants then help to support the flow of rental income and thus maintain viability and enable additional investment.

A short history of national support for social rented housing

Local authority provision

As discussed in Chapter 5, while local authorities were given the powers to build social housing in the latter part of the nineteenth century, this was not accompanied by any national subsidy until the Housing, Town Planning, etc. Act 1919 (the Addison Act) made housing a national responsibility and obliged local authorities to provide council housing with the help of government subsidy. Consequently, by 1939, social housing accounted for 10 per cent of the total stock.[7]

In the immediate post-war period, the emphasis on public sector provision increased very significantly and made up around half of all completions through to the early 1970s. There were two main strands – local authority housing, often built on authority owned or compulsorily purchased slum clearance land, plus housing produced by New Town Development Corporations which bought land in undeveloped areas and were able to fund infrastructure and multi-tenure housing by borrowing against the value uplift of urbanization.

National revenue subsidies to local authorities were open-ended and varied with costs. Authorities could also provide additional subsidies from the local rates. Rents were set to cover the local authority's annual costs of provision less these subsidies (that is, to break even on authorities' Housing Revenue Accounts). As a result of this generous approach, by 1971 when arguably the numerical shortage of housing in England and Wales had been overcome, almost 30 per cent of all households lived in social housing.[8]

Starting in the late 1960s, the position changed, as government tried to control both incomes and prices, including local authority rents. Inflation however increased rapidly so rents fell in real terms leading to major difficulties for providers in funding basic repairs and maintenance. In response, the Conservative government tried, first, to force rent rises (but the policy suffered from the fact that the increases were in absolute terms at a time of rapid inflation) and, secondly, to substitute more targeted income-related subsidies for general supply support.[9] The subsequent Labour government, as a result of its Housing Policy Review in 1977, brought in a new form of less generous residual subsidy system.[10] The Conservative Thatcher government, from 1979, further restrained local authorities by making it illegal to subsidize rents from local taxation and 'deeming'[11] increases in rents (and indeed costs) to limit national subsidies. The Thatcher government also revoked local authorities' rights to borrow against the Housing Revenue Account, a restriction which remained in place until 2018.[12] As a result, hardly any new local authority construction occurred between 1980 and 2018.

Even so, subsidies to local authority landlords continued in place to cover any difference between deemed rental income and deemed expenditure. But as new output declined in the 1980s outstanding debt also fell, and this tendency was reinforced by lower interest rates in the 1990s and 2000s. As a result, increasing numbers of authorities found their Housing Revenue Accounts in surplus, so that they were no longer eligible for national supply subsidies. These authorities were then required to use any surplus to pay for the rent rebates to lower-income council tenants. Since the late 1980s therefore supply subsidies to local authorities have mainly been limited to support for renovation under the Decent Homes Programme from 2000. More and more authorities moved into a position of 'negative subsidy' – that is, they made a contribution to central government, which was then reallocated to areas still eligible for subsidy. To address these issues in a more structured fashion, the coalition government which came into power in 2010, reallocated debt across authorities.[13] This gave some authorities headroom to borrow to invest in social housing again, although generally for improvements in the existing stock. Finally, in 2018, the Conservative government lifted the cap on Housing Revenue Account borrowing, so that local authorities are now free to borrow to build again.[14] In this context, however, it should be noted that the only national subsidy is the right to borrow through the Public Loans Board at low risk interest rates.

An increased role for housing associations

While charitable organizations and employers have had a role in providing affordable housing for centuries and local authorities in some areas encouraged housing associations to build by providing free or cheap land, a formal national subsidy framework to encourage housing associations to increase their role in social housing was not put in place until the 1970s. The legislation was introduced by the Conservatives but passed into law unchanged by the Labour government of 1974. The first subsidy arrangement was over-generous in an inflationary world as it provided for a residual subsidy to cover the gap between first year 'fair' rents[15] and first year costs into the future. Not surprisingly the government soon started to claw back the resultant surpluses.

The financial framework under which housing associations operated changed dramatically in 1988 when rent control for new lettings was abolished in both the housing association and private rented sectors. Importantly, the 1988 Act gave associations the right to borrow on the private finance market and the power to set their own rents at levels that would cover costs and build reserves to ensure that they could borrow on the market at relatively low risk interest rates.[16] They were also enabled to bid for subsidy in the form of capital grants to provide affordable homes. Housing associations thus became the only providers of new social housing based on a mixed funding regime of capital grants together with market-provided debt finance. Technically, the subsidy is a loan which is subordinated to the borrowing from financial institutions, repayable only on sale of the property (which requires special permission). This technicality reduces the costs of private borrowing and also in principle gives central government the capacity to claw back subsidy (as indeed was done in the 1980s).

Funding from the private sector initially came from a relatively small number of financial institutions involved in the provision of mortgages across the housing sector. The risk premium was originally quite high at over 200 basis points above LIBOR. However, it declined rapidly, to between 30 and 70 basis points, in part because of the safety net of housing benefit, in part because of the comfort provided by the regulatory regime, and because of continuing capital subsidy, and the fact that rents were usually well below market levels and so could be increased in the face of financial difficulties.[17] Since the GFC housing associations have found retail debt finance less advantageous. As a result, associations have moved more to the bond market both directly and through aggregators where they have been able to raise large-scale finance at very competitive rates.[18]

When the system was first put in place average capital subsidy rates were running at over 90 per cent. Through both increases in rents and competition between housing associations for subsidy, the proportion of costs paid by subsidy fell to around 50 per cent. However, in 2010, the new coalition government introduced a system which enabled subsidy rates to be significantly lowered. This was based on an Affordable Rent regime by which rents were to be set at up to 80 per cent of market rates in the local area. Also, in 2011, the Localism Act introduced a new form of tenancy for social landlords called 'flexible tenure' which enabled the use of fixed-term tenures for new tenancies; these were generally set at five years after a probationary period. These flexible tenancies have become the norm in Affordable Rent properties in many local authority areas, although the evidence is that households meeting contractual requirements can expect to have their contracts renewed.

The introduction of the Affordable Rents model was a core element in the coalition government's policy to reduce supply subsidies.[19] The October 2010 Spending Review announced a reduction in the capital funding available up to 2014/15 for the development of new social housing to £4.5 billion (down from £8.4 billion over the period of the previous Spending Review which included additional post-financial crisis support). Local authorities were also enabled to build using this scheme after the introduction of self-financing in April 2012. Social landlords could thus offer a growing proportion of new social sector tenants intermediate rental contracts that are more flexible, at rent levels between current market and traditional social rents. The terms of existing social tenancies and their rent levels remained unchanged.

The main objective of the new regime was to provide a mechanism by which affordable housing output could be maintained without large-scale capital grant. The existing use values of homes built, or transferred from the social rented stock into the Affordable Rents regime, would be higher than for the existing social rented stock, enabling higher borrowing levels. Further, the additional finance raised from the higher rents could be reinvested in the development of new affordable housing or improvement of existing units. The 2011–15 Affordable Homes Programme (AHP),which included affordable home ownership as well as affordable rented properties, generated around 190,000 additional units – a little less than 40 per cent of the annual output achieved by its predecessor, the National Affordable Housing Programme (NAHP), but with only 'about one-sixth of the annual public subsidy in grant'.[20] A further programme under basically the same rules was put in place for the next three years with a budget of £2.9bn which was supplemented the following year with additional funding for social rented properties and the expectation that 275,000 affordable homes would be built by 2021.

A final twist has been, for the first time, to introduce limited government guarantees for housing association borrowing from 2012–2015[21] with another scheme announced in 2019,[22] further to increase borrowing capacity and therefore the ability to build. This mirrors policies found in a number of European countries.

The role of social sector housebuilding

Figure 11.1 summarizes the tenure pattern of new building in the post-war period and disaggregates further the information in Figure 6.2. It shows how local authority building was restarted much more quickly than private development, reflecting government priorities. Then,

Figure 11.1: Housebuilding by tenure, United Kingdom (numbers), 1951–2017

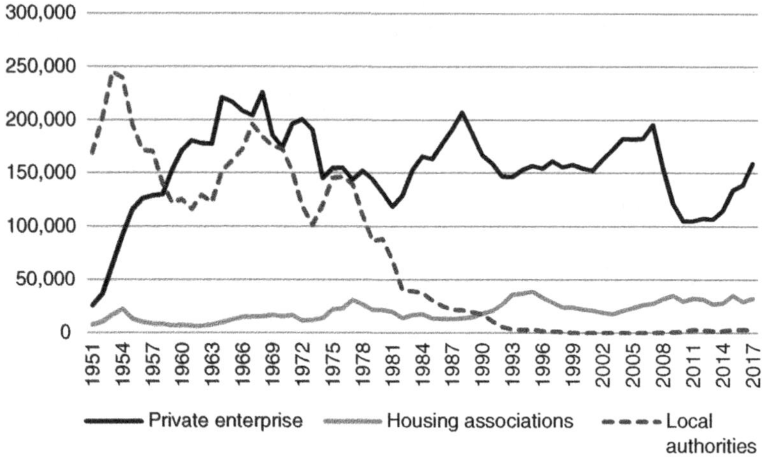

Source: Ministry of Housing, Communities and Local Government

for 20 years, the social and market sectors produced relatively similar output rates (although it should be remembered that slum clearance was also a significant factor affecting net supply). It also clarifies how local authority output stabilized and started to fall well before the Thatcher government and how the role of housing associations increased after the 1988 Act. Finally, it reflects the fact that market output did not expand consistently to offset the reduction in social sector numbers[23] – partly because of the reductions in subsidy available; partly because numerical shortages had been overcome; but also because of market and regulatory failures.

Since the turn of the century the attributes of the affordable housing provided mainly by housing associations has changed very significantly (Figure 11.2). Low-cost home ownership schemes, mainly in the form of shared ownership, which had been in place as an option since 1980 (see Chapter 13) were increasingly favoured by governments of both colours. In the last decade there has also been a major shift toward affordable rented properties (as described previously) at the expense of social rented homes. The figure also shows that the number of 'affordable homes' has increased very much more than the housing completion numbers by tenure would suggest. On this broader definition, there have been about 55,000 new affordable homes per annum since the mid-2000s, but around 40 per cent of these units have been for low-cost shared ownership or, increasingly, for intermediate rental, at rents of up to 80 per cent of market levels.[24] These initiatives

Figure 11.2: Additional affordable homes, England (numbers), 1991/92–2017/18

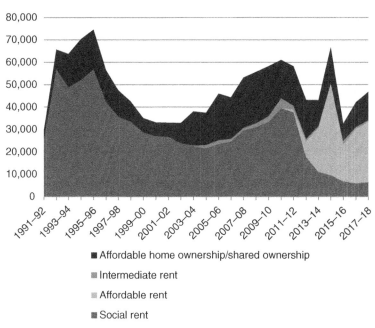

Source: Ministry of Housing, Communities and Local Government

are not generally affordable to lower-income households without additional demand side subsidy.

An additional complication: policies to change tenure within the existing stock

There have been two main government policies which have resulted in large-scale changes in ownership of subsidized housing – the Right to Buy which has so far transferred over two million dwellings from the council sector initially to owner occupation and large-scale voluntary transfers from local authorities to housing associations.

Right to Buy

The Right to Buy was introduced in 1980 across the UK and enables local authority tenants to purchase their properties at a discount on the market price which increases with the length of time the purchaser has been a secure tenant. The scale of the discount has varied over the years and for different types of property but was initially between 30 per cent and 60 per cent and in England is now 35 per cent plus 1 per cent for each additional year over five in a secure tenancy.[25] This policy alone has reduced the social sector stock from its 1979 level by around 20 per cent. Table 4.1 showed how significantly the Right to Buy impacted on the stock of socially rented housing, especially in the 1980s and 1990s. However, it should be remembered that the majority of tenants who purchased would have remained in their property for a considerable time, so the loss of stock did not immediately impact on potential tenants. The big problem was that there was little capacity to replace losses over time.

In terms of subsidizing lower-income households, what did it mean? Crucially, there was no commitment to use capital receipts for housing and no policy to replace sold dwellings. In the main the revenues from sales went straight to the Treasury and, so, these funds were lost to tenants as a whole and were simply eaten up in general government expenditure.[26] Over time this was modified to allow local authorities to retain some of the receipts in order to fund the replacement of lost units. This is a complicated process and authorities have not always been able to spend their receipts effectively, but at least some subsidy remains in the sector.[27]

However, from the point of view of the tenant, there was a transfer from the remaining social tenants (because debt remained in place) to the individual purchaser, who also obtained a different mix of rights and responsibilities. Those buying were often at the upper end of the spectrum of incomes in the social sector and so it was a windfall to the relatively better off. Importantly, the scale of the transfer in many areas added an additional tier to the owner occupied market allowing younger and lower-income households to buy.[28] But over time, a significant minority of Right to Buy dwellings have been transferred to the private rented sector, where rents are often very much higher than in the social sector and where the tenants may be eligible for income-related subsidies. At the worst, the local authority leases the properties back to provide temporary accommodation for homeless households at a premium cost.[29]

Large-scale voluntary transfers

In addition to concentrating new building in the housing association sector, the Conservative government introduced a policy of large-scale voluntary transfers, by which all or part of a local authority's housing stock is transferred, through a privately debt-financed management buyout, to a newly formed housing association. The objectives were at least fourfold: first, ideologically it was thought that specialist housing providers would be more efficient than local authorities with their wide range of responsibilities. Secondly, by introducing private finance into the system there would be external pressure to help ensure efficiency. Thirdly, over time rents could be raised providing a larger revenue stream to support borrowing and investment; and, fourthly, despite the fact that, in some cases, dowries were paid to enable the housing stock to be brought up to standard, the Treasury did receive significant revenues which could be used for general purposes. But, again, there were implications for the scale of income-related subsidies required to support tenants as this process enabled rents to increase significantly.[30]

As a result of both new construction and transfers, the housing association sector, which owned only 1 per cent of the total housing stock in 1979, accounted for over 10 per cent of the total stock in England in 2018. Local authorities owned over five million units, 93 per cent of the social housing stock in 1979, while in 2018, either directly or through Arms-Length Management Organisations (ALMOs), they owned less than 40 per cent of the social sector stock, accounting for only 7 per cent of the total stock.

Ownership of social housing is now spread among some 1,650 registered providers, most of which are housing associations together with around 165 local authorities which have not transferred any or all of their stock to housing associations. Local authorities generally only own social rented property within their own boundaries. The majority of housing associations own only in one or two local areas, but a small proportion hold dwellings across the country. The largest association owns approximately 125,000 units. Among housing associations, between 10 and 15 per cent are involved in building new accommodation. At the other extreme some only manage stock owned by other organizations. Housing associations are increasingly organized in group structures which bring together large-scale voluntary transfers, traditional associations providing for general needs, those providing for special needs, and subsidiaries operating in the intermediate and market sectors.

Rent regimes for social housing

It is clear from the previous discussion that over the decades there have been many different forms of rent regime in place. In the local authority sector, the approach until the 1980s was fundamentally that of charging cost rents (less subsidy where applicable) pooled across the whole stock so that the Housing Revenue Account would remain in balance. These rents were sometimes constrained by rent freezes which limited the local authority's capacity to undertake repairs and maintenance. Evidence on rent structures showed that individual rents were highly correlated with the age of the dwelling and had no direct relationship to market rents or to the quality of the dwelling (although some authorities used a points system to reflect dwelling attributes). Rent levels were increased by reducing subsidy in line with notional rents and once the local authority was no longer eligible for subsidy by requiring them to cover an increasing proportion of the costs of rent rebates.[31]

In the housing association sector, from 1974, there was a quite different regime based on private sector 'fair rents'; this was in place until 1988 when associations became free to set their own rents as long as they remained below market levels. As such, association rents were generally much higher than those for local authority properties, especially as all new build became concentrated in this sub-sector.

In the early 2000s, the Labour government decided to introduce a rent restructuring regime across the whole of the social sector, so that by 2012, individual rents would be determined by a formula based on the nominal earnings of local workers, dwelling size and property values. The objective was to ensure, at least in principle, that rents would be set coherently across the sector and would not be related to the original construction funding as in the past. However, these new 'target' rents still had little direct relationship to the market or tenant valuation of the stock because of additional constraints. Those in smaller dwellings pay relatively high rents, while those in large dwellings and in high-priced areas are disproportionately protected from market pressures. Under this regime, rents in the local authority sector rose approximately in line with inflation. In the housing association sector, they rose somewhat more rapidly but well below average income increases.[32] However, rent structures, while different from the past, continue to have limited relationship to market rents – although what the rent buys is anyway very different from what is available in the private rented sector in terms of location, type of unit, quality, and security of tenure.[33]

For average rents the implied subsidies, based on comparisons with market rents, are higher for family housing and particularly low for small units; they are very high in London and to a lesser extent in the South East and the South, while rents can be close to (or even higher than) market levels in northern regions.[34]

At the same time as the rent restructuring scheme was introduced, the Labour government enabled housing associations to provide intermediate rented housing with rents up to 80 per cent of market levels aimed at those who would not be eligible for social rented accommodation but needed some subsidy to be able to afford adequate accommodation. This approach has now been applied to rent determination more generally.[35] Properties provided through the Affordable Rents Programme are based on the same principles, of a maximum of up to 80 per cent of market levels. This applies for those bidding for grant under the Affordable Homes Programme. Across the country affordable rents tend to be between 20 per cent and 25 per cent above social rents. Only London and the South East lie outside this range, with affordable rents in London being 40 per cent higher than social rents and those in the South East around 30 per cent higher. Social rents are also highest in these regions.

Comparisons between affordable and market rents are complicated by the fact that the latter are measured gross of service costs while affordable and social rents are measured net. Even so, average affordable rents are above 80 per cent of the market in the three northern regions plus the East Midlands. The reasons why the ratio is above 80 per cent is mainly a compositional issue but does suggest that the 80 per cent rule is being followed quite closely in these regions. The next group of affordable rents between 70 per cent and 80 per cent lie more in the centre of the country. London is the massive outlier with affordable rents still running at less than 50 per cent of market rents.

A final complication is that as part of the new regulatory approach to rent setting introduced in 2002, average rent increases were to be set by the regulator. Initially these were set at the growth in the Retail Prices Index plus an additional 0.5 percentage point, (RPI + 0.5 per cent), to allow for relative cost increases. In 2013, the government put in place a ten-year rent regime to begin in 2015 based on the Consumer Prices Index, (CPI + 1 per cent), to provide greater certainty for the sector. That certainty was short-lived. In the Summer Budget of 2015, the Chancellor announced that rents in social housing would be reduced by 1 per cent a year for four years resulting in a 12 per cent reduction in average rents by 2020/21. The measure was forecast to save £1.4 billion, primarily through reduced housing benefit expenditure. Around 1.2 million tenants not in receipt of housing benefit in the social rented sector were expected to gain by £700 per year at 2015 prices.[36] Housing associations stated that this would negatively impact on their development programmes, but the evidence appears to be that, instead, they have managed to reduce costs rather than output. In 2017, the government announced that increases to social housing rents will be limited to the CPI plus 1 per cent for five years from 2020. Further consultation on a new rent direction took place between

September and November 2018. The response to the consultation was to confirm this position.

Overall the evidence on social sector rent determination and the outcomes from the range of financial subsidy systems is that (i) in almost all areas there is some subsidy, although it is much lower in low demand areas than in pressure areas such as London; (ii) the extent of subsidy has generally been reduced since the early 1970s when rents were subject to rent controls (although the increases have been significantly offset by income-related benefits for the majority of tenants); (iii) there is very little consistency in how individual rents are set and regulated increases can sometimes be higher than market rent rises in similar areas.

Other subsidy approaches

One of the effects of the current rental arrangements is that existing tenants are implicitly paying more towards the social sector's new build programme as rents are increased to 'affordable' levels, valuations are upgraded, and more borrowing is made possible. In addition, housing associations have become increasingly involved in building for the market sector as a means of cross-subsidizing social and affordable development. This further increases their borrowing and exposes them more to the risks of market downturns. However, these risks are mitigated to some extent by the wider range of options now available – for example, associations can transfer unsold properties into private renting which they operate themselves; they may also be able to transfer for sale properties into shared ownership or even rent to buy. Even so, rating agencies and indeed aggregators such as The Housing Finance Corporation have shown some concern.

The main source of non-governmental subsidy to affordable housing has been from landowners in the form of Section 106 planning obligations, introduced nationally in the Town and Country Planning Act 1990. These were discussed in Chapter 10, but to recap, the Act allowed local planning authorities to negotiate contributions from developers (in cash and kind) towards the infrastructure and community facilities needed to support new development, and affordable housing was formally included for the first time by making it a 'material consideration' for the granting of planning permission. The agreements are implemented through enforceable private contracts between planning authorities and developers. The affordable housing provided must be in line with the local authority's Local Plan which identifies the need for affordable housing in the area and the mix of that housing (including social rented/low-cost home ownership) which should be provided. As long as developers fund contributions by paying less for land, obligations become a de facto tax on development value borne by the landowner, locally negotiated and 'hypothecated' for local needs – in effect a hybrid charge and tax.

In 2016/17 about £4bn's worth of planning obligations were for affordable housing, with over 50 per cent of this total located in London and the South East.[37] Other national subsides are not allowed to be combined with planning obligations, so there is a trade-off between numbers achieved and the depth of subsidy needed per unit. In 2017/18 almost half of the 47,000 plus affordable homes delivered were under Section 106 with nil grant.[38] Inherently, the system tends to favour low-cost home ownership and intermediate tenures – although 60 per cent of the relatively small number of social rented houses was also delivered in this way.

International experience

The most common definition of social rented housing across countries is in terms of ownership, for which most countries can provide data. Owners include mainly local authority and non-profit housing organizations, although in some countries the range of owners is becoming more diverse. However, perhaps a more useful definition relates to the terms on which the housing is provided and let. In this context, it is normally defined as housing which has been provided with the assistance of subsidy, is let at below market rents and is allocated administratively.

Social housing in Europe

Here we look first at Europe where social housing has generally been a significant element in overall provision. In particular, after the Second World War during the development of welfare states, housing was considered to be an important pillar of the contract between the state and its citizens especially in North Western Europe. In most of these countries, social housing was open to a large proportion of the population. It was also an acknowledged entitlement in the socialist Central and Eastern European countries. More generally, social housing was seen as an effective means of overcoming shortages arising from war damage and rapid urbanization for example in Italy and Portugal. Large-scale housing schemes also helped rebuild construction industries and increase employment. The exceptions were in parts of Southern and South Eastern Europe, where the model was often very different, limiting social provision to local initiatives and, at the national level, concentrating on regulation and self-support mechanisms.[39]

Thereafter, social housing systems have evolved quite differently across Europe.[40] They now vary in size, in how they are financed, and in the degree to which they target specific groups: typically, low-income and socially vulnerable households and sometimes key workers. Ownership and institutional settings also vary as does the relative importance of different levels of governance – state, region, municipalities – and their degree of cooperation.

Over the last 30 years we have seen the decline of social housing in many European countries as the range of housing opportunities has increased and political regimes have changed. Even so, perhaps the most fundamental rationale for the continuation of traditional social rented housing has been that in Western/Northern European countries it is local authorities that retain the legal housing responsibility, often first introduced in the nineteenth century. In this context there remains a small group of countries where social housing accounts for more than a fifth of the housing stock led by the Netherlands at around one in three; and followed by Austria, Scotland and Denmark. There is then a middle group which includes England, France and Sweden[41] at between 15 and 20 per cent; while across the rest of Europe the proportion ranges from around 10 per cent down to almost nothing.

The Netherlands, France and Germany provide good examples of the different ways that social housing is delivered. The Netherlands are perhaps the closest to Britain in their approach in that they use market finance very effectively. The country has the highest proportion of social housing in Europe all provided by housing associations with financial guarantees by government. Even so, the costs of finance have been comparable to those in the UK where no overall guarantee exists.[42] The private and social sectors are treated equivalently and all rents below approximately 700 euros per month, based on a points system, are controlled. Above that level they are freely determined. Housing associations are generally financially strong and able to invest quite widely, although these powers have lately been restricted. The sector is financially stable and is making net contributions to the Exchequer.

France has had a consistent commitment to social housing, including a continuing special circuit of subsidized housing finance. Local housing providers are similar to housing associations with strong links (sometimes including ownership) to local authorities. Over the last decade France has managed to maintain both funding and the scale of the sector, although current policy looks to sell off significant numbers of social homes.[43]

Germany, on the other hand, has privatized almost all the social sector stock either by large scale sales to private equity or because social housing subsidies have traditionally been time limited. While formally the sector is relatively much smaller than in the past, a proportion of those units that have transferred are let at sub-market rents. In all three countries land continues to be made available by local authorities or on mixed tenure sites to enable additional social housing to be provided.

Eastern Europe

The socialist model was one of state ownership with the allocation of housing and related services implemented by municipalities and employers. Even before 1989, this model had begun to change in some Eastern European countries. Thereafter privatization and, where relevant, restitution became the norm, to the point where most such countries now have only a tiny municipal rented sector with very few resources even to maintain that stock and little capacity to raise rental revenues.[44] Problems of under-investment in the existing stock, particularly relating to energy efficiency, have been transferred to the private sector where many households also have few resources to address them. Policy makers across transition economies are looking to develop new models of housing and energy support but these are mainly in their infancy.

European overview

European housing policies have generally moved towards more market-oriented models since the late 1970s.[45] Liberalization of both rental and credit markets together with the privatization of social dwellings has occurred in most countries. Targeting has become a core theme, both in terms of these smaller investment programmes and through the shift towards income-related subsidies. Universalistic models have been questioned and reoriented towards more targeted approaches.

A major concern across much of Europe is that of the residualization of social rented housing. It occurs in countries which still maintain a universalist approach such as Denmark and the Netherlands, where mid-income households largely tend to prefer – and can afford – home ownership. It is inherent in countries where policy directly targets low-income and vulnerable households such as the UK and Ireland. This increased residualization raises issues of economic sustainability for social landlords: unless income-related allowances are particularly generous, the lower the income of the tenants, the lower the rents that can be charged and the higher the risk of inadequate cash flows to maintain the properties and to invest in new stock. Concentrating allocations on vulnerable, or 'problematic', tenants raises similar issues of social and political sustainability. Recent migration waves and the refugee crisis have contributed to increasing housing demand in the social sector in many countries and is resulting in a range of initiatives to expand provision, although mainly on a short-term basis.

Overall, in countries such as the Netherlands, France and the UK, where there is embedded capital in the social sector, it appears to be relatively resilient and to have the potential to play a greater role in meeting housing needs. In countries with either less of a history of social housing or where the traditional state sector has been dismantled, alternative sources of funding (such as free land on market developments in Spain) are sometimes being made available and in others, notably in the transitional countries, there is growing political will to introduce new policies. But these initiatives are relatively limited.

Social housing in market-based economies

Typical examples usually given are North America and Australia/ New Zealand. These countries have long histories of public and social housing but the proportions of households accessing this type of subsidized housing are usually quite small. In general, the emphasis has been on supporting home ownership rather than rented housing. Even so there are significant initiatives to develop affordable housing both through national policies and local initiatives.

The US introduced the Low-Income Housing Tax Credit system (LIHTC) in 1986 which has, since that date, generated some 2.6 million units for very low-income rental housing. The housing is privately developed, owned and operated; privately financed through lenders and equity investors; and privately managed by developers from both the non-profit and for-profit sectors. It works by giving private developers a tax incentive to invest in eligible projects which can be transferred and traded. For the 15-year compliance period a majority of units must be let to households with incomes below 60 per cent of the area median income. Federal funding is given to state agencies who then make the individual allocations. Once an allocation of LIHTCs is awarded to a project, a developer may sell the tax credits either through direct investment in the project or syndication. Investors in LIHTCs have very different motivations: banks are enabled to meet requirements under the US Community Reinvestment Act which is designed to encourage them to meet the credit needs of low and moderate-income neighbourhoods within the communities in which they operate. Other investors invest directly for the returns generated, while still others invest for tax sheltering purposes. Returns are low because the investment is in the credit not the housing and because of competition for that product. It is regarded as an exemplary programme which has successfully applied market discipline to the public–private partnership structure of the enterprise. Moreover, while there have been periods of cut back there are also periods when funding has been increased.[46]

In Australia the introduction of the National Rental Affordability Scheme (NRAS) in 2008 represented a significant shift in the provision of housing assistance, for the first time leveraging private investment into the supply of affordable rental housing (at 20 per cent below market levels) at a national scale.[47] It was a mixed market approach, able to integrate affordable rental accommodation within wider market developments. The allocation decisions were based on a combination of financially feasible project applications and state government directed housing priorities, and the approach worked well in delivering quality and spatial objectives. NRAS generated nearly 30,000 units in the six years up to 2014. Despite positive assessments there were concerns about complex administration, poor targeting, administrative delays and value for money. The scheme was discontinued after the government changed in 2014.

The US, Canada, Australia and New Zealand all have planning policy instruments which potentially can enable identified land to be used for affordable housing with implicit cross subsidy from market provision.[48] These powers work well in some US states although they are illegal in others. In Canada, Vancouver adopted the approach in 1988 but it has produced very small numbers of units so far. Ontario adopted the approach only in 2018. In Australia and New Zealand powers exist but their use is quite limited and usually involves a density bonus.

More generally it is how land can be provided which helps determine the capacity to provide affordable housing. Hong Kong and Singapore, both of which have very successful housing policies, achieve this in part by land nationalization and continued state commitment to affordable housing. Many other countries struggle with both ineffective planning regimes and inadequate finance.[49]

In conclusion

Social housing, owned by the state, local authorities or non-profit organizations, has been a traditional approach to providing affordable housing for both lower-income working and vulnerable households, concentrated in urban areas. It was the core mechanism for dealing with post-war shortages in Europe especially in countries that were committed to a welfare state model of support. It was equally important as an element in the 'social wage' in more socialist countries. In rural environments on the other hand self-build and family support tended to dominate.

The biggest problem in terms of affordability is that sub-market rents must inherently always generate shortages and it is often the more vulnerable or the newcomers who are excluded. Income-related housing support, which has only been regarded as administratively practicable since the early 1970s, is one way to address this issue – and we turn to this in the next chapter.

A second major issue is that, as incomes rose and with it the demand for housing and greater freedom of choice, owner occupation became the preferred tenure for the majority of stable and secure households. Social housing tended to become more residualized. Shortages of funds for improvement and regeneration in many countries have also been important in making at least some parts of the sector undesirable and generated ghettos of poverty and vulnerability.

Yet, it remains the case that state provision and subsidy are one of the most effective ways in which additional new housing can be provided. This is an important reason why there has been a resurgence of interest from the UK government over the last few years, with increased emphasis on increasing social housing investment to meet government targets, using mixed methods of finance and land provision as well as direct grants. This aspiration is reflected in a range of reports aimed at supporting the expansion of social and affordable housing. For instance, the latest report from Shelter (2019) *A Vision for Social Housing*[50] calls for an average of some 150,000 social homes to be provided per annum over the next 20 years. All that is currently missing are the resources.

Subsidizing the Housing Costs of Lower-Income Tenants

Introduction

There are two main discussions that have taken place concerning the principles associated with subsidizing the housing costs of low-income tenants: is there a case for housing-specific subsidy; and if so, should that be directed at people or dwellings? There is a further question about whether subsidy should cover those in owner occupation. None of the issues are straightforward.

Within the housing literature there is general acceptance that housing-specific subsidies are necessary; in other words, we cannot solve the problem simply by modifying the income distribution or by regulation. Once this is accepted, a core element of the housing subsidy debate has been about whether it is better to use supply side subsidies to increase the provision of sub-market rental housing and to limit the rents charged or whether it is better to provide income-related demand side subsidies to help individual households pay for the housing they need. This debate has also been strongly linked to the more political question of how important the government's role (at national as well as local level) should be in providing the dwellings and setting the appropriate allocation principles. In other words, the debate is significantly a reflection of the post-war European experience of large-scale government ownership of housing.

Within the welfare literature, however, the discussion is more around how housing costs affect both the structure and cost of social security overall and therefore how they can impede more fundamental objectives. In the housing context, these objectives include how to ensure both an efficient market for housing and sufficient support so that households can afford adequate housing as well as the other necessities of life. As such the debate has tended to be more about affordability in the marketplace, although the issues are just as relevant in the context of mixed housing systems.

As noted in Chapter 11, the starting point in advanced economies has always been supply side subsidies because of the capacity to deliver to those in housing need. But as demand side subsides have become increasingly important, the issues become more intertwined with those of general welfare and income distribution as well as, more practically, the capacity to target assistance.

Finally, there is an issue around whether support should be available to households in all tenures or be restricted to tenants. In principle, this argument tends to be concentrated on whether owner occupiers are buying a different product, including investing in an asset which is not generally regarded as a necessity of life, and therefore should not be assisted. At a more practical level, as we have already noted in previous chapters, owner occupiers are generally better off and, even when their incomes are low, often have both assets and relatively low housing costs because they are elderly and have paid off their mortgages.

In the UK, as in many other contexts, our housing policy includes a bit of everything, in that we support socially owned housing at below market rents and prices through supply subsidies and allocate that housing mainly to lower-income households; we provide income-related benefits for both social and private tenants; and we give, increasingly limited, support to owner occupiers who suffer sudden income loses.

Supply versus income-related subsidies

We noted in Chapter 11 that one reason for subsidizing the supply of housing for lower-income tenants was that, until the 1970s, there was little capacity to deliver income-related benefits which took account of both the detail of household requirements – in terms, for instance, of household composition – and of their housing costs This was a very practical reason for choosing to subsidize housing and one which was accepted by most Northern European countries. As computerization became more straightforward and data became more available, the introduction of housing-related benefits for all eligible tenants became a possibility and many European and other more developed countries saw this as an option.[1,2]

Once the option existed, debate in the literature concentrated mainly on the relative merits of supply and demand side subsidies. Academics from more market-oriented economies normally took the view that targeted income-related benefits are to be preferred to public sector investment, while others see a mix as the better approach in practice.[3] The arguments for demand side subsidies are (i) that they enable the market to respond to the increased capacity to pay among those in receipt of housing allowances and so expand the supply of appropriate housing, including using the existing stock more effectively and (ii) that subsidy can be more effectively targeted on those in housing need. Most importantly, it can ensure that all those in need are assisted and can adjust assistance as household circumstances change.

The arguments for supply side subsidies include that: (i) the market is generally rather unresponsive, so rents may rise as a result of demand subsidies rather than supply be expanded; (ii) non-profit social landlords – both local authorities and social landlords more generally – have wider objectives than private landlords which include meeting a broader range of the needs of low-income and vulnerable households. In particular, residence-based services can be more cost effective to deliver together than separately through the market (iii) government can specify what should be provided, where and for whom, in line with politically agreed social objectives.[4]

A core issue is whether this should be an either/or debate or if the more appropriate approach is some mixture of the two. In practice, supply subsidies are always limited, so that there are 'insiders' who are receiving support and 'outsiders' who are dependent on the market. So it cannot just be supply. But equally, financial support is not enough, and the evidence presented in this book shows how difficult it is for the market to provide enough housing to meet needs. So, if the objective is to ensure everyone eligible for assistance is helped, this must entail a mixture of demand and supply side approaches – which indeed is the case in most European countries.

Even so, since the 1970s there have also been political pressures across countries to cut back on supply subsidies, in part because numerical shortages had been overcome but also because it was seen as increasingly possible to provide income-related benefits for those not accommodated in social housing and indeed for those unable to afford even social sector rents (see Chapter 5). These payments to individuals are available to a greater or lesser degree in most Northern European countries[5] and have become increasingly important as social rents go up to support additional borrowing to maintain social sector investment. In particular, the revenue from these demand side subsidies provides a relatively secure income stream to social providers which helps to reduce the cost of funds.

Housing and welfare

In the UK the question of how to develop housing-specific income support had been part of the debate around the form that social security in general should take, initiated in the Beveridge Report in 1942.[6] When Beveridge published his report on developing an effective post-war social security system, he recognized that the objective of ensuring everyone would be able to achieve a reasonable standard of living through the national insurance system he was proposing was put at risk by 'rents' – because of the extent to which the costs of minimally acceptable housing varied across the country. No other element of the necessities of life was seen as having price variations that were significant enough to undermine the nationally based system.

He stated that:

> The attempt to fix rates of insurance benefit and pension on a scientific basis with regard to subsistence needs has brought to notice a serious difficulty in doing so in the conditions of modern Britain. This is the problem of rent. In this, as in other respects, the framing of a satisfactory scheme of social security depends on the solution of other problems of economic and social organization.[7]

He further argued that a flat-rate benefit with an average allowance for housing would leave people in more expensive homes with income below a subsistence level, once they had paid their rent, and people in cheaper homes with a surplus. The alternative – of paying the actual rent as part of the insurance benefit – was seen as creating perverse incentives for people to move into more expensive accommodation.

When the Labour government introduced the national insurance system, an allowance was included for rent but this did not vary with actual rent payments. This was an acceptable approach for most tenants who were already relatively protected because their rents were not market determined. Problems of housing affordability were addressed in the public sector through rents based on 'pooled historic cost' – that is, setting rents plus government and ratepayer subsidy to cover the annual costs of building and maintaining the housing within each local authority area (see Chapter 11). Moreover, subsidy favoured higher cost areas, so variations in actual rents across the country were much less than those observed in the market sector. In the private rented sector, the vast majority of the stock was subject to rent controls, with rents increasingly below market levels. In the main, this left uncovered only households in furnished accommodation not subject to rent control and those unable to access housing effectively at all, who often lived within another household.

The introduction of rebates and allowances

The decision to introduce rent rebates and rent allowances in the early 1970s, accepted the basic welfare principles of a nationally based needs allowance; but also accepted that housing costs varied too much for these to be included.

The immediate reasons for the move towards income-related benefits were fourfold:

- The government wished to introduce a new form of rent determination in the social sector more related to the value of the property.[8]
- The government was also looking to raise average levels of public sector rents so that they could more effectively cover the management and maintenance costs within the existing stock as well as to take account of the very rapid inflation then occurring.
- Rent controls were being modified and to a significant extent dismantled in the private rented sector, meaning that more and more households were paying market rents which were out of line with their reasonable capacity to pay.
- It was becoming practicable to obtain the data necessary to make individual assessments and to administer the system reasonably effectively. Local authorities were given that responsibility.

The result was a scheme that not only took account of individual circumstances but meant that housing support was seen as a 'residual', taking the strain within the overall welfare system. This approach meant that Beveridge's concerns about the distortionary effects of households' housing decisions were left unchecked, except to the extent that, in the private rented sector, some basic limits on the size of the dwelling in relation to household needs were introduced.

There were concerns that in the private rented sector, there were incentives for new tenants to come to an agreement with the landlord to pay a higher rent and claim the benefit (as all increases in rent were covered in full). However, the numbers on benefits were not expected to be large enough to push up rents in general. Another issue however was that, if you could find accommodation, the state would, at the limit, simply pay the whole rent so there was a built-in incentive to form separate households. To the extent that people took advantage of this, it meant that both more housing was required and the costs to government were increased.[9]

The current situation

The allocation of subsidy between supply and demand instruments

Perhaps the most important statistic in the context of supply versus demand subsidies is that in 1975/76 supply subsidies accounted for 82 per cent of all government housing subsidies with only 18 per cent going to income-related support. By 2015/16, just 4.3 per cent of the total bill went on supply subsidies, while 95.7 per cent was spent on housing benefit and some limited mortgage interest support. The overall totals during that period also rose by around 15 per cent in real terms – measured in 2016/17 prices – so housing benefit accounted for more than the total subsidy bill 40 years earlier.[10] Of course, this does not reflect the extent to which housing associations and other social landlords have been able to use past subsidy and rent increases to provide additional housing and so underestimates the current value of supply subsidies in economic as opposed to financial terms. However, it does make clear that there has been an extraordinary shift away from the direct subsidization of bricks and mortar towards support for individual households. Based on past estimates, this shift has probably gone too far in terms of the relative value for money for government achieved by supply versus demand side subsidies.[11]

The changing composition of housing benefit payments

Even though the scale of total housing benefit payments has grown so much and is only now apparently coming more under control, large numbers of policy changes have limited the availability of individual income-related housing support, changing the picture almost out of recognition.

In the social rented sector, the income support system has remained as envisaged in the1970s for the majority of tenants, in that a social rent for the housing allocated to that household is presumed to be reasonable and therefore fully covered. The exceptions (as noted in Chapter 5) are those who are deemed to be under-occupying and have to pay a supplement even though most have little chance of moving, and those, usually larger families, who are affected by the welfare cap.

In the private rented sector, the distribution of rents for those not on benefits in defined 'Broad Rental Market Areas' is used to determine the maximum support for which tenants are eligible. Currently, tenants are only able to claim for rents up to the third decile of the rent distribution for the relevant sized property in that area. This provides some incentive to move within the area but more generally leaves large proportions of households paying a proportion of their rent even if they have no non-benefit income.[12] Further, the four-year freeze on eligible rents introduced in 2015 meant that, as actual rents went up, those paying around or above the third decile set at the beginning of the freeze were not being compensated for any increase.

A further change, which is clearly causing very significant hardship to lower-income households,[13] is the transfer of Council Tax benefits (which are based on similar principles to housing benefit) to local authorities, without transferring additional funding. Local authorities may opt to introduce schemes that cover up to 100 per cent of Council Tax for eligible tenants, as was the case in the past. However, many are requiring household contributions of between 10 per cent and 40 per cent and sometimes higher. In turn, this is leading to court orders which, of themselves, increase the costs that households have to pay and at the limit lead to evictions.

Austerity policies underlie many of these changes, but there is also a clear objective to increase incentives to move to cheaper accommodation or to cheaper locations. Most fundamentally, the principle of ensuring that 'residual' income is enough to pay for other basic necessities has been undermined very significantly. Rather it is now implicitly assumed that people have choice and, therefore, it is their own decision to use money for housing rather than other necessities.

The importance of these changes

A report by the Institute for Fiscal Studies (IFS) published in 2017,[14] gives the best estimates currently available of how much some of these changes have impacted on lower-income tenants. They showed that among private renters in the bottom 40 per cent of incomes, the fraction whose housing benefit did not cover all of their rent had increased quite steadily, from 74 per cent in the mid-1990s to 90 per cent in the mid-2010s. The biggest change occurred among low-income working-age households with children, where it rose from 63 per cent to 90 per cent over the same period. In the social housing sector, the increase jumped from 56 per cent in 2010-2012 to 68 per cent in 2013-2015.

The IFS estimated that reforms since 2011 have cut the housing benefit entitlements of 1.9 million privately renting households and 600,000 social renting households – in other words two-thirds of low-income private renters and one-sixth of low-income social renters are now affected. This and other evidence show that the principles behind our system of social security have been undermined and that many people are facing a growing problem of poverty, because payments do not cover what the system itself determines is the required minimum income for a reasonable life. Moreover, the evidence continues to show that, given current housing conditions, most tenants probably cannot reasonably be expected to adjust their location and housing consumption to enable them to cover other costs.

Overseas experience

The OECD Affordable Housing Dataset developed in 2016[15] reviews the range of housing allowances available across OECD countries. It suggests that most countries have at least one housing allowance system in place and many have more than one. Private tenants are nearly always covered by these schemes, but social tenants may be excluded if their rents take account of income as in the US and Australia. In most North Western European countries, housing support has been developed that makes an allowance for housing costs within mainstream social security benefits. Housing allowance systems are based on the 'gap' principle whereby, for a given income, the housing allowance meets a certain proportion of rent above a minimum contribution and up to a maximum level. In circumstances where unmet housing costs take residual income below the social assistance (what we would call social security) minimum, the social assistance system itself often steps in. The clearest example of this structure is in Germany, where housing allowances (*Wohngeld*) are available for people in work or in receipt of social insurance (unemployment) benefits. Those dependent on social assistance on the other hand receive support for housing costs through that system.

The biggest difference with the UK, however, is that most other North Western European systems are more generous because their welfare systems are based on a proportion of earnings.[16] These higher benefits in countries such as Germany, Sweden and France allow most people to pay for their accommodation, with a top-up available, if necessary. In part this is possible because rents are generally a lower proportion of income in most of Europe (particularly Germany) except for areas of high housing pressure. But it is also the case that, because of higher social security benefits in relation to earnings, an acceptable basic standard of residual income can generally be maintained, while enabling a proportional approach to additional support.

In comparison, it is argued that in the UK we have a system where jobseeker's allowance and income support are set at very low levels and so housing benefit is expected, at the limit, to cover almost all housing costs.[17] The problem is that austerity and other changes mean that this is actually no longer the case.

How the tenure of housing for lower-income households has changed

The biggest structural shift in where low-income households live has occurred as a result of the decline in the social rented sector and the subsequent rapid growth of private renting. In 1979 when social housing was at its height, over one-third of dwellings in Great Britain were in the social sector. While some poorer households (especially single people, those who had moved areas, or those who were living in high housing pressure locations) did find it difficult to obtain social rented housing, the large majority of such households were accommodated in low-rent dwellings, owned mainly by local authorities. Importantly so were many better off households.[18]

In 1979, when the Thatcher government came to power private renting accounted for little more than 11 per cent of all dwellings. Within the sector about a quarter were living rent free in accommodation that went with their work. A significant proportion of those living in the remaining 8 per cent were older tenants who were still protected by rent control.[19] The easy access part of the sector was less than 5 per cent of all housing and accommodated new entrants to the housing market and marginalized households. More generally private renting was regarded as almost an 'inferior good', which might be expected to continue to decline.[20] This began to change slowly after deregulation in the late 1980s, with some beginning to see it as a tenure of choice because of easy access and low costs of moving. Such households might well be prepared to share and to live in relatively low-quality housing before moving on to more stable accommodation.[21]

Since 1979, there have been massive changes in tenure structure which have affected lower-income households as much as the better off. At the turn of the century, social housing had declined from its peak by nearly a third, to around 21 per cent of dwellings in Great Britain. As a matter of policy, it had also become far more concentrated on housing lower-income and more vulnerable households. The private rented sector, while larger numerically was still actually smaller in proportional terms at less than 10 per cent in 2001 than it had been in 1980.

Since the turn of the century the picture has shifted again, in a way not predicted by policy makers or most commentators, towards a far greater role of private renting. By 2017 over five million dwellings in Great Britain were privately rented, accounting for almost 20 per cent of the total stock. Rates of growth have been similar across not just England but also Wales and Scotland. In London this has resulted in more than one in four households becoming private tenants.[22] At the same time, social renting has further declined, to just over 17 per cent. Moreover, the majority of these dwellings were owned by housing associations where rents were generally higher than in the local authority sector.

At the present time the growth in private renting has shown signs of slowing and perhaps to a very limited degree reversing as owner occupation slowly picks up. And, while there is considerable talk of increasing new build in the social sector, this has so far only helped slow the decline. If anything, therefore, the options available to lower-income households who cannot access ownership are probably still becoming worse, at least in high pressure areas notably London.

The suitability of the private rented sector for lower-income tenants

The private rented sector in the UK (as compared to many other countries with different regulatory systems[23]) has not been seen as suitable for most family households or indeed for older or single households who are looking for longer-term stable accommodation. The main reasons for this view of the sector relate to the regulatory framework under which the private rented sector operates. This is based on Assured Shorthold Tenancies (ASTs) which run for a minimum of six months – among the shortest in the world. They also enable market-determined rents both at the beginning of the tenancy and within the tenancy as well as no-fault eviction at the end of the tenancy. Thus, at worst, the tenants face continual uncertainty about how long they can stay and what they are going to be paying. They also find it hard to complain about anything wrong with the property as this may increase the chances of having to leave. The situation changed very considerably in Scotland in 2018 where the law now requires indefinite tenancies and the removal of no-fault eviction, although the impact of the changes is not yet clear.[24]

The make-up of the private rented sector in 2017/18[25] shows that the view of its role as for younger, single, more mobile households no longer reflects reality.[26] It is indeed still the sector accommodating the largest proportions of single people, with sharing households making up somewhat over a third of the sector. However, approximately 20 per cent of those in the private rented sector are couple households with dependent children – just above the overall national average and well above the proportion in the social rented sector, at 13 per cent. Lone parents with dependent children account for over 10 per cent of those in the private rented sector as compared to less than 6 per cent overall and not that far short of the 13 per cent found in the social sector.

The other major attribute of those in the private rented sector is that 77 per cent are in work as compared to 60 per cent for households overall and only around 40 per cent of social tenants. This reflects the age structure of tenants in the sector and its rapid growth over the last two decades. The available data (mainly from the EHS and the Family Resources Survey) do not, however, make it easy to distinguish between lower-income households potentially in shorter term need – for whom private renting might be acceptable – and those likely to require assistance throughout their lives who would probably be better accommodated in the social sector.

The issues of affordability in private renting are as much about high rents as they are about low incomes (see Chapter 3), in part because these high rents mean that even those on above average incomes may be eligible for assistance. This in turn implies that the marginal rate of 'tax' is extremely high when benefits are withdrawn as incomes increase. In the social sector the issues are far more about low incomes as rents, while they have grown in real terms, mainly remain well below market levels.

Homelessness

At the limit, households may not be able to find suitable accommodation which they can afford and may become homeless.[27] This is an area of policy where, at least in principle, there is a fairly well-defined framework. Unlike many other countries, since 1977, there has been clarity about where responsibilities lie: in that year local authorities were given well-defined duties to ensure that defined categories of homeless and potentially homeless households would be supported into longer-term secure accommodation. Within this framework local authorities have freedom to achieve this in ways that they regard as locally appropriate. But what has sometimes been lacking is: (i) the administrative capacity to make the system work effectively and (ii) the resources to pay for what is required.

For many people, certainly for instance in the United States, homelessness is perceived as meaning that someone does not have a roof over their head. In the UK, people in this position are designated as street homeless or indeed roofless and treated in a more holistic fashion. A count of people sleeping rough in this way is undertaken on a particular night each year. This count shows increasing numbers in England since 2010 – from under 2,000 to around 4,700 in November 2018.[28] This does not fully reflect the scale and nature of the problem, in part because people are difficult to find and in part because, in practical terms, it is how long someone is sleeping rough that matters most to their health and wellbeing. What is very clear is that, while this type of homelessness is the most obvious, the problems are usually not simply about a lack of a roof over their head but relate to other health and social care issues. Housing policy in this context mainly consists of trying to provide hostel accommodation and organize the support necessary for each individual. Problems are associated with engagement as well as the severity of the difficulties – only rarely is there an issue of eligibility for social support.[29] Current policy initiatives, as in many countries – notably the United States and now Australia and New Zealand – include Housing First which sees providing a stable, secure home as a necessary first step to addressing other issues.[30]

The more general definitions of homelessness, for policy and resource purposes, in the UK mainly relate to whether authorities have a duty of care. The legal definition set out in the Housing Act 1996, which has been used in law since 1977, provides a clear test of who is or is not homeless. Someone is homeless if they have no accommodation that they are entitled to occupy; or, they have accommodation they are entitled to occupy but it is of such poor quality that they cannot reasonably be expected to occupy it. Until 2018, local authorities had to treat someone as homeless if they are threatened with homelessness within 28 days. Now, under the Homelessness Prevention Act 2018 this has been extended to two months in the expectation that this will give both the local authority and the household more time to prevent the homelessness occurring. Some 70 per cent of households for whom a local authority accepts a duty of care are, at the time of acceptance, living in London.

The vast bulk of the recently recorded increase in statutory homelessness is attributable to the sharply rising numbers made homeless from the private rented sector, with relevant cases having quadrupled in England since 2009/10, from less than 5,000 per year to over 18,000. As a proportion of all statutory homelessness acceptances, such cases had consequentially risen from 11 per cent in 2009/10 to 31 per cent by 2015/16, remaining at this unprecedented level in 2016/17. This is clearly a matter of declining income-related support in that the LHA reforms in 2011 which limited housing benefit and then the freeze on amounts payable appear to be major drivers of this association between loss of private tenancies and homelessness. More generally, among homeless households, there are increasing numbers of what might be called mainstream working people who are simply unable to find and maintain suitable (or even unsuitable) accommodation. Affordability is increasingly seen as the cause of the growth in the numbers of those who are statutory homeless.

Two big issues arise here: is it the government's responsibility to pay the costs and do the problems have to be solved where they are identified? This second point is a version of the Beveridge issue – does current location dominate issues of cost and indeed opportunity? On the question of payment, the government, in practice, defines temporary accommodation provided for homeless households as social housing and so does not apply any restrictions to the rent covered by income support. However, those who are in work and homeless must pay the relevant proportion of their income towards the rent charged on temporary accommodation. From the point of view of local authorities, there is a range of sources of central government subsidy but, even so, local authorities feel that the costs they must pay are increasing.

The new Homelessness Reduction Act 2017 puts a great deal more emphasis on prevention to try to limit the numbers of acceptances. This makes sense as long as there is some potential in the local housing system to find more, lower priced, accommodation. However, in London and some other parts of the country this prerequisite simply does not exist.

On the second issue – where homeless households should be accommodated – while case law makes it clear that people should not be moved long distances from their children's schools or from other necessary support systems, there is an increasing emphasis on accommodating those in need of temporary accommodation away from the authority in which they are declared homeless. In London for instance, around 40 per cent of homeless families presenting in 2017/18 were accommodated outside their borough. This may, in some cases, give households increasing job and housing opportunities but is very much against the traditional principles set out in the 1977 Housing (Homeless Persons) Act.

Overall, it is too early to say whether the Homelessness Reduction Act will be successful. There has certainly been an immediate sharp decline in the numbers of households who are accepted as homeless after prevention has failed. However, it is also accepted that the statistics are still experimental and it is not clear whether this is a short-term effect or indeed whether those who are accepted will end up staying in temporary accommodation for longer.

Homelessness is a problem that is increasing across many countries significantly because of affordability issues.[31] On the whole it affects a relatively small proportion of lower-income households, and policies to alleviate the problem often receive a more than proportionate level of funding. Even so, homelessness remains a clear and increasingly concerning symptom of housing market and wider economic and social tensions.

In conclusion

The nature of the relationships between housing and affordability in the rental sector in Britain has significantly changed as a result of three main factors:

- the relative decline in the size of the social sector where rents are below market levels, and even in this sector the fact that rents had risen consistently in real terms until the four-year policy based decline from 2015 to 2019;
- the growth of the private rented sector as accommodation for families and more vulnerable households as well as for those for whom it is a matter of choice; the insecurity of such accommodation; and notably the high rents, especially in London, which have put pressure on household budgets; and
- changes in policy which mean that it is no longer the case for large proportions of those in receipt of benefits that they have (after allowing for housing costs) sufficient residual income – in the government's own terms – to cover their necessary expenditures.

Together with increasing job insecurity and income mal-distribution, these three factors have worsened the situation for large numbers of lower-income households while, in the main, providing fewer opportunities for such households to improve the conditions they face. In terms of income support for lower-income tenants, the fundamental question remains as to whether we can solve or alleviate the Beveridge conundrum of rent variation within a nationally based system that is itself not particularly generous, while leaving in place appropriate incentives. At the present time there appears to be a stronger emphasis on the importance of incentives. Yet, it is not obvious that lower-income tenants have as much choice as such policies imply, so people are left with inadequate income to support a normal life. The alternative would be to aim to move towards a more generous social security model which does not concentrate assistance so heavily on housing, as is found in many European countries. But this looks unrealistic in public expenditure terms. Even more fundamental is whether income inequality (excluding welfare payments) can be mitigated in order to reduce the overall costs of both housing and income support.

Increasing Home Ownership

Introduction

At the end of the First World War, approximately 23 per cent of households in England were home owners, with almost all others located in the private rented sector; but, by the start of the Second World War, ownership had risen to 32 per cent and public housing to 10 per cent.[1] The construction boom of the interwar period (see Figure 6.1) took place in both the public and private sectors, aided by the introduction of significant building subsidies from central government for the first time. The rise in home ownership in the 1930s was also supported by the availability of cheap finance and the rapid growth of building society lending. But the expansion in housing and property ownership more generally also had political motives. Lloyd George's commitment to 'Homes for Heroes' recognized the poor physical condition of British soldiers, compared with their US counterparts; the average height of (non-officer) volunteers and conscripts was five feet six inches;[2] the height was lower among those who came from industrial compared with rural environments and among those living in overcrowded conditions. The relationship between poor housing and health had been recognized since the second half of the 19th century (see Chapter 11), but it was not until 1919 that municipal housing began to grow on a significant scale.

The expansion took place at a time of European revolutionary movements and real fears that major political unrest would spread to Britain. Although mainland Britain did not experience a revolution,[3] the number of working days lost to industrial disputes rose sharply in the early 1920s, even before the 1926 General Strike, and easily surpassed the levels recorded in the era of unrest in the 1970s. The phrase 'property-owning democracy' was first used by Conservative MP, Noel

Skelton, in 1923.[4] Writing against the background of industrial unrest and the extension of the vote in 1918, Skelton proposed broadening the property ownership base as a necessary complement to the extension of the electoral base, advocating this as an alternative to the collective ownership model supported by Socialists. The idea was subsequently taken up by party leader Stanley Baldwin. At this time, the concept referred to the ownership of industrial production, but the emphasis within the Conservative Party shifted towards home ownership after the Second World War and in the 1950s and was generally accepted by other parties in the 1960s and 1970s as mortgage markets opened up, making it easier to buy.

Importantly, home ownership became a means through which a larger proportion of the population could have a stake in society, extended in the 1980s by Prime Minister Thatcher's introduction of the generally highly popular Right to Buy programme. Conservatives recognized early that home owners were more likely to vote for the Party: at that time, the promotion of ownership was not primarily concerned with reducing economic inequalities, although it did spread wealth further down the income scale. Attempts to expand home ownership remain at the forefront of housing policy. In 2005, in its response to the Barker Review of Housing Supply, the Labour government committed itself to extending home ownership towards 75 per cent by 2010 in England.[5] Policies to reverse the decline that in fact occurred – home ownership had fallen to under 63 per cent by 2015/16 – are still central to housing policy today.

Home ownership policy (and housing policy more generally) has always been driven by political considerations as much as by the purely economic. Economists may wish to promote tenure 'neutrality' in the sense of taxation and subsidies, but the wider political issues still have to be recognized and some policies widely recommended by economists are effectively off limits politically.[6] It should also be recognized that there are reasons for households to favour home ownership other than the tax and capital gains benefits they may receive. Core reasons why people are seen to prefer to own rather than rent include the capacity to match expenditures on housing more directly to lifetime income patterns; greater freedom to do what they wish to the property rather than accept what a landlord provides; greater security and satisfaction; and more fundamentally because ownership and occupation are integrated so that households are their own landlords.[7] These reasons for tenure choice suggest that owner occupation is less likely to be an appropriate tenure for those who are young and mobile or have insecure jobs because of the higher transaction costs and higher risks associated with the early years of debt, but that it is likely to be the preferred tenure for older, more stable households.

These arguments are reflected in evidence across countries with very different overall owner occupation rates. Thus, in one study in the 1990s for instance, owner occupation rates among stable middle aged and older households were around 80 per cent not just in the UK with its high overall rate at that time, but also in countries such as Germany and Japan.[8] There may also be strong reasons for governments to favour owner occupation as long as households are able to pay off their mortgages since the costs of owner occupation in retirement are far lower while tenants face continuing increases.

In addition, the desire to expand home ownership these days is driven by concerns about wealth inequality, potential externalities in terms of health and education, and from concerns about the differential quality of the housing stock between renting and owning and the limited security of tenure in the former. Nevertheless, we observed in Chapter 8, in the US, that inappropriate attempts to raise home ownership can lead to increases in default rates and to wider effects for the macroeconomy; ownership has to be sustainable.

It should also be noted that action to increase home ownership is restricted by the direction of monetary, fiscal and environmental policies. These are aimed primarily at wider objectives, with housing only playing a secondary role; as a result, macro policies are not necessarily consistent with expanding home ownership. Finally, home ownership is strongly affected by events in labour markets – we noted in Chapter 4 the relative decline in the earnings of young households. Given all these constraints – political, macroeconomic and labour market, the scope for reversing the decline in ownership by housing-specific policies is limited.

How has owner occupation evolved?

We have already noted that by the Second World War almost a third of households in England owned their own homes, up from around a quarter in 1918 (see Table 4.1). Over the next three decades, home ownership rose to over 50 per cent. In part this was made possible by decontrol in the private rented sector which enabled large numbers of dwellings to be transferred into ownership and in part by the continued expansion in mortgage provision for those with stable incomes and some savings. From the late 1960s there was considerable innovation in the mortgage market (including the provision of fixed interest rate mortgages provided by local authorities). As inflation took hold in the

1970s housing also became a reasonable hedge against that inflation; many of the risks associated with borrowing – although high at the beginning of the loan – were relatively short-lived because the real value of the loan fell so rapidly for those who could overcome the initial barriers to entry. Again, home ownership grew, although more slowly than in the two earlier decades.

Then, in the 1980s, and to a lesser extent the 1990s, came the second big shift in the housing stock from one tenure to another, as a result of the Right to Buy – with over 1.5 million homes transferred from public ownership to their tenants. Partly as a result, by the early 1990s, around two-thirds of dwellings were owner occupied and the upward trend continued until the beginning of the new century. Home ownership peaked in England in 2003 in proportional terms and in 2005 in numbers terms. It has fallen in most subsequent years, with significant numbers of dwellings moving into the private rented sector. A particular issue is what has happened to Right to Buy properties: a survey by Inside Housing suggested that perhaps 40 per cent of Right to Buy properties were owned by private landlords at the end of 2017.[9] The rate of decline in owner occupation has generally been greater than seen in some other European countries and as a result the rate is now, in 2019, below the median proportion for the EU.

The importance of tax reliefs

From the introduction of income taxation in 1799, housing was treated as an investment good in the UK, so that costs could be set against income for both landlords and owner occupiers and, for owner occupiers, that income was imputed as the rent a tenant would pay the landlord. This tax, which was known as Schedule A, was removed for owner occupiers in 1963, in part because the methods of calculation of both income and expenditure were increasingly unrelated to reality and, in part, because the government wanted to incentivize home ownership. This change took place at approximately the same time as capital gains tax was introduced but with the primary residence exempted. Both changes clearly benefitted owner occupation.

The next change was, however, in the other direction, although it took place very slowly. As there was no longer an imputed rental income against which to set it, the case for removing mortgage interest tax relief became stronger, especially as the amount of housing debt had increased with inflation and deregulation (see Chapter 7). Initial moves to restrict mortgage interest tax relief were made in the late 1960s and, in 1974, it was limited to the first £25,000 of the mortgage (although more than one person could claim relief until 1988). It was not until 1990/91 that relief was limited to the basic rate of income tax and then from 1993/94 was separated from the tax rate and started to be withdrawn by lowering the rate until it reached zero in 2000. Thus, owner occupied housing is now mainly treated as a consumption rather than an investment good, except that purchases by most buyers are subject to stamp duty and inheritance tax is charged, with some (significant) exemptions.

Private renting until the last few years, however, continued to be treated as an investment good, with costs set against income. This is now changing, so that tax relief on expenses has been increasingly limited and relief on mortgage interest will be phased out in 2020 to be replaced by a 20 per cent tax credit (a somewhat similar approach to that taken with respect to owner occupation in the 1990s). As a result of all these modifications housing overall is more highly taxed than in the past, but the latest changes may well mean that owner occupation is to be preferred over rentals.

Support for low-cost home ownership

Until the 1960s the general assumption was that home ownership was the tenure for those with stable incomes, able to support a mortgage that would be paid off before the household retired without direct government support. However, as the benefits of home ownership became more generally recognized, governments, both Conservative and Labour, started to introduce policies that could help people further down the income scale to become home owners. In the Housing Subsidies Act 1967 the Labour government introduced an option mortgage scheme by which people could choose between the standard mortgage with tax relief or they could forgo that relief in return for a government subsidy. This helped those whose incomes were too low to benefit fully from tax relief.[10]

During the 1960s and 1970s (and in relation to the Right to Buy in the 1980s) local authorities played a major role in the home loan market, accounting at its height for up to 16 per cent of that market. During the 1970s, they typically offered loans of up to 97 per cent of the value of a home, with repayments spread over 25 or 30 years. Mortgages were granted to local people only and targeted areas that councils were keen to see regenerated. From 1958, authorities also had the power to guarantee mortgages, facilitating loans up to 100 per cent, in part to support their regeneration investment. And, most importantly, authorities had the right to sell properties and during the 1970s 150,000 dwellings were sold to tenants. During the 1960s and 1970s, a number of local authorities and housing associations also introduced their own shared ownership schemes for lower-income households by which a proportion – often 50 per cent – was owned by the purchaser and the rest by the authority or association, sometimes purchased from the private sector, sometimes based on local authority provision.[11]

The Housing Act 1980 saw a step change in the government's wish to incentivize home ownership as part of a property-owning democracy. It introduced a wide range of national initiatives not only to encourage owner occupation but also to help with regeneration and new supply as subsidies to social renting were reduced. These initiatives included not only the expansion of shared ownership and do-it-yourself shared ownership but also the sale of public land for low-cost homes for purchase; build and improvement for sale; homesteading (where purchasers were helped to renovate their homes in the expectation that others in the neighbourhood would follow); and guarantees.[12] While many of these initiatives have continued, notably shared ownership and a range of rent to buy products, even taken together, none has been more important than the Right to Buy.

A rather different aspect of support for home ownership has been the government's willingness to introduce products and subsidies to help those who find themselves in difficulties with their mortgage – particularly as a result of macroeconomic conditions. The problem first became serious during the crisis at the end of the 1980s and early 1990s when large numbers of households were not able to pay their mortgage instalments. The government introduced income-related interest subsidies for those facing unemployment and demanded that mortgage lenders introduce policies of forbearance. As the system moved back towards normality, the government supported the introduction of Mortgage Payment Protection Insurance (MPPI), an insurance against a range of risks faced by individual mortgagors. Unhappily, the support turned out to be relatively ineffective and led to a mis-selling scandal. In later crises however low interest rates have meant that problems have been much more limited and the government has turned the subsidy into an interest bearing loan.[13]

Help to Buy schemes

Recent Help to Buy schemes attempt to provide further support, in addition to shared ownership, in raising the required deposit and lowering monthly payments. The initial schemes involved developers putting up part of the equity, but this reduced their capacity to expand output. Those introduced since 2013 include Help to Buy Equity Loans, Help to Buy Mortgage Guarantees (now closed), and Help to Buy ISAs (which provide a government savings boost). Equity Loans are quantitatively the largest intervention: the scheme provides a government loan of up to 20 per cent of the market value (40 per cent in London) to purchasers of a newly built home. Approximately 80 per cent of loans have been taken up by first-time purchasers. The buyer is required to provide at least a 5 per cent deposit and a primary lender provides a maximum of the remaining 75 per cent through a conventional loan (55 per cent in London). By the end of March 2019, approximately 221,000 loans had been completed in England: 17 per cent purchased flats, 21 per cent terraced properties, 32 per cent semi-detached homes and 30 per cent detached houses. Therefore, purchases were, by no means, confined to the lower end of the market. In 2018, the median purchase price by first-time buyers under the scheme outside London exceeded £240,000, which was similar to the overall national average purchase price for all properties. In the same year, the median household income for first-time buyers under the scheme was more than £48,000 (£64,000 in London).

Help to Buy Equity Loans – as a demand subsidy, although equally intended to support the market and particularly new build at a time when confidence and the low capital base of most developers was limiting – have been criticized because of the potential effect on house prices. The National Audit Office evaluation report suggested however that any effect has been very small.[14] Two independent reviews for the government[15] also indicated that the scheme has had limited effect on overall house prices once property type is taken into account, partly because it was tied to new housing which is a relatively small part even of transactions. Land prices also did not increase. Other recent research[16] based on more general data has been more critical and argues that the positive price effects on newly built dwellings may have been significant in locations – notably in outer London – where new supply is price inelastic.

A possible tax reform

If a policy aim is to increase home ownership among younger households and those who missed out in their twenties or thirties, it is unlikely that this will be achieved by a strong growth in housing supply alone. Expansion will require a degree of intergenerational redistribution as well, which can probably best be addressed through taxation reform.

Tax changes are particularly attractive from a purely economic perspective because they potentially affect a wider group of owners than just aspiring first-time buyers and so their price effects are expected to be larger. Reform of the property tax system overall has been widely advocated by economists – the Mirrlees Review, discussed in Chapter 7, provides a good example[17] – but major tax reform is generally considered off limits politically and practically for the reasons set out in the Introduction. In fact, it is not the case that significant tax reforms have never taken place and the best example is the removal of mortgage interest tax relief discussed earlier. However, the key features were that abolition was phased over three decades, starting with limiting the amount of mortgage debt covered and continuing much later with reductions in the rate until the relief finally disappeared at a time of low mortgage interest rates. Importantly because of the economic environment almost no-one saw significant increases in their repayments.

The merits and demerits of Stamp Duty Land Tax were discussed in Chapter 7, but since the tax yielded well over £8 billion in 2018/19 and payments are heavily concentrated in the South, particularly London, it is not hard to see why the government is reluctant to introduce fundamental reform. Nevertheless, revenues have been reduced by certain policy changes, notably to help first-time buyers, who now pay no tax on properties purchased below £300,000. On the other hand, higher rates are now chargeable on second homes, including Buy to Let properties and purchases by non-residents.

However, the major reform most commonly advocated relates to the Council Tax system with the suggestion that the current system should be replaced with a tax more directly related to the value of the property. By contrast, under the current Council Tax system, dwellings are divided into eight property bands (A–H), using valuations from 1991. One of the criticisms of the present system is that no uprating has taken place since that date; another fundamental issue is that the system is regressive because of the limitation to eight bands and the ratios set between bands, with those living in the most expensive properties paying proportionately less than those in lower priced homes. For illustration, Table 13.1 looks at one alternative, based on the introduction of an annual property tax in England equal to 0.5 per cent of market values.[18]

Some assumptions are needed; the Family Resources Survey for 2016/17 provides information on the Council Tax band for each property in the Survey, but not the property value itself. Therefore, we take the midpoint of the band and increase valuations from 1991 to 2016/

Table 13.1: The effects of the introduction of an annual 0.5 per cent property tax in England (per cent of gross household income)

By age group			By region		
Age group	% of gross household income	Sample size	Region	% of gross household income	Sample size
25–34	2.9	655	North East	3.1	454
35–44	3.3	1,298	North West	4.0	1,271
45–54	3.7	1,692	Yorks/Humber	3.7	922
55–59	4.4	822	East Mids	4.4	837
60–64	5.9	830	West Mids	4.2	958
65–74	6.6	1,863	East	5.9	1,023
75+	8.5	1,500	South East	6.9	1,481
			London	8.7	775
			South West	5.9	966

Source: authors' calculations

17 using regional house price indices. This, therefore, assumes that all properties within each region increase in value at the same rate, rather than using measures that vary by property type. The 0.5 per cent tax rate is then applied to each dwelling; the rate is arbitrary, but different rates affect the absolute values rather than the distributions, which are our main interest. Table 13.1 sets out the average percentages of gross household income that would be spent on the notional property tax at 2016/17 house prices and incomes, assuming the household does not move. The table shows the distribution by age group and by region and refers only to those currently buying with a mortgage or outright owners and so excludes renters. It should, however, be noted that there would also be significant effects in the rental sector – notably in the social sector where incomes are inherently more out of line with property values. Most commentators also suggest that changes would have to be introduced slowly, with transitional arrangements to help the asset-rich but income-poor.

The first part of the table suggests that the tax as a percentage of income would rise with age, at least on average. Since the older age groups are paying little in terms of mortgage costs – this is one of the benefits of owner occupation – the tax redresses some of the imbalance in current housing costs. However, the averages disguise a wide dispersion; taken at face value, some households own very expensive properties relative to their incomes. These would be hit heavily by an annual property charge; approximately 1.5 per cent of the sample would be estimated to pay more than 25 per cent of their incomes on the tax and a large majority of these are outright owners with approximately 80 per cent over the age of 55. The second part, as expected, indicates that the southern regions, notably London, would face considerably higher charges than the North, reflecting the differences in property values, whereas this is not necessarily the case under the current Council Tax structure, where charges are not proportionate to property values. Since property taxes are a part of the user cost of capital, the expectation is that the tax would both reduce the level of house prices and narrow the regional dispersion, both of which would help first-time buyers at the expense of existing owners. Although it is difficult to put precise estimates on the size of the price effect, our expectation is that it would be considerable.

Alternatives to mortgage debt

The evidence suggests that countries, such as the UK, with a weak response of housing supply to changes in house prices are more likely to experience greater house price volatility. Furthermore, those with liberalized mortgage markets are also likely to undergo greater price volatility (see Chapter 8). Under these conditions, if the economy experiences a cyclical downturn, housing market risk and the probability of default are likely to be relatively high. In addition, if house prices fall, the availability of housing as collateral for consumption and business loans weakens, producing a further decline in GDP. We saw in Chapter 8 that some governments have attempted to reduce the default probabilities by imposing constraints on loan to income and loan to value ratios, which also limit the debt feedback on to the macroeconomy.[19] One downside is that macro stabilization by this route heavily affects aspiring first-time buyers, even those who might generally be considered low risk. The question, therefore, arises whether there are other non–debt funding models that alleviate the problems for both the economy and first-time buyers.

Figure 7.3 showed the decline in net mortgage advances since the GFC. There seems little likelihood of an immediate return to pre-crisis funding levels, even though the number of first-time buyers has recently risen somewhat. However, conventional debt finance is likely to continue to be the main form of finance for the majority of households. But, as noted earlier, Help to Buy Equity Loans have attempted to provide a bridge to overcome deposit constraints and to help affordability as well as stimulating new housing construction. An important difference between Help to Buy and more conventional mortgage products is that the former is an example of shared equity, and, therefore, contributes less to increases in household indebtedness at the same time as reducing outgoings. In this case, the government finances up to 20 per cent of the property (40 per cent in London) and, rather than charging interest over the first five years, benefits from any increase in the property value until the equity loan is repaid but, equally, loses in the case of a price fall. Therefore, the price risk is spread between the household and the government. Furthermore, since the household has a lower level of indebtedness, the default probability is likely to be lower were unexpected shocks – such as an income reduction – to take place. Also, equity sharing potentially allows households to widen their assets rather than holding a portfolio dominated by a single home and, hence, helps to separate housing consumption and investment decisions.[20]

In general, equity finance models are instruments by which the cost of the finance is directly related to the evolution of the value of the home: the faster the price rises, the greater is the return to the investor. Shared ownership and Equity Help to Buy fall into this categorization since, in both cases, an outside agency – a housing association in the former and the government in the latter – receives a proportion of the capital increases and bears some of the costs of any decreases at the time of sale (or purchase when a shared owner 'staircases' to increase their share). Rather different is the idea of crowdfunding for property, which is currently only a tiny part of the market in the UK. Equity property crowdfunding provides one form of alternative finance which allows the public to buy an equity stake.[21] Each investor receives a proportion of the rental income achieved from the property and from the capital appreciation when the property is finally sold. Although the scheme does not raise home ownership directly, since the returns are related to the performance of the housing market, it helps the investor to accumulate a deposit and to diversify their investments.

In contrast to Help to Buy, where the return to government is in terms of a capital gain until interest charges begin after five years, under shared ownership, the investor (usually a housing association) obtains a regular return in the form of rent on its share as well as benefitting when its share is sold. Both are forms of home purchase product where the initiative has come from government with the aim of expanding home ownership – in the case of shared ownership as a long-term policy since 1980 and, in Help to Buy, as (relatively) short-term support for the market through additional sales and supply. In practice the contributions to raising home ownership have been much smaller than Right to Buy but, aided by a modest relaxation of lending criteria for first-time buyers, there has been some rise in home ownership rates among the young since 2016 to which policy initiatives have contributed.[22]

A financing instrument that both lowers price and default risk would appear attractive to the borrower and, in principle, opens up possibilities to investors beyond government, notably financial institutions, although these have so far failed to overcome regulatory and market failures to any great extent.[23] But, *prima facie*, there is a strong case for the development of instruments that can hedge the price risk through forms of risk sharing for households who are over-exposed in a single housing asset. House price linked savings accounts or bonds provide one instrument. An advantage is that these allow renters who cannot immediately afford home ownership, or do not wish to own, to share in the benefits of price increases. Potentially, variants are also attractive to institutional property funds.

However, the evidence is that even Help to Buy has not been taken up fully by those who are eligible and who would have benefitted from the scheme, in terms of lower mortgage repayments, compared with conventional debt finance.[24] A possible explanation is that participation involves giving up a proportion of any future capital gain; if the expectation of gains is high, then the implied reduction in return may exceed the savings in mortgage interest payments.[25] Furthermore, in some cases, Help to Buy has been used by purchasers to supplement their own often quite large deposits to buy larger and sometimes more expensive properties, which may of itself be valuable for the individual purchaser in that it reduces both regular outgoings and the need to move again as their family expands. In addition, shared ownership schemes were never intended to support those at the bottom end of the income distribution but rather to provide opportunities among those near the margin of ownership.

International lessons for home ownership

The UK is far from alone in experiencing falling rates of home ownership and, indeed, the international causes and policy responses are largely similar. There are no easy solutions that the UK is missing from the international experience. Figure 4.1 showed that ownership rates had fallen in the US and Australia and, in fact, ownership has declined in the majority of European countries as well during the current century – although not generally as rapidly as in the UK. The main exceptions to the decline are some Eastern European countries and countries such as the Netherlands and Poland where there has been significant support to expand the sector, especially since the financial crisis.[26] The decline in ownership rates often started well before the GFC in 2008 and increasing mortgage regulation has not been the key driver of reductions in first-time buyer numbers. Rather affordability and job and income insecurity are the starting point for the exclusion of younger households; insecurity affects the preparedness to take on debt.[27]

The one area where regulation has had some direct impact in terms of access is the growing importance of deposits and associated restrictions on borrowing. Loan to value ratios have declined, sometimes based on legal changes, sometimes on guidance, sometimes because of changes in business practice – and sometimes as a result of consumer choice.[28] Borrowing to pay for taxes, transaction costs and the deposit is now more difficult. Changes in regulation and controls clearly have some impact, especially on the size of the deposit required and the capacity to prove resilience in the face of economic and financial change (particularly interest rate rises), but it is only one part of the story. Access to parental wealth, the so-called 'Bank of Mum and Dad', has become more important in many countries, for instance in France, the United States and Australia as well as the UK. In some cases, this is simply a reversal to the norm – in Portugal, Greece, Spain and countries where mortgage markets are still developing and family support is a major source of funding. In the absence of support, the numbers of young people living with their parents has increased since the recession in a wide range of countries including Canada, France, Greece, Hungary, Italy, Portugal and the United States – as well as in the UK where Office for National Statistics data show that the proportion of men aged 20–34 living with their parents has risen from 26 per cent to 32 per cent since the turn of the century (see also Chapter 4).

Although institutional conditions, including tax regimes and rental controls differ considerably, a common theme that emerges from the international literature is the need to learn from the experience of the GFC. Maximizing the rate of home ownership is not an appropriate objective and there is likely to be a significant proportion of households for whom home ownership is not the most appropriate option, despite the fact that the (risk unadjusted) returns on housing have typically been higher than other assets and rents can be higher than mortgage payments. In the US, the Clinton Administration launched the National Home Ownership Strategy in 1995 designed to boost home ownership to an all-time high, whereas in 2003 George W. Bush enacted the American Dream Downpayment Initiative, designed to assist first-time buyers and to reduce racial inequality.[29] In Europe, there is evidence that a temporary rise in home ownership before the crash was also partially related to the relaxation of downpayment constraints.[30] However, the subsequent decline in the US was related to tighter credit conditions (discussed in Chapter 8) and stagnant real incomes. High levels of student debt also appear to have played a role in the US. And after the GFC approximately eight million households suffered foreclosure.[31]

In conclusion

No UK review of home ownership, either official or unofficial, has proposed quick, but permanent solutions to raising home ownership and many other countries face similar problems. Instead ideas have usually concentrated on the promotion of an overall environment under which sustainable ownership can thrive; changes in the income distribution, in the mortgage market, the development of a more neutral tax regime and a reduction in real house prices have come under particular scrutiny.[32] A long-term expansion of housing supply is typically seen as a necessary condition but does not yield an immediate significant increase.

Since there are no easy solutions, we need to be careful in trying to develop short-run fixes as these can be counter-productive in the longer run. It is undesirable to aim for a target of 75 per cent (or any other number) even if most households would prefer to be owners. We have stressed that owner occupation is a market and, broadly, reacts to incentives in a similar manner to other private sector markets. The market forces are strong and there is a limit to what can be achieved in raising home ownership among the young by direct policy action. First-time buyers may compete with existing owners and investors and, arguably, the best that can be achieved is the promotion of a more level playing field. From Chapter 3, the income elasticity of owner occupied housing demand is high in the UK relative to the price elasticity and, under these conditions, first-time buyers will struggle. The conditions imply that house prices are likely to rise faster than incomes, worsening aspiring first-time buyer access. Policies to increase housing supply are important, but are only one part of the story and, perhaps, insufficient attention has been paid to the underlying preferences that generate a high income elasticity of demand. We return to this question in the next and final chapter where we show that preferences are affected by institutional conditions, including the social norms of behaviour. These differ between countries but are hard to change.

The absence of a level playing field between tenures and households relates to three main issues: the asset bases of first-time buyers relative to existing owners and investors, arising from accumulated equity in existing properties; differential access to credit markets; and the regressive property tax system. In practice, given the political realities, the scope for action appears greatest in terms of mortgage market access. We have seen the sharp decline in real net mortgage advances in recent years, which has disproportionately affected first-time buyers and a question is whether alternative funding models can be developed which increase choice and provide a suitable degree of consumer protection. In the light of the GFC there is, perhaps, understandable caution by households with regard to new derivative products.

14

Where Do We Go from Here?

We shall not cease from exploration
And the end of all our exploring
Will be to arrive where we started
And know the place for the first time

T.S. Eliot, 'Little Gidding', 1942

Introduction

If we were to design a housing system from scratch, we certainly would not start from where we are. Of course, this is not a helpful observation, but it highlights the fact that housing is a path dependent process where even the most reforming governments are heavily constrained by the history of past policy decisions and the inherited structure of the built environment. The residential structure of cities, for example, changes only slowly because annual net additions to the housing supply are modest in relation to the existing stock of dwellings and infrastructure patterns have often been set many decades, or even centuries, ago. Both help to lock in historical patterns of social advantage and disadvantage. Since the Second World War, there have been major advances in housing conditions for the average household, but change has been gradual, subject to major cycles, and there are no quick fixes.

Moreover, housing policy is further constrained by conflicting objectives. The last chapter discussed the origins of the property-owning democracy and the limitations this puts on modifying taxation. We have also stressed the impact of monetary policy on housing and the fact that housing is always likely to take second place to wider macro objectives such as the control of inflation and stabilization policy. The position of housing is also weakened by the fact that it has no single champion within government coordinating policy under a

'Big Idea'. In the English case, housing policy is technically the remit of the Ministry of Housing, Communities and Local Government; but the Bank of England oversees policies concerning mortgage debt and interest rates; policy involving taxation or subsidies needs the agreement of the Treasury; the Department of Work and Pensions has a key role in housing affordability through the housing benefit and Universal Credit systems; the Department for Business, Energy and Industrial Policy oversees the construction industry; and the National Infrastructure and Project Authority is in charge of major initiatives, many of which involve housing.[1] In none of these departments is housing the sole (or in most cases the primary) concern. Consequently, housing policy can appear incoherent and inconsistent and, indeed, social and cultural influences – including local initiatives – can play a greater role than direct housing policy.

There is, however, a remarkable degree of agreement among housing economists on a range of required policy reforms, although the emphasis and details may differ. Broadly, these include four areas: reform of property taxation; policies for planning and land release, including the funding of infrastructure and social housing; regulation of the private rental sector and income-based subsidy provision; and financial market reforms, which include not only access to mortgages but also the relative returns on financial assets and housing.[2] All of these have been discussed in previous chapters but the fact that limited progress has been made further highlights the constraints on radical policy action.

However, our understanding of how housing markets work has improved considerably. We understand better the causes of worsening affordability and to some extent the quantitative impact of different policy interventions. In aggregate, Chapter 3 showed that this could be summarized by a fairly simple condition that captured both the demand and supply sides of the market and highlighted the role of the four key parameters that have been central to international research in housing economics: the income and price elasticities of housing demand; the price elasticity of housing supply; and the responsiveness of demand to changes in the cost of capital. The first two elasticities were major concerns in an earlier generation of research, but we will suggest that we need to return to the parameters in the light of new directions in economic research; hence the quotation at the start of the chapter. Chapter 3 also drew out the importance of the cost of capital and how the responsiveness of house prices depends on the degree of mortgage market liberalization. Those countries that have undergone reform will typically experience greater sensitivity to changes in interest rates. In addition to the four housing-specific parameters, the key influence on affordability has been the income distribution. For affordability to improve, policy either has to influence the income distribution, for example through housing benefit, or affect one or more of the four key parameters. Land use planning affects the price elasticity of supply, central bank lending constraints change the responsiveness of house prices to the cost of capital and more understanding is needed of how policy might affect the income and price elasticities of demand.

Aggregate relationships provide only so much information about what is also a distribution problem. Most households are adequately housed, are happy with their homes, and do not face affordability difficulties. This was illustrated using the affordability indicators constructed in Chapter 2. We have stressed that macro policies have distributional consequences. This clearly occurs in mortgage markets where prudential policies most heavily affect aspiring first-time buyers rather than current owners. Similarly, the property tax system favours older owners with higher-value properties. So-called under-occupancy is one outcome, but this simply reflects individual values and market incentives. As noted, affordability is not only a housing market issue but is also a result of long-term changes in the distribution of income away from younger and poorer households. Since the income elasticity of housing demand is high, income inequality widens the housing wealth distribution. We also discussed the rise in mortgage defaults in the UK in the early 1990s and more dramatically the later US sub-prime crisis, which have shown that maximizing the rate of home ownership (particularly through expanding the amount of housing debt) is not an appropriate objective. In this context it is worth noting that large-scale government interventions such as the Right to Buy, which aimed to raise the levels of owner occupation for future generations, may be significantly offset over time as the housing market changes.

In summary, aggregate trends in affordability, the distribution of outcomes across households and sustainability are all issues that have to be addressed. But although our formal tools have given us a fuller understanding of the causes of affordability problems and better measures based more robustly on economic theory and empirical evidence, it still does not follow that there are easy solutions given the range of constraints on action and the multiplicity of objectives. In the next sections, we bring together what are now considered to be the conventional, primarily market-based, solutions advocated by economists. Moreover, while still recognizing the insights from economics, there are also alternative or complementary approaches that bring in other disciplines (as noted in Chapter 1). These include insights from psychology and behavioural economics that pay greater attention to the role of institutions, broadly defined to include the role of social norms. We show how they particularly impact on the key income elasticity of housing demand and, thus, on affordability.

An absolute shortage of homes or just a distribution problem?

Before a policy consensus can emerge, we need to agree on the causes of the problem. Perhaps, the most fundamental disagreement is between those who believe that there is an absolute shortage of homes – in which case the solution is to build more – and those who think that the problem is distributional, arising from the use of housing as an asset during periods of low financial yields, expanding mortgage markets, and the tax advantages enjoyed by housing. In fact, the distinction is false and there can be both an absolute shortage and distribution issues; we would argue there are both problems. We have also suggested in this book that there has been an over-reliance on supply side policies alone – the Barker Review, for example, was never asked to investigate demand side measures.[3] However, supply and demand policies can be used as complements rather than substitutes and the failure to employ the latter reflects political priorities.

Furthermore, policy has concentrated on the low price elasticity of housing supply in the UK relative to some other countries – and the empirical evidence supports this. This is commonly attributed to the effects of the land use planning system but there are a wide range of additional explanations including, in particular, industry structure, skill shortages and development finance. Rather less attention has been paid to the result that the income elasticity of demand relative to the price elasticity is high in the UK. Few international comparative studies exist on a consistent basis, although there is some evidence that the ratio is lower in Germany.[4] Either the income elasticity of demand for housing is lower in Germany or the price elasticity higher (or both). In terms of explaining changes in affordability this is important: the greater is the ratio, the faster affordability can be expected to worsen if income expands more rapidly than the housing stock. In the long run, that is from the late 1960s, this has been more important in explaining UK house price trends than interest rates. We will return to the underlying reasons for differences in the price and income elasticities of demand.

Market solutions or intervention?

Since private housing transactions take place in a market, the market will always achieve a solution, but the problem is that the solution may not be considered acceptable either in social or economic terms. We have seen in Chapter 4 that one market outcome has been a slowing in the rate of household formation among the young. In itself this is not necessarily problematic, since it simply represents a weakening of a long-run decline in the average household size, that has been in progress since the 19th century. On the other hand, it might limit labour mobility and prevent the young from moving to locations with the best employment opportunities. We highlighted the decline in relative earnings among the young as a factor contributing to lower rates of home ownership.

Chapter 8 also discussed the role of housing market risk and how this impacts decisions and outcomes. At times of high house prices, the risk premium associated with investing in housing and the probability of a market collapse increases, were negative internal or external shocks to the economy to occur. This ensures, for example, that the ratio of house prices to incomes and other measures of affordability do not increase without bound. The danger of this 'solution' is in terms of macroeconomic stability – rather than a gradual adjustment, change is likely to be sharp and rapid and could be accompanied by a rise in mortgage defaults. It also adds to the difficulties in house price forecasting. Limitations on lending to groups perceived to be in the higher risk categories are a partial response to possible rises in default but do not address the underlying problem. We have also seen that mortgage controls disproportionately affect aspiring first-time buyers.

One role of housing policy is to attempt to mitigate some of these outcomes. However, if we decide, for example, that property tax reform or relaxation of planning controls, while economically desirable, are too difficult politically, it has to be recognized that there is a cost. The probability of a market collapse is increased, although it is impossible to predict when this will occur.

Linkages across the tenures

Each housing tenure cannot be considered in isolation since there are important inter-linkages – both within the market sector and in the housing system overall. Figure 5.1 attempted to make the market interactions clearer and showed how changes in the macroeconomy could lead to a change in affordability for low-income households. If rental and ownership markets are interlinked (see Chapter 3), then a rise in house prices would be expected to lead to an increase in gross market rents. Under given eligibility rules, the rise in gross rents leads to a rise in benefit payments; the net rent, then, influences both housing stress and affordability, as discussed in Chapter 2. The full set of interactions has, however, never been fully analyzed in the literature and there are still unknowns on which further research is required.

Do housing supply policies improve affordability?

Drawing on the results of the earlier chapters, we are in a position to discuss further what have become the conventional policy approaches in economics. These policies concern housing supply, taxation, mortgage finance, rents and subsidies.

Even in the US a degree of scepticism has arisen about the effectiveness of supply-based policies.[5] Nevertheless, the consensus is still that increases in housing supply do improve affordability, as well as providing a wider choice of better quality housing. This is also true in the UK, but the issue is by how much? We showed in Chapter 6 that increases in new supply have to be large and long-lasting to be significant and this involves a step change in construction never seen since the period after the First World War. *Gross* construction also expanded rapidly after the Second World War, but the *net* increase in the housing stock was more modest, because of high levels of demolitions under larger slum clearance programmes. The important point is that new construction represents a *flow* and is small in relation to the existing dwelling stock, Therefore, its immediate impact on affordability is always likely to be limited.

It also appears to be the case that, in the US, increases in housing supply at the top end of the market filter down to lower parts of the market, although there is limited evidence for the UK, where household formation further up the income scale together with adjustments which reduce the net effect on the housing stock tend to result in limited housing chains.[6] The building of expensive homes does release slightly cheaper homes for those further down the income distribution, but there is a limit to this process. It is unlikely that those at the bottom end of the market experience any benefit and so still require support[7] either through demand or supply subsidies, including the direct provision of social housing. Consequently, some have argued that land release should prioritize low-cost housing. Section 106 provides a UK policy example. Two further criticisms should be mentioned: first, an increase in new building at the local level simply encourages an inflow of new households to the area with little improvement to affordability for local lower-income households. Within a housing market area, there is truth in this argument; by definition, households are mobile within the area and mobility ensures that house prices change at similar rates. The implication is that supply increases need to be targeted at the housing market area as a whole, rather than at individual local authorities. Secondly, increases in new construction, if they lead to wider neighbourhood improvements, may result in an increase in the prices of existing properties and so the area as a whole becomes less affordable. Gentrification provides an important example, but more research is required on the wider spillover effects on to property prices.

Planning and affordability indicators

Chapter 9 discusses the 2019 revisions to the English NPPF. One of the innovations was to introduce a common framework across local authorities for the assessment of housing need with the inclusion of a formal affordability indictor – the ratio of median house prices to earnings, which is the measure we criticized in Chapter 2. The common method is based primarily on household projections but adjusted where the ratio of median house prices to earnings exceeds an assumed equilibrium value of 4.0. Few local authorities had ratios below 4.0 in 2018. However, if aggregate indicators are required for each local authority, the model in Chapter 3 suggests a preferable affordability measure. We found that if the ratio of income relative to the size of the housing stock is increasing then affordability will deteriorate. But since the numerator can be approximated by average earnings multiplied by the number of employees, one indicator is the local ratio of employment relative to the existing housing stock, weighted by average earnings. A variation which might prove more acceptable would be the ratio of local population relative to the housing stock, again weighted by average earnings. Comparing this indicator with the more conventional planning approach, where the required number of homes is matched to the expected increase in households, a key difference is that the alternative measures suggested here are defined in terms of *stocks* of dwellings and population, rather than *flows* and capture not only increased housing demand arising from new household formation, but also increased effective demand from existing households as a result of rising incomes.

Figure 14.1 plots, for each English local authority in 2018, the conventional measure of affordability – the house price to earnings ratio (horizontal axis) against our alternative measure based on population, earnings and the housing stock. There is certainly a positive correlation between the two measures, but the relationship is by no means perfect, and the correlation coefficient is only 0.62. The outliers are particularly interesting. The authority on the far left of the graph is Copeland in the North West of England; this is an authority where the median price to earnings ratio is low (and so conventionally affordable), but the alternative measure suggests affordability is more in line with other areas. The conflict arises from the fact that Copeland includes the Sellafield nuclear reprocessing plant and this is capitalized into local house prices. The official measures of house prices do not allow for the effect of environment factors. Similarly, although less obvious from the graph, almost all the areas outside London[8] where median house prices relative to earnings imply that affordability is significantly worse than under our alternative measure lie in holiday locations, notably in the South West of England and the South coast. Other outliers are in North Norfolk and close to the Lake District. Once again, the scenery, beaches and climate are capitalized into house prices. Therefore, some part of the officially measured shortages are capturing variations in environmental conditions.

Figure 14.1: The relationship between affordability measures (English local authorities), 2018

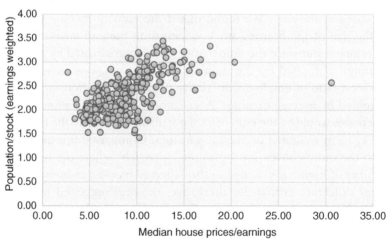

Notes: horizontal axis: the ratio of median house prices to residence-based earnings; vertical axis: the ratio of the population to the housing stock weighted by median earnings.

Source: Authors' estimates

Taxation

The majority of the population – the insiders – do not wish to see falling house prices: existing home owners benefit from capital gains; builders drip feed new properties on to the market in order to avoid disturbing the status quo; land owners benefit from rising prices; government popularity appears to be positively related to increases in house prices; the asset bases of banks and now many other institutions are heavily reliant on housing and central banks, therefore, do not wish to see rapid falls because of the impact on macro stability. The Treasury also gains from increased stamp duty and other receipts at times of rising prices (although higher prices also raise the housing benefit budget). The best we might hope for, therefore, in terms of policy adjustment is a moderation of the rate of increase and a reduction in the degree of price volatility.

By contrast those who benefit from falling house prices – the outsiders – are in a weaker position. Consequently, changes to housing taxation which economists may regard as increasing efficiency and have the potential for a major negative impact on house prices are never likely to be popular and successive governments have been unwilling to undertake significant reforms such as those advocated in the Mirrlees Review. Many current proposals are around an annual land value or property value tax. It has also been suggested that reforms could be integrated with green taxes, designed to meet carbon emissions targets.[9] If significant reforms along these lines were to be introduced, however, they would need to be implemented gradually and to take into account the asset-rich, income-poor problem for older households, possibly through a deferment of the payment.

There is a high degree of consensus among economists for the direction of change – the profession prefers neat and tidy solutions in line with economic theory that do not always match the political or social realities. Proposed innovations to housing taxation stress the benefits of tenure neutrality and emphasize the fact that taxation and subsidies are capitalized into house prices (Chapter 7). The negative effects of stamp duty on household mobility are also emphasized. But higher rates of stamp duty on Buy to Let properties and second homes and exemptions for first-time buyers are indirect attempts to address an underlying problem where existing owners have in-built advantages over first-time buyers through the accumulated equity in their homes. Political pressures mean that any changes are likely to be only partial adjustments towards a more coherent system.

If there is an unwillingness to consider tax reform, it again needs to be remembered that there is a cost; since housing is a market, the market will provide a solution and that solution is likely to promote increased market volatility. Market volatility of itself imposes significant welfare costs because of loss of supply and capacity in the housebuilding industry arising from an asymmetry between the downturn, when supply can be readily reduced (and some builders will go out of business), and the upturn when it takes considerable time to get back to normal activity levels and for entry to occur.

Innovations to mortgage markets

The international evidence is that those countries that have introduced financial deregulation – including to mortgage markets – are more likely to experience house price volatility, particularly if there are restrictions on new building. In the UK there is a strong correlation between changes in house prices and mortgage advances, although we have questioned the direction of causality. This provides one reason for the reintroduction of lending controls, in the UK now primarily based on limitations on the maximum debt to income ratio and the need to pass stress tests. Both regulatory requirements and tighter lending criteria introduced by lenders[10] have meant that net mortgage advances have fallen sharply since the GFC (Chapter 7); but the decline has fallen most heavily on aspiring first-time buyers, because existing owners have typically already accumulated sufficient equity in their homes for the controls not to be binding. Policies which reduce the inequality include additional controls on lending in the Buy to Let market; higher taxation for investors; and the introduction of Help to Buy initiatives designed to reduce both outgoings and the deposit barriers that first-time buyers face. Help to Buy Equity Loans and shared ownership are examples of equity sharing; in the former, ownership is shared with the government and in the latter with a housing association. Neither scheme is without its problems and both only appeal to a section of the population, typically those already close to becoming owners. But the question remains whether there is scope for further expansion through equity sharing with banks and other financial institutions. So far these have failed to take off in the UK or in countries such as Australia where there has been innovation in this area. There is, perhaps, an understandable reluctance to share capital gains if the expectation is that prices will continue to rise. But the concentration of personal wealth in a single, very specific asset is not without its own risks and equity sharing provides a potential route to debt and risk reduction.

Supply versus demand side subsidies

A core issue throughout the post-war period has been whether it is better to use supply or demand side subsidies to assist low-income households. The UK is different from most other countries in the extent to which it uses both together – with 60 per cent of social tenants paying below market rents and also receiving income-related housing benefit (Chapter 12). The argument for demand side benefits is that they are, at least in the UK, available to all eligible households, while supply side subsidies are both limited by the numbers of units supplied and by the fact that once the household is allocated a home, even if its circumstances change, the tenant will not generally be asked to move.

The increasing use of demand side subsidies has been a major element of government policy since the 1970s and is reflected in both the decision to increase rents in the social sector and growing housing benefit bills. Government has currently limited subsidy to social sector building to an Affordable Rents Programme, where rents can be set at up to 80 per cent of market value with over 50 per cent of this new building only receiving support from Section 106 agreements. On the other hand, austerity, the increasing numbers of low-income tenants housed in the private rented sector and concerns that benefits may cause rents to rise, have led to restrictions in both eligibility for housing benefit and the maximum amounts of benefit that can be paid. As a result, households may not be receiving enough to buy the other necessities of life. This suggests that the current situation is unsustainable and either, probably both, demand and supply subsidies need to be expanded.

The most immediate way to assist tenants is to remove some of the constraints on housing benefit. But into the longer term this is not the answer because of its fundamental flaws. The fact that (pace these constraints) those on benefit do not gain from reduced rents and do not pay increased rents and that those with similar household composition on full benefit receive the same income wherever they live, are two of the more problematic aspects of the scheme.

Into the longer term, especially given both increases in population and currently low interest rates, the case for greater investment in social housing seems unassailable. This is not to imply that housing associations and indeed local authorities should not be incentivized to use their own resources more effectively. Nor is it the case that the social sector housing model could not work better in terms of the range of providers, effective management, improving the quality of the stock and indeed allocation methods. But it is to say that the pendulum has certainly swung too far towards demand subsidies and the shift should be in the other direction.

A well-working three tenure housing system?

For most of the last century we have perceived our housing system as made up of two tenures with the third tenure being a residual and often inferior tenure form. Before the Second World War local authority housing accounted for no more than 10 per cent of the stock and private renting was the majority tenure. After 1945, private renting went into decline as a result of slum clearance, rent regulation and the growth of owner occupation, while public housing was generally seen as a far better option than private renting. Indeed, in 1965, Wilfred Beckerman in his text on what Britain would look like in 1975 saw private renting as an 'inferior' good which would soon disappear.[11] At the zenith of social housing in numbers terms, in 1980, nearly one in three households lived in the social rented sector, private renting housed around 10 per cent and owner occupation was rising and would continue to rise rapidly. Yet in 2018 we observe a much broader based system with owner occupation in England at around 63 per cent but including at least some directly subsidized dwellings; private renting at around 20 per cent; and social renting at 17 per cent.

The biggest issue, in the context of both affordability and value for money, relates to the private rented sector where rents are generally much higher than in social renting and, at least in significant parts of the sector, size and quality are on average considerably poorer. Most importantly, England in particular has one of the most highly deregulated private rented sectors in Europe – with a minimum of only six months security of tenure and the possibility of being evicted without cause thereafter; entirely market-determined rents; and at the bottom end of the scale little enforcement of basic standards. Arguably if private renting is to be a mainstream tenure, (accommodating a wide range of households who choose to rent as well as families and more vulnerable households who would more traditionally have been accommodated in the social sector), there need to be improved terms and conditions, as well as better value for money than is currently available.

There have been a small number of government initiatives mainly aimed at increasing investment in private renting, notably through Build to Rent. This type of development is funded by institutional investors who are looking for stable revenues that keep pace with incomes and is seen as filling a gap in the market by providing higher quality and better managed rented housing for those who prefer to rent. In principle, it may also provide longer contracts and stabilized rents. It also has some capacity to reduce volatility in the new build market by bringing in investors who want development built out rapidly so that they can start to generate revenue. This model is seen as being more in line with experience in other European countries. Even so, across Europe the majority of landlords are private individuals and governments are similarly looking for significant sources of money to support new private rented investment.

Institutions and path dependence: moving beyond conventional economic approaches

Useful lessons can be drawn from international comparisons, but care is needed in concluding that the experience of more successful countries can be directly applied to others. Institutional differences make this problematic. By 'institutions' we do not only mean, for example, the structure of mortgage markets or the regulation of land, but more widely, institutions include the social norms and laws built up in a society over many generations as part of a path dependent process. More precisely path dependence implies 'constraints on the choice set of the present that are derived from historical experiences of the past'.[12] Policy in the UK is often contrasted with that in Germany, which has had a lower rate of house price inflation, higher levels of construction and a generally well-functioning rental market. But these arose from a very different historical path, including population and income trends. One suggestion that has tentatively been put forward is that cultural differences can be traced back to the Reformation and the influence of Martin Luther on German work ethics.[13]

Another part of the explanation might be that Second World War bombing had a fundamental impact on German housing.[14] Bombing was not limited to the major cities but was widespread across smaller towns. In what became West Germany, 2.3 million housing units were destroyed completely or rendered permanently uninhabitable, amounting to approximately a quarter of the 1939 housing stock; a similar number suffered damage.[15] Adding in the requirements of large inflows of refugees, the housing deficit amounted to approximately five million units in West Germany at the end of 1950.

The scale of the destruction and the weaknesses of post-war capital markets made it inevitable that the private sector alone would be unable to eliminate the shortages without government support through subsidies and guarantees. Immediately after the war new units were, typically, moderately priced rental dwellings each containing two or three rooms and a kitchen. From the mid-1950s the trend was towards four-room larger apartments.[16] During the 1950s, completions averaged more than 500,000 per annum and were constructed to be suitable for the broad population rather than the lower end of the market. Although less extreme in scale, similar programmes were put in place in the UK but concentrated on public sector rather than private renting.

The construction of private rental housing after the war was not the only factor leading to continuing lower aggregate rates of home ownership in Germany than in most of Europe (although ownership rates are similar for the middle aged) – fewer subsidies to owners, limited intervention in rent setting after a period of extreme controls and lower expectations of capital gains[17] were all important. But the post-war construction programme provided the initial conditions for private renting to become established and flourish as the norm, locking in renting as the dominant tenure.

Short-term versus long-term policies?

Set against a background of long-term improvements in housing conditions, there are always likely to be short-term crises. We have a history of market volatility, often not caused by events within housing markets directly, but associated with wider macroeconomic changes, to which housing policy has to respond. But, in practice, there is a limit to what housing policy can achieve; short-run initiatives to raise home ownership levels, such as Help to Buy, fall into this category.

Arguably long-term progress has had more to do with events originating outside the housing market. Perhaps the most important factor underlying long-run improvements in housing conditions has been continuing growth in the economy. If the income elasticity of housing demand is high, then growth will be translated into a higher demand for housing services, which is more likely to be met by owner occupation, where the quality of the stock is typically higher than in the private rented sector. Furthermore, since the 19th century we can point to a set of key factors. First, housing conditions were improved by a greater understanding of the relationship between health and housing from the mid-19th century (see Chapter 5). Most early legislation concerning housing and the subsequent introduction of building standards related to health and sanitation which led to the beginnings of slum clearance programmes, which expanded rapidly from the 1930s. Secondly, advances in technology had a fundamental effect on construction methods including the principles of modernist design and urban planning. Thirdly, developments in rail and road networks in the second half of the 19th century and first half of the 20th century allowed the suburbanization of the population.[18] Fourthly, wars had a profound impact on housing: the First World War saw a subsequent large increase in housebuilding in order to produce Homes Fit for Heroes; building also expanded rapidly after the Second World War to meet shortages and as part of slum clearance programmes. The bombings also led to major urban population shifts (for example away from London's East End) including the establishment of new towns and the location of social housing.[19] Fifthly, economic globalization and the accompanying migrant flows have had important implications for housing markets, both in terms of the absolute numbers of homes required and their spatial distribution as well as prices.

Joined-up policy and policy appraisal

We noted in the Introduction the broad-based responsibility for housing across different government departments and the potential for an under-estimation of the benefits of housing because of conflicting priorities and poor data. This is also true in government project appraisal. With respect to the measurement of benefits, the Treasury's Green Book states:

> Productivity effects should be included in the calculation of UK costs and benefits where they can be objectively demonstrated. Productivity effects may arise from movement to more or less productive jobs, changes in the structure of the economy, benefits from dynamic clustering or agglomeration (benefits that arise through close location of businesses and/or people), private investment, product market competition or the generation and flow of ideas. Productivity effects will typically lead to higher wages, rather than higher employment. The benefits can be calculated from the different levels of total employment costs under different options.
>
> Interventions which increase human capital, job-search activity or provide better access to jobs can have positive labour supply and macroeconomic effects. Provided they can be supported by clear, objective evidence labour supply effects can be included in appraisal.[20]

Housing falls into these categories, since better quality and more suitably located housing has the potential to increase productivity, for example, through improved educational and health outcomes and by promoting labour mobility. However, in practice, these factors are not included in benefit–cost ratios for housing projects because of the difficulties of objective measurement, although the potential productivity gains are informally referenced in the strategic cases for intervention. Review studies have identified the key channels of influence and some progress has been made in quantification.[21] There is general agreement that, although these benefits exist, they are diffuse and best analyzed at local or metropolitan level, but providing estimates in the form required for project appraisal is complex. Nevertheless, the case for a higher priority for housing would be enhanced by their recognition. This suggests that conventional project appraisal would benefit from a wider framework. For example, any housing policy might be evaluated in terms of its contribution to: (i) productivity and growth; (ii) macro stability; (iii) affordability for target groups; (iv) the effect on wealth distribution; (v) the environment; (vi) spatial inequalities. In each case, any short-run gains need to be assessed relative to the longer term.

National or community-based policies?

These are, of course, not alternatives; few local initiatives can flourish without appropriately designed national policy frameworks. But equally, given the constraints on national housing policy, there is a case for locally driven action, which may not necessarily have much effect on the national picture but can still be of local significance and be more acceptable to the community. It may also, as for instance was the case for both shared ownership and Section 106, provide a local demonstration of how the government might move forward across the country.

Throughout history, locally based groups and determined individuals have had a strong influence, for example, Robert Owen's model community at New Lanark in the early 19th century. The philanthropic Peabody Trust built its first dwellings for the labouring poor in London in the 1860s and its work continues today as a housing association. Financed by John Ruskin, Octavia Hill's attempts to improve housing for the working classes in London date from the same period. The Joseph Rowntree New Earswick development in York was constructed in the early years of the 20th century; the Bournville Village Trust was established in 1900 to provide decent housing for the Cadbury workers. There are many other examples from this era, often arising from religious conviction, but also because of humanitarian aims more generally or because of a belief that well-housed workers are more productive.

It might be argued that these early movements were unencumbered by planning regulations and the interference of national policies, but it is hard to believe that local organizations with a similar drive have not existed throughout the twentieth century and today. Housing associations were a particularly good example well before the 1974 Act. Neighbourhood plans are currently one, nationally incentivized, attempt to involve local communities in the planning process. A further example comes from Community Land Trusts (CLTs) which aim to develop and manage affordable housing and provide an alternative model to the mainstream. In 2019, 320 CLTs were in existence and although output continues to remain modest, the number of new homes is expected to expand.

In conclusion

The earlier sections of this chapter concerned with conventional policies imply that there are no quick fixes or silver bullets. Those of a pessimistic disposition would point out that: (i) the likely growth in the housing stock is insufficient, by itself, to ensure that the level of real house prices will stabilize; (ii) the political realities are such that fundamental reform of the housing tax system is unlikely; (iii) there is little sign of a reversal of the persistent relative income losses experienced by younger age groups; (iv) the imposition of tighter lending controls impacts primarily on aspiring first-time buyers; while (v) a failure to address any of these issues is likely to lead to a continuation of the cyclical volatility that has characterized housing markets over many decades, as macroeconomic shocks are transmitted to the housing market.

Some have pointed to the role of housing as a tradable asset as a fundamental cause of the problem; at times of low returns on financial assets, housing becomes more attractive, particularly if the risks of housing investment are inadequately taken into account. There seems little doubt that this has contributed to price trends in recent years. However, we also noted (Figure 3.1) that the housing cost of capital has little long-run trend and, therefore, cannot account for the strong long-run growth rate in real house prices, which has averaged approximately 3.5 per cent per annum since 1969. To understand long-run growth we have to turn to housing's fundamental role as a consumption good. This brings us back once again to the income and price elasticities of housing demand, arguably the key parameters in earlier generations of housing research, but which have received less attention in recent years as interest has shifted to the supply side of the market and to the investment characteristics of housing. To stress the point, this is not to say that supply and investment are unimportant, but that the balance of concerns has become distorted.

As noted earlier the ratio of the income to price elasticity of housing demand is high in the UK. As an illustration of its importance, using the parameters in Table 3.1, since real household disposable income has risen by approximately 2.5 per cent per annum on average since 1969 in the UK, the rise in income alone would have increased real house prices by around 6.25 per cent per annum (the fact that prices rose by only 3.5 per cent is primarily attributable to the offsetting increase in the dwelling stock). But if, for example, the income elasticity relative to the price elasticity was only half the estimated value, real house prices might have been approximately constant with the level of housing construction that actually took place over the period (although construction could be expected to have been weaker with lower price growth). Halving the key parameter is, of course, arbitrary, but it illustrates the quantitative importance. Rising real house prices are not only a question of supply and investment demand, but particularly of consumption demand.

Three questions arise: first, what determines the income elasticity of demand for owner occupiers, which is likely to be higher than for tenants? Table 3.1 implies that this is greater than one, using UK time-series data. Secondly, what determines the price elasticity of demand, which is well below one? Thirdly, is there a possibility that the elasticities might change in the future? An understanding of these issues is crucial to future housing policy. The conventional explanation for the high income elasticity is that the underlying demands for space and other housing characteristics are highly responsive to income changes and, indeed, the parameter is important in traditional models of residential location. Moreover, the income elasticity of owner occupier demand is likely to be higher than for renting because of the different attributes of the properties in each tenure. In addition, we might expect the price elasticity of owner occupier housing demand to be fairly low in the UK, at least historically, because of the limited availability of reasonable quality rental accommodation, acting as a substitute for ownership.

A more recent line of enquiry concerns the extent to which home ownership is influenced by social norms and/or its role as a positional good,[22] which affect wellbeing. Both factors stress the *relative* position of a household in a social hierarchy where housing decisions are influenced not only by the utility obtained from an absolute level of consumption, but also from consumption relative to that of a peer group. In the case of social norms, if the peer group values home ownership highly, an individual's own wellbeing is enhanced by also becoming an owner and conforming to the norm. In the case of positional goods, wellbeing is decreased if peers consume a higher level of housing than the individual. The importance is that this may lead to a form of herd behaviour where households jockey for the premier position. A consequence – although never yet directly tested in the literature – is that the aggregate income elasticity of demand can be higher than if the household ignored the peer group; similarly, the price elasticity of demand can be lower. In models allowing for interactions between households, social interactions generate strategic complementarities:

> even if changes in fundamentals [for example in our case a change in income] create only a small change in the level of activity for each individual, each individual's small change will then raise the benefits [or costs] for everyone else pursuing that activity. … Small changes in fundamental variables can set off a cascade …[23]

Therefore, allowing for interactions is expected to raise the aggregate income elasticity of demand.

There is some evidence that social norms and positional goods matter in UK housing markets.[24] By comparison, although home ownership in Germany does appear to have a positive influence on life satisfaction, the effects are marginal relative to other factors.[25] Although no more than indicative, this is at least consistent with a lower income elasticity of demand in Germany and, therefore, weaker house price growth. Those countries with lower home ownership rates may have lower income elasticities of housing demand because ownership is less relevant as a social norm. But it should be noted that increased housing consumption arising purely from the desire to meet social norms or because of positional goods does not necessarily add to overall national welfare. Because it is a response to a relative position, one household's increase in wellbeing comes at the expense of others.

It also follows that if the housing aspirations of the peer group change (see Chapter 4), then demand by an individual household will also change. For example, if younger households come to accept renting as the norm, then there is no necessary loss of welfare (unless the quality of the housing and its management are poorer) from lower levels of home ownership overall. More technically, models that recognize the importance of social interactions are more likely to exhibit multiple equilibria; in this case the economy might shift from a high to lower equilibrium home ownership rate. This is, of course, highly speculative and more research is needed. But it raises a set of issues for housing that are only just beginning to be appreciated with potentially strong implications for home ownership, house price trends and for policy.

Finally, to go back to the beginning, in Chapter 1 we suggested that housing problems are persistent, although the methods of economic analysis have changed considerably over the years and may well reflect current fashion or indeed data availability. Early research had much to say about the income and price elasticities of housing demand but perhaps we are now beginning to appreciate even more why they are so important. This suggests a return to the roots of the discipline if we are to begin to address the long-standing problems of affordability.

APPENDICES

APPENDIX 2.1

Modelling the effects of affordability on stress

The effects of affordability on stress are modelled through a probit equation.[1] The dependent variable refers to renters under the age of 60 and includes 5,715 observations, taken from the 2015/16 EHS. The dependent variable takes a value of one if the household is in stress (as defined in the main text) and zero otherwise. Twenty-nine per cent are defined to be in stress.

The key independent variable takes a value of one if the household is paying for housing more than 25 per cent of its household gross income, net of benefits, and zero otherwise. No allowance is made for property taxes, fuel or other costs. The variable is multiplied by a dummy for the income quintile in which the household lies, which allows different effects for affordability in each quintile. The lowest quintile is omitted as the comparator, but its implied coefficient is given by row (5) in Table A2.1; for the second quintile, the total effect is row (1) + row (5) and similarly for the other quintiles. Since the coefficients are taken from a probit equation, in this form they do not have a ready interpretation; for example, they are not marginal effects. Therefore, in the main text (Table 2.1), they are shown in terms of their relative sizes.

A range of demographic, tenure and location control variables, described in the text, are also added, but not shown in Table A2.1.

Table A2.1 The probability of financial stress

Variable	Coefficient	z-value
(1) Affordability * Quintile 2	-0.266	3.6
(2) Affordability * Quintile 3	-0.376	3.9
(3) Affordability * Quintile 4	-0.666	4.4
(4) Affordability * Quintile 5	-0.920	3.9
(5) Affordability	0.867	15.2

Determining Private Market Rents

Table A3.1 is obtained from a linear OLS (Ordinary Least Squares) regression where private sector annual market rental payments, taken from the 2017/18 EHS, are regressed on regional house prices, disaggregated by property type, and a series of control variables representing the characteristics of the households, since rents reflect demand as well as supply. Among these characteristics is the length of time the household has lived in the property. Non-market rents are excluded from the sample. Data cover five Government Office Regions across the country – South East, South West, London, East Midlands and North East.

As expected, the table shows that there is a statistically significant relationship between rents and house prices in order to maintain the rental yield. But rents are also sensitive to household size and composition, the size of the property, income and employment status. The table shows that relative to households who have lived in the property for less than one year (which is the excluded category), rents are lower the longer the household has been in residence. In fact, the results suggest that rents are noticeably lower for those who have lived in the property for more than 30 years but, in practice, few households (seven) fall into this category.

Similar results are obtained using EHS data for 2015/16.

Table A3.1 The determinants of market rents (dependent
variable = annual gross rent payment, £)

Variable	Coefficient	t-value
Constant	-1615.8	2.7
House price	0.0257	25.5
Number of children	-2061.6	9.0
Household size	1680.1	9.1
Number of full-time employed persons	-1011.1	5.8
Number of rooms	503.8	4.2
Household income	0.0880	10.4
length of residence (1–2 years)	-546.0	1.6
length of residence (3–4 years)	-1312.4	3.3
length of residence (5–9 years)	-2252.8	5.7
length of residence (10–19 years)	-3424.6	6.1
length of residence (20–29 years)	-3659.0	3.6
length of residence (30+ years)	-6757.5	3.9
R^2	0.51	
Equation standard error	£4,499	
Number of Observations	1,237	

On the Growth of Mortgages and House Prices

International evidence indicates that there is an association between the growth in mortgage advances, house prices and default risk in that house prices have been more volatile in those countries where financial market liberalization is more advanced. However, some care is required in clarifying the transmission mechanism since there are important implications for policy, particularly concerning the efficacy of lending controls.[1]

Figure 7.2 showed the UK mortgage debt to income ratio. As discussed, the strong growth in the ratio took place from the early 1980s, when liberalization began. Before that date the ratio had been broadly constant. During the growth period, conventional borrowers had greater scope for choosing the amount of finance they required. Therefore, over that period, the observed volume of mortgages represented *demand* rather than *supply*. But prior to the 1980s, when mortgage advances were much weaker, demand was limited by shortages. Furthermore, after the GFC, borrowers faced lender-imposed constraints.

As a simplification, the excess demand for mortgages (written as λ) can be expressed as (8.1a).

Prior to the early 1980s: $M^d - M^s > 0$

1980s – 2007: $M^d - M^s = 0$

Post 2007: $M^d - M^s > 0$ (8.1a)

M = Outstanding stock of mortgages; M^d and M^s are mortgage demand and supply respectively

Now consider the house price equation (8.2a), taken from Table 3.1 (the fourth equation) and the definition of the cost of capital (8.3a), which includes possible credit restrictions. Additionally, the cost of capital includes a risk premium discussed in the main text.

$$ln\ (g) = 2.46\ ln\ (Y) + 0.118\ ln\ (RW) - 0.045\ CC - 1.776\ ln(HS)$$

$$(8.2a)$$

$$CC = (r + \delta + mt + pt + \lambda + \tau - \dot{PH})$$
$$(8.3a)$$

g	= Real house price (expressed relative to general consumer prices)
Y	= Real household income
RW	= Real household financial wealth
HS	= Housing stock
CC	= Cost of capital
r	= Market interest rate
δ	= Depreciation rate
mt	= Maintenance expenditure (as a percentage of the property value)
pt	= Property taxes (as a percentage of the property value)
PH	= Expected nominal capital gain on the property
λ	= Measure of credit shortages
τ	= Housing risk premium.

Equations (8.1a–8.3a) define a model that can be solved conditional on the housing stock, income, financial wealth, taxes, maintenance expenditures and market interest rates. It can be seen that, outside mortgage constrained periods, credit has no effect on house prices. But the imposition of controls on the debt to income ratio leads to an increase in λ and reduces house prices. Consequently, controls potentially affect the collateral channel to consumers' expenditure. But since debt to income limits are typically targeted at groups perceived at most risk, there are important distributional consequences.

It also follows that a fall in interest rates has a smaller positive effect on prices if $\lambda > 0$. Lower interest rates typically lead to an increase in housing demand, but also to an accompanying rise in mortgage demand. However, if $\lambda > 0$ the fall in the cost of capital, arising from the lower interest rates, is partially offset by an increase in λ, so that the price effects are weaker.

The model can be extended by taking risk into account.[2] The risk premium is defined by (8.4a).

$$\tau = [r_a^e - r + \pi]\frac{\rho_{ah} \cdot \sigma_h}{\sigma_a} + \varphi.g. \, HS(1 - \rho_{ah}^2)\sigma_h^2 \qquad (8.4a)$$

r_a^e is the expected return on the risky financial asset; r is the risk-free rate; π is the general inflation rate; HS is the housing stock; g represents

real house prices; $\rho_{ah} = \dfrac{\sigma_{ah}}{\sigma_a \sigma_h}$ is the correlation coefficient between the

returns on housing and the risky financial asset, where σ_a^2, σ_h^2 are the variances of the returns on the risky financial asset and housing and σ_{ah} is the covariance. φ is the risk aversion parameter. In practice, over the long run, the covariance in returns has been close to zero, although it has been positive in some periods and negative in others. But if the covariance is zero, then (8.4a) simplifies to (8.4a').

$$\tau = \varphi.g.HS.\sigma_h^2 \qquad (8.4a')$$

In this case the key influences on risk are the level of house prices, the degree of risk aversion and the variance of the return on housing. From this, it is clear that rising house prices raise the cost of capital and contribute to a subsequent cyclical downturn. Through the collateral channel, this adds to volatility in the wider economy. Finally, it should be noted that if the *variance* of the return on housing is low, then from (8.4a'), the risk premium is also limited. Therefore, it is not only the level of house prices that matters, but also the volatility of prices.

Notes

Preface
[1] Corporal Jim Coote was writing to his sister Louie; Jim was one of Geoff Meen's great uncles and Louie was his grandmother. As far as we know, this was the last letter Jim wrote as he was killed a few days later, aged 19, just a month before the end of the war. The letter can be found on the University of Oxford Lest We Forget Archive under 'George, Alfred and James Coote' at: http://lwf.it.ox.ac.uk/s/lest-we-forget/item?sort_by=created&sort_order=desc&page=8 [accessed 28 November 2019].

Chapter 1
[1] More precisely, in the 1911 census, total population in England and Wales divided by the number of inhabited dwellings was 5.1; in the 2011 census, the usually resident population divided by the number of household spaces was 2.4.
[2] Department of Communities and Local Government (2017).
[3] House of Lords (2016).
[4] Lyons (2014), Institute of Public Policy Research (2016), Redfern Review (2016), Affordable Housing Commission (2019), Shelter (2019).
[5] Barker (2004).
[6] For example, Berry (2014).
[7] Meen et al (2016).
[8] Dalton (2009), Gurran and Phibbs (2015).
[9] For example, Aalbers (2016).

Chapter 2
[1] Bogdon and Can (1997), Leishman and Rowley (2012).
[2] Whitehead (1991).
[3] Bramley (1994).
[4] Linneman and Megbolugbe (1992), Gyourko and Linneman (1993).
[5] Measures based on work incentives have also been developed but are not discussed here. See Young et al (2017).
[6] Bramley and Karley (2005) distinguish between households with very low incomes and limited housing options and households with higher incomes, who are still constrained in access to home ownership. The distinction is important here.
[7] Twenty shillings made up one pound.

8   See the Housing Policy Review Technical Volume I, Department of the Environment (1977a).

9   Hulchanski (1995).

10 The figure considers those households with a head under the age of 60. The sample size is 7,313.

11 Friedman (1957).

12 Hulchanski (1995).

13 See Nelson (1994), for example, for a discussion of the use of expenditure ratios in US housing policy.

14 Kahneman (2011).

15 Murphy (2014).

16 Malpezzi and Mayo (1997).

17 See Leishman and Rowley (2012) and Rowley and Ong (2012) among many others for discussions of affordability concepts and the associated measurement problems.

18 In fact, formally, based on Augmented Dickey-Fuller Statistics, there is some evidence of an upward trend, but it depends on the time period chosen.

19 By contrast Weicher (1977) indicates that worsening US affordability up to the mid-1970s, based on expenditure, arose from an increase in nominal interest rates, whilst price to income ratios had been broadly constant. Furthermore, the rise in interest rates arose from higher general inflation and benefitted existing owners to the detriment of first-time buyers. We return to this issue in the context of monetary policy in later chapters.

20 Paris (2007) provides a summary.

21 See Hancock (1993) for a derivation from first principles using indifference curves and the budget constraint.

22 Lerman and Reeder (1987).

23 For example Bourassa (1996) or Meen (2001).

24 Hancock (1993).

25 Stone (2006a).

26 Most studies calculate the numbers or percentages of households whose expenditures lie above the threshold, i.e. they employ a headcount measure. Chaplin and Freeman (1999), however, propose a more sophisticated approach, which allows for how far above the threshold costs are for each household.

27 For example, Nepal et al (2010) and Hulse et al (2014) evaluate variants and find the 30:40 rule to be the most robust.

28 Yates (2008) argues that Australia's affordability problems are not new but are structural and date back at least to the 1970s and the greater use of housing as an asset rather than as a consumption good. Using the 30:40 rule, she shows that housing stress is concentrated on low-income renters. In 2002/03, 16 per cent of all households were in stress, but 65 per cent of low-income renters.

29 Rowley and Ong (2012), Table 9.

30 Rowley et al (2015).

31 See also Borrowman et al (2017) for Australia, who show that most households who enter housing affordability stress escape within a year.

32 Michael Stone has been a particularly strong advocate; originally constructed primarily for the US, he has also conducted analysis of the UK and Australia, see Stone (2006, 2006a), Stone et al (2011), Burke et al (2011), Henman and Jones (2012). Kutty (2005) uses a similar approach, employing the US poverty threshold as a measure of minimum non-housing consumption. Thalmann (2003) uses

the residual income approach to develop indicators that distinguish affordability problems that arise from low incomes as opposed to high housing costs. The methods are applied to Switzerland.

[33] Bramley and Karley (2005).

[34] Stone et al (2011), page 36.

[35] Thalmann (2003).

[36] Stone (2006a).

[37] Stone's work for the US provides an exception for 1983, 1990, 1993, 1994 and 2006.

[38] Bogdon and Can (1997).

[39] Bogdon and Can (1997).

[40] See Bramley (2012) who estimates a similar model to that employed in this section but uses data from the British Household Panel Survey for 1997 to 2003.

[41] Australian studies on panel data, for example, Borrowman et al (2017) in fact find that the majority of households escape stress within a year. Bramley (2012) also indicates that a significant part of English stress is transitory.

[42] These are only available in the Special Licence version of the EHS.

[43] See Bramley and Karley (2005) and Bramley (2012). These studies also carry out similar logistic analysis to ours.

[44] Bramley (2012) came to a similar conclusion.

[45] Gan and Hill (2009) operationalize the concepts for Australia and the US. Bramley and Karley (2005) also introduce a related approach for England, concentrating on access to home ownership based on maximum loan to income ratios and a residual income requirement.

[46] Meen (2001). See also Bourassa (1996) for an application to affordability measures.

[47] See Jones et al (2011). This study circumvents the absence of income data at fine spatial scales by concentrating on one group – young teachers whose salaries exhibit little spatial variation. By contrast, Bramley and Karley (2005) construct their own local income distributions. It might be noted that highly localized analysis is not necessarily appropriate since it implies that households can only buy in those small areas.

[48] The sample could also include some renters, who had been owners in previous periods and, therefore, not potential first-time buyers.

[49] Wilcox and Bramley (2010) use a related methodology. See also Wilcox (2006).

[50] Ben-Shahar and Warszawski (2016). Also, Tunstall (2015) uses the Gini coefficient to measure changes in room space inequality over time.

Chapter 3

[1] Much of this research is summarized in Meen (2001) and Meen et al (2016), which set out the theoretical models underlying the research more formally.

[2] Consequently, time-varying parameter methods are sometimes advocated; see, for example, Hall et al (1997).

[3] For example, Muellbauer and Murphy (1997).

[4] However, strictly, under versions of the life cycle model that assume certainty about the future, the actual rate of growth of house prices rather than the expected growth rate is the relevant variable. The addition of expectations is an *ad hoc* adjustment to the model commonly employed in the literature. Expectations of capital gains

and explicit measures of housing risk are discussed in more detail in Chapter 8. These have important implications for the model and for policy.

[5] This can change if a measure of risk is added as discussed in Chapter 8.

[6] Himmelberg et al (2005) for the US.

[7] Under these conditions, the standard solution would be to model jointly house prices and mortgage advances; but in this case, regime switching between periods of excess mortgage demand and supply make the approach problematic.

[8] Meen (2013).

[9] In policy circles, variants of the equation are used in the UK for forecasting by the Office for Budget Responsibility, and the Ministry of Housing, Communities and Local Government.

[10] Meen (2008).

[11] This abstracts from changes in household wealth which only has a modest effect quantitatively. The cost of capital also has an effect but since, from Figure 3.1, it has no trend it does not contribute to long-run changes in the price to income ratio, although this is modified if risk is taken into account. Notice also that the coefficient of 1.5 is only an approximation. For the coefficient to be exactly equal to 1.5 the coefficient on the housing stock in Table 3.1 would have to be -1.5 and that on income 2.5. To see this, let g = real house prices; Y = real aggregate income; HH = the number of households; HS = the housing stock. Then the equation in Table 3.1 (excluding wealth and the cost of capital) can be written as: $\ln(g) = 2.61 \ln(Y/HH) -1.55 \ln (HS/HH)$. Therefore, the equation for affordability becomes: $\ln(g/(Y/HH)) = 1.61 \ln(Y/HH) -1.55 \ln (HS/HH)$. Since on the right-hand side the two coefficients on HH are approximately equal in absolute terms, they cancel out and so the equation becomes: $\ln(g/(Y/HH)) \approx 1.5 \ln(Y/HS)$.

[12] See, for example, Cheshire and Sheppard (1995, 1998).

[13] Meen and Andrew (1998); the result arises from the Theil (1954) aggregation conditions.

[14] Picketty (2014), Jordà et al (2017) and Knoll et al (2017). There is also a significant number of single country studies: Eichholtz (1997) and Eichholtz et al (2012) for Amsterdam; Friggit (2012) for Paris; Stapledon (2010) for Australia; Shiller (2005) and Fishback and Kollman (2012) for the USA.

[15] Meen (2002) provides a comparative study of the UK and USA, which standardizes model specifications.

[16] See Adams and Füss (2010) for a panel study across 15 countries; Agnello and Schuknecht (2011) show the importance of monetary indicators in explaining housing short-run booms and busts across 18 industrialized economies; Anundsen and Jansen (2013) look at the relationship between house prices and household debt in Norway; Oikarinen (2012) looks at the response of prices and transactions to demand shocks in Finland; Cuestas (2017) considers the effects of foreign capital flows on Spanish prices; Damen et al (2016) examine the effects of mortgage interest tax deduction across eight countries; Miles (2017) discusses the synchronization of international house price cycles; Vansteenkiste and Hiebert (2011) estimate price spill overs across the Euro area; Zhu et al (2017) consider prices and monetary policy also across the Euro area.

[17] For example, Green et al (2005), Glaeser et al (2008), Huang and Tang (2012) and Anundsen and Heebøll (2016). The issue is considered in more detail in Chapter 6.

[18] Although some care is needed because of German reunification.

[19] The GORs were also abolished in 2011 as administrative units and a more limited range of data has been available since then.

[20] Examples from the international literature include: Clark and Coggin (2009), Gupta and Miller (2010, 2012), Miao et al (2011), Holmes et al (2011), Barros et al (2012), Kim and Rous (2012), Cohen et al (2016) – all for the USA; Berg (2002, Sweden), Stevenson (2004, Ireland), Van Dijk et al (2011, Netherlands), Fereidouni et al (2016, Singapore and Malaysia), Luo et al (2007, Australia), Shi (2009, New Zealand), Lean and Smyth (2013, Malaysia) and Balcilar et al (2013, South Africa).

[21] For example, Kim and Rous (2012) find evidence for multiple clubs and suggest that housing supply regulation is an important determinant of club membership. Blanco et al (2016) find four clubs in Spain; in the UK, Chowdhury and Maclennan (2014) suggest two super-groups, based on the amplitude and duration of cycles, broadly corresponding to a North-South divide. However, Montagnoli and Nagayasu (2015) find four convergence clubs in the UK. Clark and Coggin (2009) suggest two super regions for the US.

[22] Chowdhury and Maclennan (2014).

[23] However, London has not conformed to this pattern in recent years.

[24] For example, Blanco et al (2016) find population growth, the size of the rental market, housing supply and geography to be important determinants in Spain. Füss and Zietz (2016) examine the effects of US national monetary policy on local price changes.

[25] For example, through cointegration or spectral techniques.

[26] These will be represented by different values for the coefficients in regional house price equations. The differences may be either random or have a distinct spatial structure.

[27] These are measured by simple average prices, rather than adjusting for quality differences. Quality adjustment does not change the central message.

[28] Cameron and Muellbauer (1998) for example.

[29] Meen (1999); the result still holds in an updated unpublished study.

[30] Fisher (1933), Simpson (1933).

[31] Gyourko et al (2008).

[32] See Watkins (2008) for a useful review of approaches to the analysis of local housing markets in economics.

[33] For example, see Watkins (2001, 2008), Jones et al (2004, 2012), Leishman (2009) and Leishman et al (2013).

[34] Bramley and Leishman (2005) provide an exception in which a panel data set for HMAs is used to construct a housing market model.

[35] For example, Can and Megbolugbe (1997), Fingleton et al (2008) and Cohen et al (2016).

[36] Leishman (2009) provides a useful summary of the issues and concepts.

[37] Maclennan and Tu (1996).

[38] For example, Leishman's (2009) study for Glasgow, where seven sub-markets are found.

[39] Cheshire and Sheppard (2004b).

[40] The seminal work is associated with Schelling (1971), but later developments to a stochastic framework can be found in Zhang (2004, 2004a). See also Meen and Meen (2003).

[41] See the 2018 English Private Landlord Survey, Ministry of Housing, Communities and Local Government (2019).

[42] The data are taken from the Valuation Office Agency.

Chapter 4

[1] Also sometimes known as 'Generation Rent' on account of the problems of accessing home ownership.

[2] See, for example, Willetts (2010).

[3] And, there have been similar trends in Scotland and Wales.

[4] It might be argued that house prices are not the most appropriate measure for assessing household formation since households may rent and rents have increased at a slower rate than house prices. But since, as Chapter 3 showed, rents are related to prices, relative house prices across locations may also provide information on relative rents. This argument is stronger in Figure 4.3, which looks at a single year. The trends over time in Figure 4.2 might also be affected, for example, by the expansion in higher education.

[5] Bramley et al (1997), Ermisch (1999).

[6] The coefficient of variation for the household representative rate was 0.04, but 0.25 for the price to earnings ratio.

[7] A point stressed by McKee and Soaita (2018) and Preece et al (2019).

[8] Preece et al (2019).

[9] Manski (2000).

[10] Ravenstein (1885).

[11] Cameron and Muellbauer (1998), Böheim and Taylor (2002).

[12] We might note that, in Denmark, debt to income ratios have risen for middle aged and older households rather than for moving younger households.

[13] The formal definition is: 'A standard number of bedrooms is calculated for each household in accordance with its age/sex/marital status composition and the relationship of the members to one another. ... This notional standard number of bedrooms is then compared with the actual number of bedrooms (including bed-sitters) available for the sole use of the household. ... Households are said to be overcrowded if they have fewer bedrooms available than the notional number needed. Households are said to be under-occupying if they have two or more bedrooms more than the notional needed' (English Housing Survey 2017/18, Glossary).

[14] House of Commons (2018), Chapters 4 and 5.

[15] The House of Commons Communities and Local Government Committee rejected proposals for stamp duty exemption for older households. One reason was that stamp duty for most owners would be covered by the released equity from their homes.

[16] See Meen (2013) for a formal model that demonstrates the increase in volatility.

[17] Later waves of the EHS have not asked the required questions.

[18] Ministry of Housing, Communities and Local Government (2019).

[19] Andrew and Meen (2003).

[20] The probabilities are derived from probit equations.

[21] A considerable amount of empirical research has been conducted, particularly in the US, on the impact of deposit constraints; see, for example, Bourassa et al (1994), Haurin et al (1994, 1997), Ermisch (1999), Andrew et al (2006), Andrew (2010, 2012).

[22] This removes some implausible values from the sample and excludes those on shared ownership schemes.

[23] The work of Oswald (1996) was particularly influential, although his results were controversial – see, for example, Green and Hendershott (2001), Borg and Brandén (2018).

Chapter 5

[1] In terms of housing choice, however, the issues are more complex both because of what is being purchased, for example the extent of security of tenure, and assumptions about future rents. These attributes differ between the private and social sectors (Whitehead and Kleinman, 1986).

[2] OECD Affordable Housing Database (OECD 2019).

[3] See the Eurostat definition of cost overburden at https://ec.europa.eu/eurostat/statistics-explained/index.php/Glossary:Housing_cost_overburden_rate. See also https://ec.europa.eu/eurostat/web/products-datasets/product?code=tespm140 for details of Eurostat statistics on the cost overburden

[4] For example, Schmid (2018) and diNapoli (2019).

[5] See for example the OECD Affordability index for details of subsidies across OECD countries (OECD 2019).

[6] Chadwick (1842).

[7] Department of the Environment (1977).

[8] See, for example, Wilson (2017) for a brief resumé of the history of rent controls in the UK.

[9] Holmans (2005) Table S15.

[10] Department of Environment (1982).

[11] See, for example, Whitehead and Kleinman (1986) and Rhodes (2015).

[12] University of the West of England (undated).

[13] See, for example, Gibb and Whitehead (2007), Malpass (2015), Whitehead (2017b).

[14] See Wilson (2017) for the detailed changes.

[15] Department of the Environment (1977).

[16] Department of the Environment (1971).

[17] It is important to note that, in the UK, the rent is legally required to be based on the individual property, not on the attributes of the tenant. This makes the situation very different to countries like Australia and New Zealand where rents are set as a proportion of tenant income.

[18] Scanlon et al (2015).

[19] As such it addressed the problems identified by Beveridge when putting in place the post-war social security system, Beveridge (1942).

[20] Department of Environment (1977a) Technical Volume III and Kemp (1998).

[21] As described in, e.g., Gibb (2016), Wilson et al (2016).

[22] The removal of what was termed the spare room subsidy came into effect in April 2013. Table 4.3 in Chapter 4 above shows that by 2017/18 only 10 per cent of social tenants had properties with two or more bedrooms above standard.

[23] See Wilson et al (2016) for details.

[24] Joyce et al (2017).

[25] National Housing Federation (2019).

[26] Department of Work and Pensions (2019), Peabody (2019).

[27] Based on a sample of 5,571 households.

[28] See Joyce et al (2017) for details of the numbers.

29   Although the government has stated that they are intending to remove the possibility of no-fault evictions (Ministry of Housing, Communities and Local Government (2019a) and Wilson and Barton (2019)).

30   Inside Housing (2017).

31   Rhodes and Rugg (2018), Rugg and Rhodes (2018).

32   Ministry of Housing, Communities and Local Government (2019).

33   Udagawa et al (2018).

34   For example, Ellis and Whitehead (2015).

Chapter 6

1   See Mulheirn (2019).

2   Ball (2003), page 897.

3   Home Builders Federation (2017).

4   Ball et al (2010).

5   See, for example, models in the tradition of Poterba (1984).

6   For US time-series studies providing estimates of the national price elasticity of supply, see Muth (1960), Follain (1979), Poterba (1984), Topel and Rosen (1988), Blackley (1999), Mayer and Somerville (2000, 2000a), Malpezzi and Maclennan (2001). Those concentrating on bubbles include Glaeser et al (2008), Goodman and Thibodeau (2008). Caldera and Johansson (2013) provide a comparison across 21 OECD countries, whereas Mayo and Sheppard (1996) compare Malaysia, Thailand and South Korea.

7   There are also issues concerning the comparability of the different indicators because of measurement errors.

8   This is discussed further in Chapter 10.

9   The international comparison by Caldera and Johansson (2013) uses residential investment.

10   A similar point was made in Lyons (2014), Figure 16.

11   This is the concept of cointegration. Starts and real house prices have different orders of integration, but starts and the growth in prices have the same orders of integration. Both are stationary processes. In principle it is possible that a combination of the level house prices and other variables (such as construction costs) are stationary, but in practice this is not the case.

12   See Ball et al (2010) for the UK and Mayer and Somerville (2000) and Riddel (2000, 2004) for the US.

13   See House of Lords (2016) for the UK and Sai-Fan Chan (1999), Ambrose and Peek (2008) for US studies.

14   Goodman (1987), Cammarota (1989), Coulson and Richard (1996), Fergus (1999).

15   Ihlanfeldt and Shaughnessy (2004), Burge and Ihlanfeldt (2006, 2006a), which are US studies.

16   Nordvik (2006) for example.

17   Zabel and Paterson (2006), Saiz (2010), Meen and Nygaard (2011).

18   But the issue is discussed in House of Lords (2016, page 22). It quotes an estimate that one million more construction workers would be needed by 2020 in the UK if 300,000 homes were to be built each year.

19   For example, Malpezzi (1996), Pryce (1999), Mayer and Somerville (2000), Mayo and Sheppard (2001), Bramley (2002), White and Allmendinger (2003), Glaeser and Gyourko (2005), Ihlanfeldt (2007), Glaeser et al (2008), Goodman and Thibodeau (2008), Ball (2011).

[20] Ball et al (2010).

[21] Mayo and Sheppard (1996), Malpezzi and Mayo (1997a), Malpezzi and Maclennan (2001), Green et al (2005), Caldera and Johansson (2013).

[22] See Caldera and Johansson (2013) who, among OECD countries, find the price elasticity to be higher in North American and some Nordic countries, but lower in other European countries including the UK.

[23] Hilber and Vermeulen (2016).

[24] The supply elasticity may be estimated directly or inferred indirectly from house price equations where assumptions are made concerning the price and income elasticities of housing demand (see Malpezzi and Maclennan 2001).

[25] For US analyses of the relationship between local prices or construction and the strength of the regulatory regime see Malpezzi (1996), Mayer and Somerville (2000a), Glaeser et al (2005), Green et al (2005), Glaeser et al (2008) and Gyourko et al (2008).

[26] Ball et al (2009).

[27] UK studies include Bramley (1993, 1993a, 1998, 1999), summarized in Bramley (2002), Bramley and Leishman (2005) and most recently Hilber and Vermeulen (2016).

[28] Meen and Nygaard (2011).

[29] Pryce (1999), Mayo and Sheppard (2001), Cunningham (2006).

[30] Lyons (2014), page 66.

[31] Barker (2004).

[32] Cheshire and Sheppard (2002, 2004a, 2005).

[33] Meen (2011).

[34] Meen (2011, Figure 1b).

[35] For example, House of Lords (2016).

[36] Australia, for example, has undergone a similar debate; see Gurran et al (2018), for a recent enquiry into strategies for increasing affordable housing supply.

[37] Murray (1999), Meen (2005), Nordvik (2006), Lee (2007).

[38] See, for example. Crosby and Wyatt (2016) for a discussion of the role of viability assessments.

[39] Cheshire et al (2014).

Chapter 7

[1] See Rohe et al (2001) and Dietz and Haurin (2003).

[2] Stephens (2000), Lunde and Whitehead (2016).

[3] Green and Wachter (2005).

[4] See, for example, Pannell (2003).

[5] This is a form of regime switching model.

[6] Scanlon and Blanc (2019).

[7] Controls also exist on debt to income and debt to value ratios for Buy to Let investors as well as restrictions on the ratio of rent receipts to mortgage interest payments.

[8] Bank of England/FCA MLAR Statistics Table 1.31.

[9] Loans between 90 per cent and 95 per cent of the purchase price have shown a similar profile but have experienced some recovery in recent years.

[10] There is some evidence that they do not generally compete for individual properties (Scanlon et al 2016).

[11] Meen (2013).

[12] Remember the example from Chapter 4 that showed how current owners could increase housing consumption without raising the debt to market value ratio.

[13] Mirrlees et al (2011), page 34.

[14] Mirrlees et al (2011), but criticisms have not been confined to the UK; see Eccleston et al (2018) for a review of the Australian system and proposals for phased property tax reforms.

[15] See the discussion in House of Commons (2018).

[16] Muellbauer (2005) provides a formal analysis of tax reform proposals in the UK; in addition, Poghosyan (2016) finds, in the US, that increases in property tax rates lead to a reduction in house price volatility.

[17] See, for example, Grey, Hepworth and Odling-Smee (1981).

[18] Pelletier and Tunc (2019).

[19] See Lenoel et al (2018) for a recent survey.

[20] Besley et al (2014) and Best and Kleven (2018) for the UK; Costello (2006) for Australia; Bérard and Trannoy (2017) for France; Petkova and Weichenrieder (2017) for Germany; Dachis et al (2012) for Canada; Van Ommeren and Van Leuvensteijn (2005) for the Netherlands.

[21] Van Ommeren and Van Leuvensteijn (2005).

[22] Hilber and Lyytikäinen (2017).

[23] These conditions are set out in more detail in the next chapter.

Chapter 8

[1] Mian et al (2017).

[2] For example, Aalbers (2017).

[3] There had also been concerns in the 1970s with the effects of house price volatility.

[4] Muellbauer and Murphy (1990), Maclennan et al (1998).

[5] King (1990).

[6] Benito et al (2006).

[7] Buiter (2008).

[8] Campbell and Cocco (2007) provide supporting evidence in contrast to Attanasio and Weber (1994) and Attanasio et al (2009).

[9] Benito et al (2006).

[10] Case et al (2005).

[11] Aoki et al (2002).

[12] Black et al (1996), DeMeza and Webb (1999).

[13] Mian and Sufi (2011).

[14] These were usually conducted using dynamic stochastic general equilibrium (DSGE) models.

[15] Particularly through the work of Bernanke and Gertler (1989) and Reinhart and Rogoff (2009).

[16] See particularly Iacoviello (2005) and Iacoviello and Neri (2010). Criticisms have been levelled at early DSGE models in that they failed to capture key features of housing markets, such as frictions, tenure choices and the inclusion of explicit mortgage markets. Over time specifications have become somewhat richer, for example Veld et al (2011).

[17] Reinhart and Rogoff (2009), Mian et al (2017).

[18] For example, Mian and Sufi (2009, 2011), Duca et al (2011, 2016), Cerutti et al (2017).

[19] For example, Ryan-Collins (2019).

[20] Mian and Sufi (2011).

[21] Reported in Van Zandt and Rohe (2011).

[22] Case and Shiller (1996).

[23] Quercia and Stegman (1992), Vandell (1995).

[24] UK studies of arrears, default and possession prior to the GFC are more limited, but include Burrows and Ford (1997), Lambrecht et al (1997), Burrows (1998) and Böheim and Taylor (2000).

[25] Mian and Sufi (2009).

[26] Mian et al (2017).

[27] Mian et al (2017).

[28] For example, Mian et al (2017, page 1804) state: 'The microeconomic evidence in the existing literature also points to a causal effect of credit supply shifts on house prices. While caution is warranted in the interpretation, we believe that the body of evidence suggests the chain of causality is more likely to run from credit supply shocks to house prices rather than vice versa'.

[29] This was demonstrated in Meen (1989) in the context of the removal of owner occupation subsidies.

[30] For example, Poterba (1984).

[31] The long-run cointegrating relationship between house prices and incomes has been heavily explored but some of this work excludes the housing stock as an additional variable.

[32] This is not to say that the international literature fails to recognize the importance of housing supply, but rather that it is not always reflected in aggregate house price equations.

[33] See, for example, Piazzesi et al (2007), Piazzesi and Schneider (2016).

[34] Akerlof and Shiller (2009). The idea dates back to the work of Keynes in the 1930s.

[35] Akerlof and Shiller (2009), page 149.

[36] Arthur et al (1997) and LeBaron et al (1999).

[37] See Ong et al (2017) and Maclennan et al (2018, 2019) for studies of the effects of housing on productivity growth in Australia.

[38] Bover el al (1989), Cameron and Muellbauer (1998, 2001).

[39] Meen and Nygaard (2011), Gibb et al (2019).

[40] Davis and Weinstein (2002), Nitsch (2003), Pereira (2009), Voigtländer and Voth (2013), Siodla (2015), Dincecco and Onorato (2016), Hornbeck and Keniston (2017).

Chapter 9

[1] Government of France (2017).

[2] Deutsche Bank (2017).

[3] For example, Rowley et al (2017), Lawson et al (2018).

[4] See, for example, the regular State of the Nation's Housing reports produced by Harvard University (Joint Center of Housing Studies 2019).

[5] See the annual reports of the National Housing Supply Council from 2009 to 2013.

[6] Rowley et al (2017), Lawson et al (2018).

[7] The Housing Policy Review Technical Volume Part I (Department of the Environment 1977a) included the first detailed estimates at national level.

[8] Ministry of Housing, Communities and Local Government (2018).

[9] Ellis (2017).

[10] See, for example, Hall et al (1973) for an assessment of both objectives and impacts.

[11] Webster (2006).

[12] As noted by Webster (2006).

[13] For example, Cullingworth (1960).

[14] In the New Towns Act, 1946.

[15] UK Government, Cabinet Papers (1965).

[16] Department of Economic Affairs (1965).

[17] Barker (2003), Department of the Environment (1977a).

[18] As exemplified in Grigson (1986) and Evans (1987).

[19] Coopers and Lybrand (1985, 1987).

[20] Notably Bramley et al (2005) and Cheshire (2009).

[21] Jackson et al (1994 and 1994a).

[22] Ministry of Housing, Communities and Local Government (2018).

[23] Ministry of Housing, Communities and Local Government (2019b, 2019c).

[24] For example, Department of Communities and Local Government (2017).

[25] See for instance the Draft London Plan and its Enquiry in Public as an example of the process (Greater London Authority, 2018 and 2019).

[26] Holmans (1970).

[27] Department of Environment (1977a).

[28] Whitehead (1998), Holmans et al (2008).

[29] Whitehead and Kleinman (1992), Bramley et al (2010), Holmans (2012), Whitehead (2016), Bramley (2018).

[30] Holmans (2012).

[31] Department of Communities and Local Government (2016).

[32] Office for National Statistics (2018, 2018a).

[33] Office for National Statistics (2018a).

[34] Pereira (2018). A compliance check has subsequently been published, which has been reviewed by the UK Statistics Authority (2019).

[35] Ministry of Housing, Communities and Local Government (2019b).

[36] See, for example, Gordon et al (2016).

[37] Greater London Authority (2018).

[38] Ellis (2017).

[39] A particular issue is that much of the land identified cannot be delivered unless infrastructure is put in place at the expected time. As infrastructure often runs late, this is of fundamental concern to the underlying rationale of the five year land supply and indeed the delivery test.

[40] Wilson et al (2017, 2018).

[41] See, for example, Gerald Eve (1991), Monk (1999), Barker (2004), Evans (2004).

[42] Monk et al (2013).

[43] Reviewed in detail in Monk (1999).

[44] Rose (1989).

[45] Zheng (2013).

Chapter 10

[1] Neuberger and Nichol (1976), Department of Environment (1977).

[2] Barker (2003, 2004).

[3] House of Lords Economic Affairs Committee (2016), HM Treasury (2017).

[4] Although it is possible that they will pick up again if there is a post-Brexit recovery.

[5] For example, Lyons (2014), KPMG and Shelter (2015) and, indeed, Department of Communities and Local Government (2017).

[6] Notably the end of new and extended towns policies and reduced subsidies and incentives to provide affordable homes (see next section and Chapter 11).

[7] For example, Whitehead (2017a) and Whitehead and Udagawa (2020).

[8] Marmaras (2015).

[9] Barker (2006).

[10] Mace et al (2016), Mace (2017), GLA (2018).

[11] For instance, the annual reports by the CPRE (2018) and indeed the draft New London Plan, GLA (2018).

[12] The latest such approach can be found in Cheshire and Buyuklieva (2019) and in the context of specific investment in Mace et al (2016) but such ideas go back a long way – see for instance Barker (2006).

[13] Ministry of Housing, Communities and Local Government (2012, 2018 and 2019).

[14] For example, McOmish (2018), CPRE (2019).

[15] Crook et al (2016).

[16] For example, Burgess (2014).

[17] Gordon et al (2016).

[18] Crook et al (2016), Chapter 3.

[19] It should be noted that the legislation also contained compulsory purchase powers for local authorities which, in modified form, are still in place today.

[20] For example, Department of Communities and Local Government (2012) and regular reports thereafter.

[21] Crook and Whitehead (2019).

[22] House of Commons, Housing, Communities and Local Government Select Committee (2018a).

[23] This was also true in the 1960s but, then, the large firms were contractors building for local authorities, who went bankrupt or were heavily restructured in the 1970s and 1980s (NHBC, 2015).

[24] For example, Ball (2010).

[25] House of Commons, Housing, Communities and Local Government Select Committee (2017).

[26] Letwin (2018).

[27] Gordon et al (2016).

[28] Travers and Whitehead (2013), Scanlon et al (2017), Wallace et al (2017).

[29] See, for example, Scanlon, Whitehead and Blanc (2017) for a discussion of housing associations' current and future role.

[30] See Wilson (2019b) for a discussion of the role of housing associations in development.

[31] ChamberlainWalker (2017), Lichfields (2017).

[32] For example, House of Commons, Communities and Local Government Committee (2017).

[33] House of Commons, Housing, Communities and Local Government Select Committee (2019).

[34] Farmer (2016), Pinoncely and Belcher (2018).

[35] Monk et al (2013).

[36] See, for example, Davies et al (2016) on the German industry, but also the regular reports by Deloitte (2018), which reflect an international approach to housing development. Also, National Housing Supply Council (annually 2009–2013) for analysis of the Australian system.

[37] See the paper by Neil Martin in Pinoncely and Belcher (2018).

[38] Smith (2017).

[39] Clifford et al (2018).

[40] House of Commons, Housing, Communities and Local Government Select Committee (2019a).

[41] De Magalhães et al (2018).

[42] Lord et al (2018) and Crook and Whitehead (2019) give many of the details.

[43] Crook et al (2016) chapter 2 sets out the detailed analysis.

[44] Greater London Authority (2018).

[45] Lord et al (2018), Crook and Whitehead (2019).

[46] As opposed to owner occupied housing which is treated more as a consumption good for taxation purposes.

[47] Ministry of Housing, Communities and Local Government (2019d).

[48] Montague (2012).

[49] British Property Federation (2017), Savills (2019).

[50] Meen et al (2016).

[51] Because developer balance sheets were too weak to maintain output even at 2013 levels; see Finlay et al (2016).

[52] Department of Communities and Local Government (2017). The latest move in this direction was signalled in March 2020, when the government published a policy document (MHCLG 2020) stating that their new Planning White Paper would speed up the planning system and expand the use of zoning tools.

[53] Whitehead (2018).

Chapter 11

[1] In any general statement of this type there are always exceptions; for example, a tenure neutral flat rate subsidy for new build in the inter-war period. Equally there are some private sector providers of social housing who are eligible for subsidy.

[2] For example, Musgrave (1959) and Hancock (1991).

[3] Galster (1997), Yates and Whitehead (1998).

[4] Whitehead (2003), Elsinga et al (2014), Scanlon et al (2014).

[5] An additional complication for government is that, given public borrowing constraints, the opportunity cost of government borrowing may be seen to be significantly greater than mechanisms which allow the borrowing to be off the government's balance sheet. So, value for money for government may differ from the direct cost of finance.

[6] Although, as we note elsewhere, market rents are also not necessarily market clearing rents and are themselves affected by differential tax regimes and income related subsidies.

[7] University of the West of England (undated); Department of the Environment (1977), Holmans (1987).

[8] Holmans (2005).

[9] Department of the Environment (1971).

[10] Department of the Environment (1977).

[11] Because so many local authorities refused to raise their rents and so continued to be eligible for subsidy the government decided to 'deem' notional increases in both costs and rents reflecting their view of appropriate increases (Wilson 1998).

[12] Holmans (1987).

[13] See Wilson (2012) for a history of HRA subsidies to that date.

[14] HM Treasury (2018a).

[15] Fair rents applied to most new lettings in the private rented sector after 1965 – they were set by independent tribunal with the objective of removing the scarcity element from market rents. They applied to housing association rents as associations were technically part of the private sector.

[16] See Pryke and Whitehead (1993 and 1994) and Whitehead (1999) for details of the changes after the 1988 Act.

[17] Priemus and Whitehead (2014).

[18] See, for example, the website of the Housing Finance Corporation – the major aggregator www.thfcorp.com/investing-and-borrowing/why-borrow.

[19] Wilson and Bate (2015a).

[20] Again, Wilson and Bate (2015a) and Barton and Wilson (2019a) provide details.

[21] Details of the scheme can be found at www.gov.uk/government/collections/affordable-homes-guarantees-programme-guidance-and-allocations.

[22] HM Treasury (2019).

[23] It should also be noted that private sector completions may include some affordable home ownership units.

[24] Barton and Wilson (2019).

[25] The Right to Buy policy was UK wide but, since 2018, no longer applies in Scotland or Wales.

[26] See, for example, Jones and Murie (2005) and Murie (2015) for details of the Right to Buy initiative.

[27] Wilson and Bate (2015b).

[28] Jones and Murie (2006).

[29] Inside Housing (2017).

[30] See Department of the Environment (1995), Kiddle (2002).

[31] Wilson (1998).

[32] Wilson (2019a).

[33] Cambridge Centre for Housing and Planning Research (2001–2010).

[34] Whitehead and Cao (2007).

[35] Ellis and Whitehead (2015).

[36] Wilson (2019a).

[37] Lord et al (2018).

[38] Ministry of Housing, Communities and Local Government (2018a).

[39] Allen et al (2004).

[40] Priemus and Boelhouwer (1999) Hegedüs et al (2013), Scanlon et al (2014).

[41] Although there is formally no such thing as a social sector in Sweden.

[42] Priemus and Whitehead (2014).

[43] Scanlon et al (2014), Chapter 8. For updates on the French housing reforms see articles regularly posted on politiquedulogement.com.

[44] Hegedüs et al (2013).

[45] In 2017 *Critical Housing Analysis* published two special issues on social housing in European countries in volume 4 issues 1 and 2 which provides more detail, www.housing-critical.com/archive/?year=2017&issue=1 and www.housing-critical.com/archive/?year=2017&issue=2.

[46] For example, Baum-Snow and Marion (2009), Keightley (2019).

[47] Rowley et al (2017).

[48] Calavita and Mallach (2010), Gurran et al (2018).

[49] RICS (2019).

[50] Shelter (2019).

Chapter 12

[1] Note in this context the capacity to bring in a universal, wholly digitally-based, welfare system across Brazil. Europe is far behind. See Garcia Freitas et al (2015).

[2] Department of the Environment (1977), Kemp (2007), OECD (2016).

[3] See, for instance, the debate between Galster (1997) and Yates and Whitehead (1998).

[4] For example, Chevin (2008).

[5] OECD (2016).

[6] Beveridge (1942).

[7] Beveridge (1942, page 15).

[8] Fair Deal for Housing (Command Paper No. 4728), (Department of Environment 1971), set out the government's approach to rent setting in the social sector and was implemented in 1972. At the same time rent rebates were introduced, followed in 1973 by rent allowances for most private and housing association tenants. As noted in Chapter 11, in practice because rent increases were specified in money terms rents actually fell in real terms because of rapidly rising inflation. However, their introduction enabled change over the following decades.

[9] Hills et al (1991), Hills (2001), Kemp et al (2002).

[10] Stephens et al (2018).

[11] Holmans and Whitehead (1997).

[12] Rugg and Rhodes (2018); see also Rhodes and Rugg (2018) for a more quantitative analysis using English Housing Survey data to examine vulnerability more broadly.

[13] For example, Murphy et al (2018) who clarify the costs of the reduction in the Council Tax payment allowance for low-income Londoners.

[14] Joyce et al (2017).

[15] OECD (2016).

[16] Kemp (2007).

[17] Griggs and Kemp (2012).

[18] Holmans (1970).

[19] Whitehead and Kleinman (1986).

[20] Beckerman (1965).

[21] Whitehead (1994).

[22] Udagawa et al (2018).

[23] Whitehead et al (2012).

[24] Whitehead and Williams (2019).

[25] Ministry of Housing, Communities and Local Government (2019e).

[26] Rugg and Rhodes (2018), Udagawa et al (2018).

[27] Housing (Homeless Persons) Act 1977.

[28] Ministry of Housing, Communities and Local Government (2019f). The latest figures show some decline.

[29] See Fitzpatrick et al (2019) for the latest position.

[30] See for instance the Housing First: England website.

[31] FEANSTA (2018).

Chapter 13

[1]   Holmans (2005).

[2]   Bailey et al (2016).

[3]   Civil war in Ireland was, of course, an exception.

[4]   See Jackson (2014) for a discussion of the history of the concept.

[5]   HM Treasury (2005).

[6]   Although see, for example, the Housing Policy Review (Department of the Environment 1977) and Grey, Hepworth and Odling Smee (1981) for a rather more optimistic view of what might have been possible.

[7]   See for instance an early attempt to ask 'why owner occupation' in Whitehead (1979) and a much later paper stressing behavioural aspects in Elsinga and Hoekstra (2005).

[8]   Freeman et al (1996), but also note how changes were already emerging among younger households, see Scanlon and Whitehead (2004).

[9]   Inside Housing (2018).

[10] See Heywood (2011) for a broadly based discussion of evolving government policy in the period of expansion of owner occupation.

[11] For details of the development of local shared ownership schemes and other initiatives as well as the national initiatives in the 1980 Housing Act see Booth and Crook (1986).

[12] For example, Booth and Crook (1986), Chapter 2.

[13] See Williams et al (2017) for a more detailed history and analysis as well as international comparisons.

[14] National Audit Office (2019).

[15] Finlay et al (2016), Whitehead et al (2018).

[16] Carozzi et al (2019).

[17] Muellbauer (2018) also provides a good example and discusses the tax options in detail.

[18] See, for example, Adam et al (2020) and Murphy et al (2019) for detailed discussions of both the rationale for change and possible reforms.

[19] Whitehead and Williams (2017) provide a comprehensive analysis of the controls that are in place in different countries.

[20] Miles (2011, 2012) provides a discussion of the benefits for both households and monetary policy. Smith et al (2009, 2013) and Whitehead (2010) present analyses of the principles and the practical limitations of market provision.

[21] Evans and Keohane (2016).

[22] Resolution Foundation (2018).

[23] Smith et al (2013).

[24] Benetton et al (2019).

[25] Benetton et al (2019) calculate a break-even rate of expected house price inflation of 7.7 per cent.

[26] European Mortgage Federation (2019), Table 11.

[27] Whitehead and Williams (2017).

[28] See Whitehead and Williams (2017), Table 2.3 for the details of the limits on loan to value ratios across Europe and Table 2.4 for a summary of the regulatory changes since 2008, as well as a discussion of the other reasons for lower rates of owner occupation among young people.

[29] Goodman and Mayer (2018).

[30] Andrews and Sánchez (2011).

[31] Goodman and Mayer (2018).

[32] The Redfern Review (2016) is a recent example.

Chapter 14

[1] Further discussion can be found in Whitehead (2018).

[2] This categorization is based on Muellbauer (2018).

[3] Although it did run parallel with a detailed examination of mortgage markets by David Miles (2004).

[4] Geiger et al (2016) show that the elasticity of house prices with respect to income in Germany is approximately 1.5. This compares with our results for the UK in Table 3.1 where the elasticity is 2.5. Our own unpublished estimates also suggest that the elasticity is lower in Germany.

[5] Summarized in Been et al (2019).

[6] Boddy and Gray (1979).

[7] Been et al (2019).

[8] Kensington and Chelsea is the authority on the far right of the graph.

[9] Muellbauer (2018).

[10] And possibly lower demand.

[11] Beckerman (1965).

[12] North (2005), page 52.

[13] Muellbauer (2018).

[14] The effects of the bombings on German population distributions and the extent to which they subsequently returned to pre-war relativities are modelled in Bosker et al (2007).

[15] Wertheimer (1958), Voigtländer (2009).

[16] Wertheimer (1958).

[17] Voigtländer (2009).

[18] Meen et al (2016).

[19] Meen et al (2016).

[20] HM Treasury (2018), page 39.

[21] Gurran et al (2015), Maclennan et al (2015, 2018, 2019), Ong et al (2017). These are all Australian studies.

[22] Cohen et al (2009), Foye et al (2018).

[23] Glaeser and Scheinkman (2001), page 84. Our own additions are in square brackets.

[24] Foye et al (2018).

[25] See Zumbro (2014), although the model does not test for social norms or positional goods.

Appendix 2.1

[1] Perhaps the closest study in the literature is Yates (2007) for Australia, who, in multi-variate logit estimation, found little relationship between financial stress and housing stress, although the measures of financial stress were rather different from those employed here.

Appendix 8.1

[1] Meen (1989) provides an early version of the analysis.

[2] Meen et al (2020).

References

Aalbers, M. (2016) *The Financialization of Housing: A Political Economy Approach*. Routledge Studies in the Modern World Economy, London: Routledge.

Aalbers, M. (2017) 'The variegated financialization of housing', *International Journal of Urban and Regional Research*, 41(4): 542–554.

Adam, S., Hodge, L., Phillips, D. and Xu, X (2020) *Revaluation and Reform: Bringing Council Tax in England into the 21st Century*, London: Institute for Fiscal Studies.

Adams, Z. and Füss, R. (2010) 'Macroeconomic determinants of international housing markets', *Journal of Housing Economics*, 19(1): 38–50.

Affordable Housing Commission (2019) *Defining and Measuring Housing Affordability – An Alternative Approach*, https://static1.squarespace.com/static/5b9675fc1137a618f278542d/t/5cf55923f41ae70001170311/1559583017920/Defining+and+measuring+housing+affordability.pdf [accessed 19 November 2019].

Agnello, L. and Schuknecht, L. (2011) 'Booms and busts in housing markets: Determinants and implications', *Journal of Housing Economics*, 20(3): 171–190.

Akerlof, G. and Shiller, R. (2009) *Animal Spirits: How Human Psychology Drives the Economy, and Why it Matters for Global Capitalism*, Princeton and Oxford: Princeton University Press.

Allen, J., Barlow, J., Leal, J., Maloutas, T. and Padovani, L. (2004) *Housing and Welfare in Southern Europe*, Oxford: Wiley.

Ambrose, B. and Peek, J. (2008) 'Credit Availability and the Structure of the Homebuilding Industry', *Real Estate Economics*, 36(4): 659–692.

Andrew, M. (2010) 'The changing route to owner occupation: The impact of student debt', *Housing Studies*, 25(1): 39–62.

Andrew, M. (2012) 'The changing route to owner occupation: The impact of borrowing constraints on young adult home ownership transitions in Britain in the 1990s', *Urban Studies*, 49(8): 1659–1678.

Andrew, M. and Meen, G. (2003) 'Housing transactions and the changing decisions of young households in Britain: The microeconomic evidence', *Real Estate Economics*, 31(1): 117–138.

Andrew, M., Haurin, D. and Munasib, A. (2006) 'Explaining the route to owner occupation: A transatlantic comparison', *Journal of Housing Economics*, 15(3): 189–216.

Andrews, D. and Sánchez, A. (2011) 'The evolution of home ownership rates in selected OECD countries: Demographic and public policy influences', *OECD Journal: Economic Studies*, 2011: 207–243.

Anundsen, A. and Heebøll, C. (2016) 'Supply restrictions, subprime lending and regional US house prices', *Journal of Housing Economics*, 31: 54–72.

Anundsen, A. and Jansen, E. (2013) 'Self-reinforcing effects between house prices and credit', *Journal of Housing Economics*, 22(3): 192–212.

Aoki, K., Proudman, J. and Vlieghe, G. (2002) 'House Prices, Consumption and Monetary Policy: A Financial Accelerator Approach', *Bank of England Working Paper No. 169*. London.

Arthur, W., Holland, J., LeBaron, B., Palmer, R. and Tayler, P. (1997) 'Asset pricing under endogenous expectations in an artificial stock market', in W. Arthur, S. Durlauf and D. Lane (eds.), *The Economy as an Evolving Complex System* (pp 15–44), Reading, MA: Addison-Wesley.

Attanasio, O. and Weber, G. (1994) 'The UK consumption boom of the late 1980s: Aggregate implications of microeconomic evidence', *Economic Journal*, 104(427): 1269–1302.

Attanasio, O., Blow, L., Hamilton, R. and Leicester, A. (2009) 'Booms and busts: Consumption, house prices and expectations', *Economica*, 76(301): 20–50.

Bailey, R., Hatton, T. and Inwood, K. (2016) 'Health, height and the household at the turn of the 20th Century', *Economic History Review*, 69(1): 35–53.

Balcilar, M., Beyene, A., Gupta, R. and Seleteng, M. (2013) 'Ripple' effects in South African house prices', *Urban Studies*, 50(5): 876–894.

Ball, M. (2003) 'Markets and the structure of the housebuilding industry: An international perspective', *Urban Studies*, 40(5–6): 897–916.

Ball, M. (2010) *The Housebuilding Industry: Promoting Recovery in Housing Supply*, London: Department of Communities and Local Government.

Ball, M. (2011) 'Planning delay and the responsiveness of English housing supply', *Urban Studies*, 48: 349–362.

Ball, M., Allmendinger, P. and Hughes, C. (2009) 'Housing supply and planning delay in the South of England', *Journal of European Real Estate Research*, 2: 151–169.

Ball, M., Meen, G. and Nygaard, C. (2010) 'Housing supply price elasticities revisited: Evidence from international, national, local and company data', *Journal of Housing Economics*, 19: 255–268.

Barker, K. (2003) *Review of Housing Supply: Securing Our Future Housing Needs, Interim Report – Analysis*, London: HM Treasury.

Barker, K. (2004) *Review of Housing Supply: Delivering Stability: Securing Our Future Housing Needs, Final Report*, London: HM Treasury.

Barker, K. (2006) *Barker Review of Land Use Planning*, London: HM Treasury.

Barlow Commission (1940) *Report of the Royal Commission on the Distribution of the Industrial Population*, Cmd 6153, London: HMSO.

Barros, C., Gil-Alana, L. and Payne, J. (2012) 'Comovements among U.S. state housing prices: Evidence from fractional cointegration', *Economic Modelling*, 29(3): 936–942.

Barton, C. and Wilson, W. (2019) *What Is Affordable Housing?*, Commons Briefing Paper 07747, House of Commons Library, London: Parliament.

Baum-Snow, N. and Marion, J. (2009) 'The effects of low income housing tax credit developments on neighborhoods', *Journal of Public Economics*, 93(5–6): 654–666.

Beckerman, W. (1965) *The British Economy in 1975*, Cambridge: Cambridge University Press.

Been, V., Gould Ellen, I. and O'Regan, K. (2019) 'Supply skepticism: Housing supply and affordability', *Housing Policy Debate*, 29(1): 25–40.

Benetton, M., Bracke, P., Cocco, J. and Garbarino, N. (2019) 'Housing consumption and investment: Evidence from shared equity mortgages', *Bank of England Staff Working Paper No. 790*. London.

Benito, A., Thompson, J., Waldron, M. and Wood, R. (2006) 'House prices and consumer spending', *Bank of England Quarterly Bulletin*, Summer: 142–154.

Ben-Shahar, D. and Warszawski, J. (2016) 'Inequality in housing affordability: Measurement and estimation', *Urban Studies*, 53(6): 1178–1202.

Bérard, G. and Trannoy, A. (2017) 'The impact of a rise in the real estate transfer taxes on the French housing market', *AMSE Working Paper No. 1732*. Aix, France: Aix-Marseille School of Economics.

Berg, L. (2002) 'Prices on the second-hand market for Swedish family houses: Correlation, causation and determinants', *International Journal of Housing Policy*, 2(1): 1–24.

Bernanke, B. and Gertler, M. (1989) 'Agency costs, net worth, and business fluctuations', *American Economic Review*, 79(1): 14–31.

Berry, M. (2014) 'Neoliberalism and the city: Or the failure of market fundamentalism', *Housing, Theory and Society*, 31(1): 1–18.

Besley, T., Meads, N. and Surico, P. (2014) 'The incidence of transactions taxes: evidence from a stamp duty holiday', *Journal of Public Economics*, 119: 61–70.

Best, M. and Kleven, H. (2018) 'Housing market responses to transaction taxes: Evidence from notches and stimulus in the UK', *The Review of Economic Studies*, 85(1): 157–193.

Beveridge, W. (1942) *Social Insurance and Allied Services*, Cmd 6404, London: Her Majesty's Stationery Office.

Black, J., DeMeza, D. and Jeffreys, D. (1996) 'House prices, the supply of collateral and the enterprise economy', *Economic Journal*, 106(434): 60–75.

Blackley, D. (1999) 'The long-run elasticity of new housing supply in the United States: Empirical evidence for 1950 to 1994', *Journal of Real Estate Finance and Economics*, 18(1): 25–42.

Blanco, F., Martín, V. and Vazquez, G. (2016) 'Regional house price convergence in Spain during the housing boom', *Urban Studies*, 53(4): 775–798.

Boddy, M. and Gray, F. (1979) 'Filtering theory, housing policy and the legitimation of inequality', *Policy & Politics*, 7(1): 39–54.

Bogdon, A. and Can, A. (1997) 'Indicators of local housing affordability: Comparative and spatial approaches', *Real Estate Economics*, 25(1): 43–80.

Böheim, R. and Taylor, M. (2000) 'My home was my castle: Evictions and repossessions in Britain', *Journal of Housing Economics*, 9(4): 287–319

Böheim, R. and Taylor, M. (2002) 'Tied down or time to move? Investigating the relationships between housing tenure, employment status and residential mobility in Britain', *Scottish Journal of Political Economy*, 49(4): 369–392.

Booth, P and Crook, T. (1986) *Low Cost Home Ownership*, Aldershot: Gower Publishing Company.

Borg, I. and Brandén, M. (2018) 'Do high levels of home ownership create unemployment? Introducing the missing link between housing tenure and unemployment', *Housing Studies*, 33(4): 501–524.

Borrowman, L., Kazakevitch, G. and Frost, L. (2017) 'How long do households remain in housing affordability stress?', *Housing Studies*, 32(7): 869–886.

Bosker, M., Brakman, S., Garretsen, H. and Schramm, M. (2007) 'Looking for multiple equilibria when geography matters: German city growth and the WWII shock', *Journal of Urban Economics*, 61(1): 152–169.

Bourassa, S. (1996) 'Measuring the affordability of homeownership', *Urban Studies*, 33(10): 1867–1877.

Bourassa, S., Haurin, D., Haurin, J. and Hendershott, P. (1994) 'Independent living and home ownership: An analysis of Australian youth', *Australian Economic Review*, 27(3): 29–44.

Bover, O., Muellbauer, J. and Murphy, A. (1989) 'Housing, wages and UK labour markets', *Oxford Bulletin of Economics and Statistics*, 51(2): 97–136.

Bramley, G. (1993) 'The impact of land use planning and tax subsidies on the supply and price of housing in Britain', *Urban Studies*, 30(1): 5–30.

Bramley, G. (1993a) 'Land use planning and the housing market in Britain: The impact on housebuilding and house prices', *Environment and Planning A*, 25(7): 1021–1051.

Bramley, G. (1994) 'An affordability crisis in Britain: Dimensions, causes and policy impact', *Housing Studies*, 9(1): 103–124.

Bramley, G. (1998) 'Measuring planning: Indicators of planning restraint and its impact on the housing market', *Environment and Planning B*, 25(1): 31–57.

Bramley, G. (1999) 'Housing market adjustment and land-supply constraints', *Environment and Planning A*, 21: 1169–1188.

Bramley, G. (2002) 'Planning regulation and housing supply in a market system', in A. O'Sullivan and K. Gibb (eds.), *Housing Economics and Public Policy*, Oxford: Basil Blackwell.

Bramley, G. (2012) 'Affordability, poverty and housing need: Triangulating measures and standards', *Journal of Housing and the Built Environment*, 27(2): 133–151.

Bramley, G. (2018) *Housing Supply Requirements across Great Britain*, London: National Housing Federation and Crisis.

Bramley, G. and Karley, N. (2005) 'How much extra affordable housing is needed in England?' *Housing Studies*, 20(5): 685–715.

Bramley, G. and Leishman, C. (2005) 'Planning and housing supply in two-speed Britain: Modelling local market outcomes', *Urban Studies*, 42(12): 2213–2244.

Bramley, G., Munro, M. and Lancaster, S. (1997) *The Economic Determinants of Household Formation: A Literature Review*, London: Department of the Environment, Transport and the Regions.

Bramley, G., Fitzpatrick, S., Karley, K., Monk, S. and Pleace, N. (2005) *Evaluation of English Housing Policy, 1975–2000, Theme 1 Supply, Need and Access*, London: Office of the Deputy Prime Minister.

Bramley, G., Pawson, H., White, M., Watkins, D. and Pleace, N. (2010) *Estimating Housing Need*, London: Department of Communities and Local Government.

British Property Federation (2017) *Build to Rent: Unlocking the Potential of an Emerging Property Market*, London: British Property Federation.

Buiter, W. (2008) 'Housing Wealth Isn't Wealth', *CEPR Discussion Paper DP6920*. London: CEPR.

Burge, G. and Ihlanfeldt, K. (2006) 'Impact fees and single-family home construction', *Journal of Urban Economics*, 60: 284–306.

Burge, G. and Ihlanfeldt, K. (2006a) 'The effects of impact fees on multifamily housing construction', *Journal of Regional Science*, 46(1): 5–23.

Burgess, G. (2014) *The Nature of Planning Constraints*, Cambridge: Cambridge Centre for Housing and Planning Research, University of Cambridge.

Burke, T., Stone, M. and Ralston, L. (2011) *The Residual Income Method: A New Lens on Housing Affordability and Market Behaviour*, AHURI Final Report No. 176, Melbourne: Australian Housing and Urban Research Institute.

Burrows, R. (1998) 'Mortgage indebtedness in England: An epidemiology', *Housing Studies*, 13(1): 5–22.

Burrows, R. and Ford, J. (1997) 'Who needs a safety net? The social distribution of mortgage arrears in England', *Housing Finance*, 34: 17–24.

Calavita, N. and Mallach, A. (2010) *Inclusionary Zoning in an International Perspective*, Cambridge, MA: Lincoln Institute.

Caldera, A. and Johansson, A. (2013) 'The price responsiveness of housing supply in OECD countries', *Journal of Housing Economics*, 22(3): 231–249.

Cambridge Centre of Housing and Planning Research (CCHPR) (2001–2010 annually) *Guide to Local Rents*, www.cchpr.landecon.cam.ac.uk/Research/Start-Year/2001/Guide-to-Local-Rents/2010 [accessed 22 December 2019].

Cameron, G. and Muellbauer, J. (1998) 'The housing market and regional commuting and migration choices', *Scottish Journal of Political Economy*, 45(4): 420–446.

Cameron, G. and Muellbauer, J. (2001), 'Earnings, unemployment, and housing in Britain', *Journal of Applied Econometrics*, 16: 203–220.

Cammarota, M. (1989) 'The impact of unseasonable weather on housing starts', *Journal of the American Real Estate and Urban Economics Association*, 17(3): 300–313.

Campaign for the Protection of Rural England (2018) *The State of the Green Belt*, London: CPRE.

Campaign for the Protection of Rural England (2019) *The State of Brownfield*, London: CPRE.

Campbell, J. and Cocco, J. (2007) 'How do house prices affect consumption? Evidence from micro data', *Journal of Monetary Economics*, 54(3): 591–621.

Can, A. and Megbolugbe, I. (1997) 'Spatial dependence and house price index construction', *Journal of Real Estate Finance and Economics*, 14(1,2): 203–222.

Carozzi, F., Hilber, C. and Yu, X. (2019) 'The economic impacts of Help to Buy', www.sprweb.com/Public/Events/Nick-Tyrrell-Research-Prize/Public/Events/Nick-Tyrrell-Research-Prize/Nick-Tyrrell-Research-Prize.aspx?hkey=73f723eb-08db-4b96-843e-56e4ca98c905 [accessed 29 November 2019].

Case, K. and Shiller, R. (1996) 'Mortgage default risk and real estate prices: The use of index-based futures and options in real estate', *Journal of Housing Research*, 7(2): 243–258.

Case, K., Quigley, J. and Shiller, R. (2005) 'Comparing wealth effects: The stock market versus the housing market', *The B.E. Journal of Macroeconomics*, 5(1): Article 1.

Cerutti, E., Dagher, J. and Dell'Ariccia, G. (2017) 'Housing finance and real estate booms: A cross country perspective', *Journal of Housing Economics*, 38: 1–13.

Chadwick, E. (1842) *Sanitary Conditions of the Labouring Population*, Report to Her Majesty's Principal Secretary of State for the Home Office from the Poor Law Commissioners, London: House of Commons Sessional Paper.

ChamberlainWalker (2017) *The Role of Land Pipelines in the UK Housebuilding Process*, ChamberlainWalker Economics Ltd.

Chaplin, R. and Freeman, A. (1999) 'Towards an accurate description of affordability', *Urban Studies*, 36(11): 1949–57.

Cheshire, P. (2009) *Urban Land Markets and Policy Failures*. Land Use Futures, Discussion Papers, Foresight, London: Department for Business Innovation and Skills.

Cheshire, P. and Buyuklieva, B. (2019) *Homes on the Right Tracks*, London: Centre for Cities.

Cheshire, P. and Sheppard, S. (1995) 'On the price of land and the value of amenities', *Economica*, 62(246): 247–267.

Cheshire, P. and Sheppard, S. (1998) 'Estimating the demand for housing, land and neighbourhood characteristics', *Oxford Bulletin of Economics and Statistics*, 60(3): 357–382.

Cheshire, P. and Sheppard, S. (2002) 'The welfare effects of land use planning', *Journal of Urban Economics*, 52(2): 242–269.

Cheshire, P. and Sheppard, S. (2004a) 'Capitalising the value of free schools: The impact of supply characteristics and uncertainty', *Economic Journal*, 114(499): 397–424.

Cheshire, P. and Sheppard, S. (2004b) 'Land markets and land market regulation: Progress towards understanding', *Regional Science and Urban Economics*, 34(6): 619–637.

Cheshire, P. and Sheppard, S. (2005) 'The introduction of price signals into land use planning decision-making', *Urban Studies*, 42(4): 647–663.

Cheshire, P., Nathan, M. and Overman, H. (2014) *Urban Economics and Urban Policy: Challenging Conventional Policy Wisdom*, Massachusetts: Edward Elgar.

Chevin, D. (2008) *Moving Up a Gear*, London: Smith Institute.

Chowdhury, R. and Maclennan, D. (2014) 'Regional house price cycles in the UK, 1978–2012: A Markov switching VAR', *Journal of European Real Estate Research*, 7(3): 345–366.

Clark, S. and Coggin, T. (2009) 'Trends, cycles and convergence in US regional house prices', *Journal of Real Estate Finance and Economics*, 39(3): 264–283.

Clifford, B., Ferm, J., Livingstone, N. and Canelas, P. (2018) *Assessing the Impacts of Extending Permitted Development Rights to Office-to-Residential Change of Use in England*, London: RICS.

Cohen, J., Ioannides, Y. and Thanapisitikul, W. (2016) 'Spatial Effects and House Price Dynamics in the USA', *Journal of Housing Economics*, 31: 1–13.

Cohen, T., Lindblad, M. and Paik, J. (2009) 'Renting to owning: An exploration of the theory of planned behavior in the homeownership domain', *Basic and Applied Social Psychology*, 31(4): 376–389.

Coopers and Lybrand (1985) *Land Use Planning and the Housing Market; Summary Report*, London: Department of Environment.

Coopers and Lybrand (1987) *Land Use Planning and Indicators of Housing Demand*, London: Coopers and Lybrand.

Costello, G. (2006) 'The impact of stamp duty reductions on demand in the Perth housing market', *Pacific Rim Property Research Journal*, 12(2): 198–212.

Coulson, N. and Richard, C. (1996) 'The dynamic impact of unseasonable weather on construction activity', *Real Estate Economics*, 24(2): 179–194.

Crook, A., Henneberry, J. and Whitehead, C. (2016) *Planning Gain: Providing Infrastructure and Affordable Housing*, Oxford: Wiley Blackwell.

Crook, A. and Whitehead, C. (2019) 'Capturing development values: Why is it so difficult?' *Town Planning Review*, 90(4): 359–381.

Crosby, N. and Wyatt, P. (2016) 'Financial viability appraisals for site-specific planning decisions in England', *Environment and Planning C*, 34(8): 1716–1733.

Cuestas, J. (2017) 'House prices and capital inflows in Spain during the boom: Evidence from a cointegrated VAR and a structural Bayesian VAR', *Journal of Housing Economics*, 37: 22–28.

Cullingworth, J. (1960) *Housing Needs and Planning Policy*, London: Routledge and Kegan Paul.

Cunningham, C. (2006) 'House price uncertainty, timing of development, and vacant land prices: Evidence for real options in Seattle', *Journal of Urban Economics*, 59(1): 1–31.

Dachis, B., Duranton, G. and Turner, M. (2012) 'The effects of land transfer taxes on real estate markets: Evidence from a natural experiment in Toronto', *Journal of Economic Geography*, 12(2): 327–354.

Dalton, T. (2009) 'Housing policy retrenchment: Australia and Canada compared', *Urban Studies*, 46(1): 63–92.

Damen, S., Vastmans, F. and Buyst, E. (2016) 'The effects of mortgage interest deduction and mortgage characteristics on house prices', *Journal of Housing Economics*, 34: 15–29.

Davies, B., Turner, E., Marquardt, S. and Snelling, C. (2016) *German Model Homes*, London: Institute for Public Policy Research.

Davis, D. and Weinstein, D. (2002) 'Bones, bombs, and break points: The geography of economic activity', *American Economic Review*, 92(5): 1269–1289.

Deloitte (2018) *European Construction Monitor, 2017–2018*, https://www2.deloitte.com/content/dam/Deloitte/pl/Documents/Reports/pl_European_Construction_Monitor_2017-2018.PDF [accessed 29 December 2019].

De Magalhães, C., Freire-Trigo, S., Gallent, N., Scanlon, K. and Whitehead, C. (2018) *Planning Risk and Development*, Research Report, London: RTPI.

DeMeza, D. and Webb, D. (1999) 'Wealth, enterprise and credit policy', *Economic Journal*, 109(455): 153–163.

Department of Communities and Local Government (2012) *Accelerating the Release of Surplus Public Sector Land*, London: DCLG.

Department of Communities and Local Government (2016) *2014-Based Household Projections in England, 2014 to 2039*, London: DCLG.

Department of Communities and Local Government (2017) *Fixing Our Broken Housing Market.* Cm 9352, www.gov.uk/government/publications/fixing-our-broken-housing-market [accessed 3 December 2019].

Department for Economic Affairs (1965) *The National Plan for Economic Development*, (PREM 13/274), London: Her Majesty's Stationery Office.

Department of the Environment (1971) *Fair Deal for Housing*, Cmnd 4728, London: Her Majesty's Stationery Office.

Department of the Environment (1977) *Housing Policy Review*, Cmnd 6851, London: Her Majesty's Stationery Office.

Department of the Environment (1977a) *Housing Policy Technical Volume Parts I, II and III*, Cmnd 6851. London: Her Majesty's Stationery Office.

Department of the Environment (1982) *English House Condition Survey, 1981 Part 1,* London: Her Majesty's Stationery Office.

Department of the Environment (1995) *Evaluating Large Scale Voluntary Transfers of Local Authority Housing (Housing Research Report)*, London: Her Majesty's Stationery Office.

Department of Work and Pensions (2019) *Housing Costs and Universal Credit*, www.gov.uk/housing-and-universal-credit [accessed 11 December 2019].

Deutsche Bank (2017) *Germany Monitor: Bundestag Elections 2017. Housing Policy in Germany: Changing Direction*, www.dbresearch.com/PROD/RPS_EN-PROD/PROD0000000000450490/Housing_policy_in_Germany_ per centC2 per cent96_Changing_direction.PDF [accessed 14 December 2019].

Dietz, R. and Haurin, D. (2003) 'The social and private micro-level consequences of home ownership', *Journal of Urban Economics*, 54(3): 401–450.

Dincecco, M. and Onorato, M. (2016) 'Military conflict and the economic rise of urban Europe', *Journal of Economic Growth*, 21(3): 259–282.

DiNapoli, T. (2019) *Housing Affordability in New York State*, New York: Office of the New York State Controller.

Duca, J., Muellbauer, J. and Murphy, A. (2011) 'House prices and credit constraints: Making sense of the US experience', *Economic Journal*, 121(552): 533–551.

Duca, J., Muellbauer, J. and Murphy, A. (2016) 'How mortgage finance reform could affect housing', *American Economic Review*, 106(5): 620–624.

Eccleston, R., Verdouw, J., Flanagan, K., Warren, N., Duncan, A., Ong, R., Whelan, S. and Atalay, K. (2018) *Pathways to Housing Tax Reform*, AHURI Final Report No. 301, Melbourne: Australian Housing and Urban Research Institute.

Eichholtz, P. (1997) 'A long run house price index: The Herengracht Index, 1628–1973', *Real Estate Economics*, 25(2): 175–192.

Eichholtz, P., Straetmans, S. and Theebe, M. (2012) 'The Amsterdam rent index: The housing market and the economy, 1550–1850', *Journal of Housing Economics*, 21(4): 269–282.

Ellis, H. (2017) *The Rise and Fall of the 1947 Planning System*, London: TCPA.

Ellis, K., and Whitehead, C. (2015) *Affordability: A Step Forward, Establishing Principles for Rent Setting*, London: Affinity Sutton.

Elsinga, M. and Hoeksta, J. (2005) 'Home ownership and housing satisfaction', *Journal of Housing and the Built Environment*, 20: 401–424.

Elsinga, M., Stephens, M. and Knorr-Siedow, T. (2014) 'The privatisation of social housing: Three different pathways', in K. Scanlon, C. Whitehead and M. Fernández Arrigoitia (eds.), *Social Housing in Europe*, Oxford: Wiley Blackwell.

Ermisch, J. (1999) 'Prices, parents and young people's household formation', *Journal of Urban Economics*, 45(1): 47–71.

European Mortgage Federation (2019) *Hypostat 2019*, Brussels: EMF.

Evans, A. (1987) *House Prices in the South East – A Review*, London: The Housebuilders Federation.

Evans, A. (2004) *Economics and Land Use Planning*, Oxford: Blackwell.

Evans, K. and Keohane, N. (2016) *Locked Out: How Property Crowdfunding Could Help the Next Generation of Homeowners*, London: Social Market Foundation.

Farmer, M. (2016) *The Farmer Review of the UK Construction Labour Model*, London: Construction Leadership Council.

FEANSTA (2018) *The Third Overview of Housing Exclusion in Europe 2018*. www.feantsa.org/download/full-report-en1029873431323901915. pdf. [accessed 23 December 2019].

Fereidouni, H., Al-Mulali, U., Lee, J. and Mohammed, A. (2016) 'Dynamic relationship between house prices in Malaysia's major economic regions and Singapore house prices', *Regional Studies*, 50(4): 657–670.

Fergus, J. (1999) 'Where, when, and by how much does abnormal weather affect housing construction?', *Journal of Real Estate Finance and Economics*, 18(1): 63–87.

Fingleton, B. (2008) 'Housing supply, housing demand, and affordability', *Urban Studies*, 45(8): 1545–1563.

Finlay, S., Ipsos MORI, in partnership with Williams, P., Whitehead, C. and the London School of Economics (2016) *Evaluation of Help to Buy Equity Loan Scheme*, London: Department of Communities and Local Government.

Fishback, P. and Kollman, T. (2012) 'New multi-city estimates of the changes in home values, 1920–1940', NBER Working Paper No. 18272.

Fisher, E. (1933) 'Speculation in suburban lands', *American Economic Review, Papers and Proceedings*, 23(1): 152–162.

Fisher, I. (1933) 'The debt-deflation theory of the Great Depressions', *Econometrica*, 1(4): 337–357.

Fitzpatrick, S., Pawson, H., Bramley, G., Wood, J., Watts, B., Stephen, M. and Blenkinsopp, J. (2019) *The Homelessness Monitor*, London: Crisis.

Follain, J. (1979) 'The price elasticity of the long-run supply of new housing construction', *Land Economics*, 55(2): 190–199.

Foye, C., Clapham, D. and Gabrieli, T. (2018) 'Home-ownership as a social norm and positional good: Subjective wellbeing evidence from panel data', *Urban Studies*, 55(6): 1290–1312.

Freeman, A., Holmans, A. and Whitehead, C. (1996) *Is the UK Different? International Comparisons of Tenure Patterns*, London: Council of Mortgage Lenders.

Friedman, M. (1957) *A Theory of the Consumption Function*, Princeton: Princeton University Press.

Friggit, J. (2002) *Long Term Home Prices and Residential Property Investment Performance in Paris in the Time of the French Franc, 1840–2001*. Conseil Général des Points et Chaussées.

Füss, R. and Zietz, J. (2016) 'The economic drivers of differences in house price inflation rates across MSAs', *Journal of Housing Economics*, 31: 35–53.

Galster, G. (1997) 'Comparing demand-side and supply-side policies: Sub market and spatial perspectives', *Housing Studies*, 12(4): 561–577.

Gan, Q. and Hill, R. (2009) 'Measuring housing affordability: Looking beyond the median', *Journal of Housing Economics*, 18(2): 115–125.

Garcia Freitas, F., Whitehead, C. and Santa Rosa, J. (eds) (2015) *Finance and Subsidy Policies in Brazil and European Union: A Comparative Analysis*, Brasilia: Cities Alliance.

Geiger, F., Muellbauer, J. and Rupprecht, M. (2016) 'The housing market, household portfolios, and the German consumer', ECB Working Paper 1904, Frankfurt: European Central Bank.

Gerald Eve (1991) *The Relationship between House Prices and Land Supply*, Gerald Eve and the Department of Land Economy, University of Cambridge, London: Her Majesty's Stationery Office.

Gibb, K. (2016) 'Housing benefit: Slow on the take-up?', *Contemporary Social Science*, 11(1): 40–51.

Gibb, K. and Whitehead, C. (2007) 'Towards the more effective use of housing finance and subsidy', *Housing Studies*, 22(2): 183–200.

Gibb, K., Meen, G. and Nygaard, C. (2019) 'Long-run urban dynamics: understanding local housing market change in London', *Housing Studies*, 34(2): 338–359.

Glaeser, E. and Gyourko, J. (2005) 'Urban decline and durable housing', *Journal of Political Economy*, 113(2): 345–375.

Glaeser, E. and Scheinkman, J. (2001) 'Measuring social interactions' in *Social Dynamics*, S. Durlauf and H. P. Young (eds.), Cambridge, Massachusetts: The MIT Press.

Glaeser, E., Gyourko, J. and Saks, R. (2005) 'Why have housing prices gone up?', *American Economic Review*, 95(2): 329–333.

Glaeser, E., Gyourko, J. and Saiz, A. (2008) 'Housing supply and housing bubbles', *Journal of Urban Economics*, 64(2): 198–217.

Goodman, A. and Thibodeau, T. (2008) 'Where are the Speculative Bubbles in US Housing Markets?', *Journal of Housing Economics*, 17(2): 117–137.

Goodman, J. (1987) 'Housing and the weather', *Journal of the American Real Estate and Urban Economics Association*, 15(1): 639–663.

Goodman, L. and Mayer, C. (2018) 'Home ownership and the American Dream', *Journal of Economic Perspectives*, 32(1): 31–58.

Gordon, I., Mace, A. and Whitehead, C. (2016) *Defining, Measuring and Implementing Density Standards in London: London Plan Density Research Project 1*. London: LSE London.

Government of France (2017) *Housing Strategy*, www.gouvernement.fr/en/the-government-s-housing-strategy [accessed 14 December 2019].

Greater London Authority (2018) *Draft New London Plan*, www.london.gov.uk/what-we-do/planning/london-plan/new-london-plan/download-draft-london-plan-0 [accessed 14 December 2019].

Greater London Authority (2019) *Enquiry in Public for the Draft New London Plan*, www.london.gov.uk/what-we-do/planning/london-plan/new-london-plan/examination-public-draft-new-london-plan [accessed 14 December 2019].

Green, R. and Hendershott, P. (2001) 'Home Ownership and Unemployment in the US', *Urban Studies*, 38(9): 1509–1520.

Green, R. and Wachter, S. (2005) 'The American mortgage market in historical and international context', *Journal of Economic Perspectives*, 19(4): 93–114.

Green, R., Malpezzi, S. and Mayo, S. (2005) 'Metropolitan-specific Estimates of the Price Elasticity of Supply of Housing, and their Sources', *American Economic Review*, 95(2): 334–339.

Grey, A., Hepworth, N. and Odling-Smee, J. (1981) *Housing, Rents, Costs and Subsidies: A Discussion Document*, London: CIPFA.

Griggs, J. and Kemp, P. (2012) 'Housing allowances as income support: Comparing European welfare regimes', *International Journal of Housing Policy*, 12(4): 391–412.

Grigson, W. (1986) *House Prices in Perspective – A Review of South East Evidence*, London: SERPLAN.

Gupta, R. and Miller, S. (2010) '"Ripple Effects" and forecasting home prices in Los Angeles, Las Vegas, and Phoenix', *The Annals of Regional Science*, 48(3): 763–782.

Gupta, R. and Miller, S. (2012) 'The time-series properties of house prices: A case study of the Southern California Market', *Journal of Real Estate Finance and Economics*, 44(3): 339–361.

Gurran, N. and Phibbs, P. (2015) 'Are governments really interested in fixing the housing problem? Policy capture and busy work in Australia', *Housing Studies*, 30(5): 711–729.

Gurran, N., Gilbert, C., Gibb, K., van den Nouwelant, R., James, A. and Phibbs, P. (2018) *Supporting Affordable Housing Supply: Inclusionary Planning in New and Renewing Communities*, AHURI Final Report No. 297, Melbourne: Australian Housing and Urban Research Institute.

Gurran, N., Rowley, S., Milligan, V., Randolph, B., Phibbs, P., Gilbert, C., James, A., Troy, L. and van den Nouwelant, R. (2018) *Inquiry into Increasing Affordable Housing Supply: Evidence-Based Principles and Strategies for Australian Policy and Practice*, AHURI Final Report No. 300, Melbourne: Australian Housing and Urban Research Institute.

Gurran, N., Phibbs, P., Yates, J., Gilbert, C., Whitehead, C., Norris, M., McClure, K., Berry, M., Maginn, P. and Goodman, R. (2015) *Housing Markets, Economic Productivity, and Risk: International Evidence and Policy Implications for Australia Volume 1: Outcomes of an Investigative Panel*, AHURI Final Report No. 254, Melbourne: Australian Housing and Urban Research Institute.

Gyourko, J. and Linneman, P. (1993) 'The Affordability of the American Dream: An Examination of the Last 30 Years', *Journal of Housing Research*, 4(1): 39–72.

Gyourko, J., Saiz, A. and Summers, A. (2008) 'A new measure of the local regulatory environment for housing markets', *Urban Studies*, 45(3): 693–729.

Hall, P., Gracey, H., Drewett, R. and Thomas, R. (1973) *The Containment of Urban England*, London: Allen and Unwin.

Hall, S., Psaradakis, Z. and Sola, M. (1997) 'Switching error-correction models of house prices in the United Kingdom', *Economic Modelling*, 14(4): 517–528.

Hancock, K. (1991) 'The Economic Principles of Affordability', paper given at the Housing Studies Association Conference. York: University of York.

Hancock, K. (1993) 'Can't pay? Won't pay? The economic principles of affordability', *Urban Studies*, 30(1): 127–145.

Haurin, D., Hendershott, P. and Kim, D. (1994) 'Housing decisions of American youth', *Journal of Urban Economics*, 35(1): 28–45.

Haurin, D., Hendershott, P. and Wachter, S. (1997) 'Borrowing constraints and the tenure choice of young households', *Journal of Housing Research*, 8(2): 137–154.

Hegedüs, J., Lux, M. and Teller, N. (eds.) (2013) *Social Housing in Transition Countries*, New York and Abingdon: Routledge.

Henman, P. and Jones, A. (2012) *Exploring the Use of Residual Measures of Housing Affordability in Australia: Methodologies and Concepts*, Melbourne: Australian Housing and Urban Research Institute Final Report No. 180.

Heywood, A. (2011) *The End of the Affair: Implications of Declining Home Ownership*, London: Smith Institute.

HM Treasury (2017) *Autumn Budget, 2017*, London: HM Treasury.

HM Treasury (2018) *The Green Book: Central Government Guidance on Appraisal and Evaluation*, www.gov.uk/government/publications/the-green-book-appraisal-and-evaluation-in-central-governent [accessed 29 November 2019].

HM Treasury (2018a) *Budget 2018*, www.gov.uk/government/topical-events/budget-2018 [accessed 22 December 2019].

HM Treasury (2019) *Spring Statement*, www.gov.uk/government/publications/spring-statement-2019-written-ministerial-statement [accessed 22 December 2019].

HM Treasury and Office of the Deputy Prime Minister (2005) *The Government's Response to Kate Barker's Review of Housing Supply*, London: HM Treasury and ODPM.

Hilber, C. and Lyytikäinen, T. (2017) 'Transaction taxes and household mobility: Distortion on the housing or labour market?' *Journal of Urban Economics*, 101: 57–73.

Hilber, C. and Vermeulen, W. (2016) 'The impact of supply constraints on house prices in England', *Economic Journal*, 126(591): 358–405.

Hills, J. (2001) 'Inclusion or exclusion? The role of housing subsidies and benefits', *Urban Studies*, 38(11): 1887–1902.

Hills, J., Berthoud, R. and Gibb. K. (1991) 'The future of housing allowances', *Critical Social Policy*, 11(31): 94–97.

Himmelberg, C., Mayer, C. and Sinai, T. (2005) 'Assessing high house prices: Bubbles, fundamentals and misperceptions', *Journal of Economic Perspectives*, 19(4): 67–92.

Holmans, A. (1970) 'A forecast of effective demand for housing in Great Britain in the nineteen seventies', *Social Trends*, 1: 33–42.

Holmans, A. (1987) *Housing Policy in Britain: A History*, London: Croom Helm.

Holmans, A. (2005), *Historical Statistics of Housing in Britain*, Cambridge: Cambridge Centre for Housing and Planning Research, University of Cambridge.

Holmans, A. (2012) *Household Projections, their History and Uses*, Cambridge: Cambridge Centre of Housing and Planning, University of Cambridge.

Holmans, A. and Whitehead, C. (1997) *Funding Affordable Social Housing*, London: National Housing Federation.

Holmans, A., Monk, S. and Whitehead, C. (2008) *Homes for the Future: A New Analysis of Housing Need and Demand in England*, London: Shelter.

Holmes, M., Otero, J. and Panagiotidis, T. (2011) 'Investigating regional house price convergence in the United States: Evidence from a pair-wise approach', *Economic Modelling*, 28(6): 2369–2376.

Home Builders Federation (2017) *Reversing the Decline of Small Housebuilders*, www.hbf.co.uk/fileadmin/documents/Policy/Publications/HBF_SME_Report_2017_Web.pdf [accessed 28 November 2019].

Hornbeck, R. and Keniston, D. (2017) 'Creative destruction: Barriers to urban growth and the Boston Great Fire of 1872', *American Economic Review*, 107(6): 1365–1398.

House of Commons, Communities and Local Government Committee (2017) *Capacity in the Home Building Industry*, 10th Report of Session 2016-17, HC46, London: UK Parliament.

House of Commons, Communities and Local Government Select Committee (2018) *Housing for Older People*, Second Report of Session 2017–19, HC 370, London: UK Parliament.

House of Commons, Housing, Communities and Local Government Select Committee (2018a) *Land Value Capture*, Tenth Report of Session 2017–19, HC 766, London: UK Parliament.

House of Commons, Housing, Communities and Local Government Select Committee (2019) *Modern Methods of Construction*, Fifteenth Report of Session 2017–19, HC 1831, London: UK Parliament.

House of Commons, Housing, Communities and Local Government Select Committee (2019a) *High Streets and Town Centres in 2030*, Fifteenth Report of Session 2017–19, HC 1010, London: UK Parliament.

House of Lords (2016) *Building More Homes*, Economic Affairs Committee, First Report of Session 2016/17, HL Paper 20, London: UK Parliament.

Huang, H. and Tang, Y. (2012) 'Residential land use regulation and the US house price cycle between 2000 and 2009', *Journal of Urban Economics*, 71(1): 93–99.

Hulchanski, J. (1995) 'The concept of housing affordability: Six contemporary uses of the housing expenditure-to-income ratio', *Housing Studies*, 10(4): 471–491.

Hulse, K., Reynolds, M. and Yates, J. (2014) *Changes in the Supply of Affordable Housing in the Private Rental Sector for Lower Income Households, 2006–11*, AHURI Final Report No. 235, Melbourne: Australian Housing and Urban Research Institute.

Iacoviello, M. (2005) 'House prices, borrowing constraints, and monetary policy in the business cycle', *American Economic Review*, 95(3): 739–764.

Iacoviello, M. and Neri, S. (2010) 'Housing market spillovers: Evidence from an estimated DSGE model', *American Economic Journal: Macroeconomics*, 2(2): 125–164.

Ihlanfeldt, K. (2007) 'The effect of land use regulation on housing and land prices', *Journal of Urban Economics*, 61(3): 420–435.

Ihlanfeldt, K. and Shaughnessy, T. (2004) 'An empirical investigation of the effects of impact fees on housing and land markets', *Regional Science and Urban Economics*, 34(6): 639–661.

Inside Housing (2017) *Inside Housing Spotlight*, Issue 7.12.17, www.insidehousing.co.uk/insight/insight/revealed-the-scale-of-ex-rtb-home-conversions-to-private-rent-53525 [accessed 11 December 2019].

Inside Housing (2018), 'Right to Buy to Let', www.insidehousing.co.uk/insight/insight/right-to-buy-to-let-44479 [accessed 29 November 2019].

Institute of Public Policy Research (2016) *Final Report of the London Housing Commission: Building a New Deal for London*, www.ippr. org/publications/building-a-new-deal-for-london [accessed 19 November 2019].

Jackson, A., Morrison, N. and Royce, C. (1994) *The Supply of Land for Housing, Changing Local Authority Mechanisms*, Discussion Paper 42, Cambridge: Department of Land Economy, University of Cambridge.

Jackson, A., Monk, S., Royce, C. and Dunn, J. (1994a) *Land Supply and Housing: A Case Study*, Discussion Paper 44, Cambridge: Department of Land Economy, University of Cambridge.

Jackson, B. (2014) 'Property-owning democracy: A short history', in M. O'Neill and T. Williamson (eds.), *Property-Owning Democracy: Rawls and Beyond* (pp 33–52), Chichester: John Wiley & Sons.

Joint Center of Housing Studies of Harvard University (2019) *The State of the Nation's Housing, 2019*, Boston: the Center.

Jones, C. and Murie, A. (2006) *The Right to Buy: Analysis and Evaluation of a Housing Policy*, Oxford: Blackwell.

Jones, C., Coombes, M. and Wong, C. (2012) 'A system of national tiered housing-market areas and spatial planning', *Environment and Planning B*, 39(3): 518–532.

Jones. C., Leishman, C. and Watkins, C. (2004) 'Intra-urban migration and housing submarkets: Theory and evidence', *Housing Studies*, 19(2): 269–283.

Jones, C., Watkins, C. and Watkins, D. (2011) 'Measuring local affordability: Variations between housing market areas', *International Journal of Housing Markets and Analysis*, 4(4): 341–356.

Jordà, O., Knoll, K., Kuvshinov, D., Schularick, M. and Taylor, A. (2017) 'The rate of return on everything, 1870–2015', *Federal Reserve Bank of San Francisco Working Paper 2017–25*. San Francisco.

Joyce, R., Mitchell, M. and Keiller, A. (2017) *The Costs of Housing for Low Income Tenants*, London: Institute for Fiscal Studies.

Kahneman, D. (2011) *Thinking, Fast and Slow*, New York: Farrar, Straus and Giroux.

Keightley, M. (2019) *An Introduction to the Low-Income Housing Tax Credit*, Washington DC: Congressional Research Service.

Kemp, P. (1998) *Housing Benefit, Time for Reform*, York: Joseph Rowntree Foundation.

Kemp, P. (ed.) (2007) *Housing Allowances in a Comparative Perspective*, Bristol: Policy Press.

Kemp, P., Wilcox, S. and Rhodes, D. (2002) *Housing Benefit Reform: Next Steps*, York: Joseph Rowntree Foundation.

Kiddle, C. (2002) *The Impact of the Large Scale Transfer of Local Authority Stock on the Housing Association Sector*, Cambridge: Cambridge Centre for Housing and Planning Research, University of Cambridge.

Kim, Y. and Rous, J. (2012) 'House price convergence: Evidence from US state and metropolitan area panels', *Journal of Housing Economics*, 21: 169–186.

King, M. (1990) 'Discussion of Muellbauer and Murphy: Is the UK's balance of payments sustainable?', *Economic Policy*, 5(11): 383–387.

Knoll, K., Schularick, M. and Steger, T. (2017) 'No Place Like Home: Global House Prices, 1870–2012', *American Economic Review*, 107(2): 331–352.

KPMG and Shelter (2015) *Building the Homes We Need*. London: KPMG.

Kutty, N. (2005) 'A new measure of housing affordability: Estimates and analytical results', *Housing Policy Debate*, 16(1): 113–142.

Lambrecht, B., Perraudin, W. and Satchell, S. (1997) 'Time to default in the UK mortgage market', *Economic Modelling*, 14(4): 485–499.

Lawson, J., Pawson, H., Troy, L., van den Nouwelant, R. and Hamilton, C. (2018) *Social Housing as Infrastructure: An Investment Pathway*, AHURI Final Report No. 306, Melbourne: Australian Housing and Urban Research Institute.

Lean, H. and Smyth, R. (2013) 'Regional house prices and the ripple effect in Malaysia', *Urban Studies*, 50(5): 895–922.

LeBaron, B., Arthur, W. and Palmer, R. (1999) 'Time series properties of an artificial stock market', *Journal of Economic Dynamics and Control*, 23(9), 1487–1516.

Lee, Chul-In (2007) 'Does provision of public rental housing crowd out private housing investment? A panel VAR approach', *Journal of Housing Economics*, 16(1): 1–20.

Leishman, C. (2009) 'Spatial change and the structure of urban housing sub-markets', *Housing Studies*, 24(5): 563–586.

Leishman, C. and Rowley, S. (2012) 'Affordable housing', in D. Clapham, A. Clarke and K. Gibb (eds.) *The Sage Handbook of Housing*, London: Sage.

Leishman, C., Costello, G., Rowley, S. and Watkins, C. (2013) 'The predictive performance of multilevel models of housing sub-markets: A comparative analysis', *Urban Studies*, 50(6), 1201–1220.

Lenoel, C., Matsu, J. and Naisbitt, B. (2018) *International Evidence Review on Housing Taxation*, UK Collaborative Centre for Housing Evidence, https://housingevidence.ac.uk/publications/international-evidence-review-on-housing-taxation/ [accessed 28 November 2019].

Lerman, D. and Reeder, W. (1987) 'The affordability of adequate housing', *Journal of the American Real Estate and Urban Economics Association*, 15(4): 389–404.

Letwin, O. (2018) *Independent Review of Build-out: Final Report*, Cm 9720, London: MHCLG and HM Treasury.

Lichfields (2017), *Stock and Flow, Planning Permissions and Housing Output*, London: Nathaniel Litchfield and Partners.

Linneman, P. and Megbolugbe, I. (1992) 'Housing affordability: Myth or reality?', *Urban Studies*, 29(3/4): 369–392.

Lord, A., Dunning, R., Dockerill, B., Carro, A., Burgess, G., Crook, A., Watkins, C. and Whitehead, C. (2018) *The Incidence, Value and Delivery of Planning Obligations in England in 2016–2017*, London: Department of Communities and Local Government.

Lunde, J. and Whitehead, C. (2016) *Milestones in European Housing Finance*, Oxford: Wiley-Blackwell.

Luo, Z., Liu, C. and Picken, D. (2007) 'Housing price diffusion pattern of Australia's state capital cities', *International Journal of Strategic Property Management*, 11(4): 227–242.

Lyons, M. (2014) *Mobilising across the Nation to Build the Homes our Children Need.* The Lyons Housing Review www.thinkhouse.org. uk/archive/lyons.pdf, [accessed 28 November 2019].

McKee, K. and Soaita, D. (2018), *The 'Frustrated' Housing Aspirations of Generation Rent.* UK Collaborative Centre for Housing Evidence Research Report, https://housingevidence.ac.uk/publications/the-frustrated-housing-aspirations-of-generation-rent/, [accessed 28 November 2019].

Mace, A. (2017) 'The metropolitan green belt – changing an institution', *Progress in Planning*, 121: 1–28.

Mace, A., Blanc, F., Gordon, I. and Scanlon, K. (2016) *A 21st Century Metropolitan Green Belt.* HEIF (5), London: The London School of Economics.

Maclennan, D. and Tu, Y. (1996) 'Economic perspectives on the structure of local housing markets', *Housing Studies*, 11(3): 387–406.

Maclennan, D., Muellbauer, J. and Stephens, M. (1998) 'Asymmetries in housing and financial market institutions and EMU', *Oxford Review of Economic Policy*, 14(3): 54–80.

Maclennan, D., Ong, R. and Wood, G. (2015) *Making Connections: Housing Productivity and Economic Development*, AHURI Final Report No. 251, Melbourne: Australian Housing and Urban Research Institute.

Maclennan, D., Crommelin, L., van den Nouwelant, R. and Randolph, B. (2018) *Making Better Economic Cases for Housing Policies*, City Futures Research Report, Sydney: University of New South Wales.

Maclennan, D., with Randolph, B., Crommelin L., Witte, E., Klestov, P., Scealy, B. and Brown, S. (2019) *Strengthening Economic Cases for Housing Policies*, City Futures Research Report, Sydney: University of New South Wales.

McOmish, D. (2018) *Potential Impacts of Brownfield Development: An Assessment*, London: Historic England.

Malpass, P. (2015) 'Histories of social housing, a comparative approach', in K. Scanlon, C. Whitehead, and M. Fernandez Arrigoitia (eds.), *Social Housing in Europe*, Oxford: Wiley Blackwell.

Malpezzi, S. (1996) 'Housing prices, externalities, and regulation in US metropolitan areas', *Journal of Housing Research*, 7(2): 209–241.

Malpezzi, S. and Maclennan, D. (2001) 'The long-run price elasticity of supply of new residential construction in the United States and the United Kingdom', *Journal of Housing Economics*, 10(3): 278–306.

Malpezzi, S. and Mayo, S. (1997) 'Getting housing incentives right: A case study of the effects of regulation, taxes and subsidies on housing supply in Malaysia', *Land Economics*, 73(3): 372–391.

Malpezzi, S. and Mayo, S. (1997a) 'Housing and urban development indicators: A good idea whose time has returned', *Real Estate Economics*, 25(1): 1–11.

Manski, C. (2000) 'Economic analysis of social interactions', *Journal of Economic Perspectives*, 14(3): 115–136.

Marmaras, E. (2015) 'British town planning on the eve of the Second World War', in *Planning for London for the Post-War Era*, pp 7–14, Basle: Springer International.

Mayer, C. and Somerville, C. (2000) 'Residential construction: Using the urban growth model to estimate housing supply', *Journal of Urban Economics*, 48: 85–109.

Mayer, C. and Somerville, C. (2000a) 'Land use regulation and new construction', *Regional Science and Urban Economics*, 30(6): 639–662.

Mayo, S. and Sheppard, S. (1996) 'Housing supply under rapid economic growth and varying regulatory stringency: An international comparison,' *Journal of Housing Economics*, 5(3): 274–289.

Mayo, S. and Sheppard, S. (2001) 'Housing supply and the effects of stochastic development control', *Journal of Housing Economics*, 10(2): 109–128.

Meen, D. and Meen, G. (2003) 'Social behaviour as a basis for modelling the urban housing market: A review', *Urban Studies*, 40(5–6): 917–935.

Meen, G. (1989) 'The ending of mortgage rationing and its effects on the housing market: A simulation study', *Urban Studies*, 26(2): 240–252.

Meen, G. (1990) 'The removal of mortgage market constraints and the implications for econometric modelling of UK house prices', *Oxford Bulletin of Economics and Statistics*, 52(1): 1–24.

Meen, G. (1995) 'Is housing good for the economy?', *Housing Studies*, 10(3): 405–424.

Meen, G. (1999) 'Regional house prices and the ripple effect: A new interpretation', *Housing Studies*, 14(6): 733–753.

Meen, G. (2001) *Modelling Spatial Housing Markets: Theory, Analysis and Policy*, Boston: Kluwer Academic Publishers.

Meen, G. (2002) 'The time-series properties of house prices: A transatlantic divide?', *Journal of Housing Economics*, 11(1): 1–23.

Meen, G. (2008) 'Ten new propositions in UK housing macroeconomics: An overview of the first years of the century', *Urban Studies*, 45(13): 2759–2781.

Meen, G. (2011) 'A long-run model of housing affordability', *Housing Studies*, 26(7–8): 1081–1104.

Meen, G. (2013) 'Home-ownership for future generations', *Urban Studies*, 50(4): 637–656.

Meen, G. and Andrew, M. (1998) 'On the aggregate housing market implications of labour market change', *Scottish Journal of Political Economy*, 45(4): 393–419.

Meen, G. and Andrew, M. (2008) 'Planning for housing in the post-Barker era: affordability, household formation and tenure choice', *Oxford Review of Economic Policy*, 24(1): 79–98.

Meen, G. and Nygaard, C. (2011) 'Local housing supply and the impact of history and geography', *Urban Studies*, 48(14): 3107–3124.

Meen, G., Mihailov, A. and Wang, Y. (2020) 'On the long-run solution to aggregate housing systems', University of Reading Department of Economics Discussion Paper, Reading: University of Reading.

Meen, G., Gibb, K., Leishman, C. and Nygaard, C. (2016) *Housing Economics: A Historical Approach*, London: Palgrave Macmillan.

Mian, A. and Sufi, A. (2009) 'The consequences of mortgage credit expansion: Evidence from the US mortgage default crisis', *Quarterly Journal of Economics*, 124(4): 1449–1496.

Mian, A. and Sufi, A. (2011) 'House prices, home-equity based borrowing, and the US household leverage crisis', *American Economic Review*, 101(5): 2132–2156.

Mian, A., Sufi, A. and Verner, E. (2017) 'Household debt and business cycles worldwide', *Quarterly Journal of Economics*, 132(4): 1755–1817.

Miao, H., Ramchander, S. and Simpson, M. (2011), 'Return and volatility transmission in US housing markets', *Real Estate Economics*, 39(4): 701–741.

Miles, D. (2004) *The UK Mortgage Market: Taking a Longer View*, London: HM Treasury.

Miles, D. (2011) 'Mortgages, Housing and Monetary Policy – What Lies Ahead?', www.bankofengland.co.uk/-/media/boe/files/speech/2011/mortgages-housing-and-monetary-policy-what-lies-ahead-speech-by-david-miles [accessed 29 November 2019].

Miles, D. (2012) 'Demographic change and housing markets', *Scottish Journal of Political Economy*, 59(5): 444–466.

Miles, W. (2017) 'Has there actually been a sustained increase in the synchronization of house price (and business) cycles across countries?', *Journal of Housing Economics*, 36: 25–43.

Ministry of Housing, Communities and Local Government (2012, 2018 and 2019) *National Planning Policy Framework*, London: MHCLG.

Ministry of Housing, Communities and Local Government (2018) *Technical Consultation on Updates to National Planning Policy and Guidance*, https://assets.publishing.service.gov.uk/government/uploads/system/uploads/attachment_data/file/751810/LHN_Consultation.pdf [accessed 14 December 2019].

Ministry of Housing, Communities and Local Government (2018a), *Affordable Housing Supply April 2017*, https://assets.publishing.service.gov.uk/government/uploads/system/uploads/attachment_data/file/758389/Affordable_Housing_Supply_2017-18.pdf. [accessed 22 December 2019].

Ministry of Housing, Communities and Local Government (2019) *English Private Landlord Survey 2018 Main Report*, www.gov.uk/government/publications/english-private-landlord-survey-2018-main-report [accessed 11 December 2019].

Ministry of Housing, Communities and Local Government (2019a) *A New Deal for Renting: Resetting the Balance of Rights and Responsibilities between Landlords and Tenants*, www.gov.uk/government/consultations/a-new-deal-for-renting-resetting-the-balance-of-rights-and-responsibilities-between-landlords-and-tenants [accessed 11 December 2019].

Ministry of Housing, Communities and Local Government (2019b) *Government Response to the Technical Consultation on Updates to National Planning Policy and Guidance*, https://assets.publishing.service.gov.uk/government/uploads/system/uploads/attachment_data/file/779792/LHN_Gov_response.pdf, [accessed 14 December 2019].

Ministry of Housing, Communities and Local Government (2019c) *Housing and Economic Needs Assessment*, www.gov.uk/guidance/housing-and-economic-development-needs-assessments [accessed 14 December 2019].

Ministry of Housing, Communities and Local Government (2019d) *House Building: New Build Dwellings, England: December Quarter 2018*, London: Housing Statistical Release, March.

Ministry of Housing, Communities and Local Government (2019e) English Housing Survey 2017 to 2018: Headline Report, www.gov.uk/government/statistics/english-housing-survey-2017-to-2018-headline-report

Ministry of Housing, Communities and Local Government (2019f) *Rough Sleeping in England: Autumn 2018*, London: Housing Statistical Release, February.

Ministry of Housing, Communities and Local Government (2020) *Planning for the Future*, London: MHCLG.

Mirrlees, J., Adam, S., Besley, T., Blundell, R., Bond, S., Chote, R., Gammie, M., Johnson, P., Myles, G. and Poterba, J. (2011) *Tax by Design*, Oxford: Oxford University Press.

Monk, S. (1999) *The Use of Price in Planning for Housing: A Literature Review*, Discussion Paper 105, Cambridge: Department of Land Economy, University of Cambridge.

Monk, S., Whitehead, C., Burgess, G. and Tang, C. (2013) *International Review of Land Supply and Planning Systems*, York: Joseph Rowntree Foundation.

Montagnoli, A. and Nagayasu, J. (2015) 'UK house price convergence clubs and spillovers', *Journal of Housing Economics*, 30: 50–58.

Montague, A. (2012) *Review of the Barriers to Institutional Investment in Private Rented Homes*, London: Department of Communities and Local Government.

Muellbauer, J. (2005) 'Property taxation and the economy after the Barker review', *Economic Journal*, 115(502): C99–117.

Muellbauer, J. (2018) 'Housing, debt and the economy: A tale of two countries', *National Institute Economic Review*, 245(1): R20–R33.

Muellbauer, J. and Murphy, A. (1990) 'Is the UK's balance of payments sustainable?', *Economic Policy*, 5(11): 347–395.

Muellbauer, J. and Murphy, A. (1997) 'Booms and busts in the UK housing market', *Economic Journal*, 107(445): 1701–1727.

Mulheirn, I. (2019) *Tackling the UK Housing Crisis: Is Supply the Answer?* UK Collaborative Centre for Housing Evidence, https://housingevidence.ac.uk/wp-content/uploads/2019/08/20190820b-CaCHE-Housing-Supply-FINAL.pdf [accessed 30 December 2019].

Murie, A. (2015) 'The Right to Buy, History and Prospect', History and Politics Policy Papers, www.historyandpolicy.org/policy-papers/papers/the-right-to-buy-history-and-prospect [accessed 22 December 2019].

Murphy, L. (2014) 'Houston, we've got a problem: The political construction of a housing affordability metric in New Zealand', *Housing Studies*, 29(7): 893–909.

Murphy, L., Snelling, C. and Stirling, A. (2019) *A Poor Tax: Council Tax in London: Time for Reform*, London: Institute for Public Policy Research.

Murray, M. (1999) 'Subsidized and unsubsidized housing stocks 1935 to 1987: Crowding out and cointegration', *Journal of Real Estate Finance and Economics*, 18(1): 107–124.

Musgrave, R. (1959) *The Theory of Public Finance*, New York: McGraw-Hill.

Muth, R. (1960) 'The demand for non-farm housing', in: A. Harberger (Ed.) *The Demand for Durable Goods*, Chicago: University of Chicago Press.

National Audit Office (2019) *Help to Buy Equity Loan Scheme: Progress Review*, www.nao.org.uk/wp-content/uploads/2019/06/Help-to-Buy-Equity-Loan-scheme-progress-review.pdf [accessed 29 November 2019].

National Housing Federation (2019) 'Housing benefit freeze: 9 in 10 homes unaffordable for families', www.housing.org.uk/press/press-releases/housing-benefit-freeze-9-in-10-homes-unaffordable-for-families/ [accessed 11 December 2019].

National Housing Supply Council (annually, 2009–13) *State of Supply Annual Reports*, Canberra: NHSC.

Nelson, K. (1994) 'Whose shortage of affordable housing?', *Housing Policy Debate*, 5(4): 401–442.

Nepal, B., Tanton, R. and Harding, A. (2010) 'Measuring housing stress: How much do definitions matter?', *Urban Policy and Research*, 28(2): 211–224.

Neuberger, H. and Nichol, B. (1976) *The Recent Course of Land and Property Prices and the Factors Underlying It.* London: Department of the Environment.

NHBC Foundation (2015) *Homes through the Decades*, Milton Keynes: NHBC.

Nitsch, V. (2003) 'Does history matter for urban primacy? The case of Vienna', *Regional Science and Urban Economics*, 33(4): 401–418.

Nordvik, V. (2006) 'Selective housing policy in local housing markets and the supply of housing', *Journal of Housing Economics*, 15(4): 279–292.

North, D. (2005) *Understanding the Process of Economic Change*, Princeton: Princeton University Press.

OECD (2016) *Affordable Housing Database*, Paris: OECD.

OECD (2019) *HC1.2 Housing Costs over Income*, OECD Social Policy Division, www.oecd.org/els/family/HC1-2-Housing-costs-over-income.pdf [accessed 11 December 2019].

Office for Fair Trading (2008) *Homebuilding in the UK: A Market Study*, https://webarchive.nationalarchives.gov.uk/20140402181400/http:/www.oft.gov.uk/shared_oft/reports/comp_policy/oft1020.pdf [accessed 28 November 2019].

Office for National Statistics (2018) *Household Projections for England: 2016-Based*, www.ons.gov.uk/peoplepopulationandcommunity/populationandmigration/populationprojections/bulletins/2016base dhouseholdprojectionsinengland/2016basedhouseholdprojectionsin england [accessed 14 December 2019].

Office for National Statistics (2018a) *Methodology Used to Produce Household Projections for England: 2016-Based*, www.ons.gov.uk/peoplepopulationandcommunity/populationandmigration/populationprojections/methodologies/methodologyusedtopr oducehouseholdprojectionsforengland2016based [accessed 14 December 2019].

Oikarinen, E. (2012) 'Empirical Evidence on the Reaction Speeds of House Prices and Sales to Demand Shocks', *Journal of Housing Economics*, 21(1): 41–54.

Ong, R., Wood, G., Whelan, S., Cigdem, M., Atalay, K. and Dodson, J. (2017) *Inquiry into Housing Policies, Labour Force Participation and Economic Growth*, AHURI Final Report No. 285, Melbourne: Australian Housing and Urban Research Institute.

Oswald, A. (1996), 'A Conjecture on the explanation for high unemployment in the industrialised nations: Part 1', Warwick University Economic Research Papers No. 475.

Pannell, R. (2003) 'Denmark: Probably the best housing finance system in the world', *CML Housing Finance*, Winter.

Paris, C. (2007) 'International perspectives on planning and affordable housing', *Housing Studies*, 22(1): 1–9.

Peabody (2019) *Understanding the Impact of Universal Credit*, www.peabody.org.uk/news-views/2019/sep/universal-credit-impact [accessed 11 December 2019].

Pelletier, D. and Tunc, C. (2019) 'Endogenous life-cycle housing investment and portfolio allocation', *Journal of Money, Credit and Banking*, 51(4): 991–1019.

Pereira, A. (2009) 'The opportunity of a disaster: The economic impact of the 1755 Lisbon earthquake', *The Journal of Economic History*, 69(02): 466–499.

Pereira, R. (2018) 'What Our Household Projections Really Show', *National Statistical*, October, Office of National Statistics, https://blog.ons.gov.uk/2018/10/19/what-our-household-projections-really-show/ [accessed 14 December 2019].

Petkova, K. and Weichenrieder, A. (2017) 'Price and quantity effects of the German real estate transfer tax', *CESifo Working Paper No. 6538*. Munich: Ifo Institute.

Piazzesi, M. and Schneider, M. (2016) 'Housing and macroeconomics', in J. Taylor and H. Uhlig (eds.), *Handbook of Macroeconomics Vol. 2*, Amsterdam: Elsevier.

Piazzesi, M., Schneider, M. and Tuzel, S. (2007) 'Housing, consumption and asset pricing', *Journal of Financial Economics*, 83(3): 531–569.

Picketty, T. (2014) *Capital in the 21st Century*, Cambridge, MA: Harvard University Press.

Pinoncely, V. and Belcher, E. (2018) *Made for London: Realising the Potential for Modern Methods of Construction*. London: Centre for London.

Poghosyan, T. (2016) 'Can property taxes reduce house price volatility? Evidence from US regions', IMF Working Paper WP/16/216.

Poterba, J. (1984) 'Tax subsidies to owner occupied housing: An asset market approach', *Quarterly Journal of Economics*, 99(4): 729–752.

Preece, J., Crawford, J., McKee, K., Flint, J. and Robinson, D. (2019) 'Understanding changing housing aspirations: A review of the evidence', *Housing Studies*, doi.org/10.1080/02673037.2019.1584665.

Priemus, H. and Boelhouwer, P. (1999) 'Social housing finance, trends and opportunities', *Urban Studies,* 36(4): 633–645.

Priemus, H. and Whitehead, C. (2014) 'Interactions between the financial crisis and national housing markets', *Journal of Housing and the Built Environment*, 29(2): 193–200.

Pryce, G. (1999) 'Construction elasticities and land availability: A two-stage least-squares model of housing supply using the variable elasticity approach', *Urban Studies*, 36(13): 2283–2304.

Pryke, M. and Whitehead, C. (1993) 'The provision of private finance for social housing: An outline of recent developments in funding existing housing associations in England', *Housing Studies*, 8(4): 274–291.

Pryke, M. and Whitehead, C. (1994) 'The influence of private finance on the provision of social housing in England', *Journal of Housing and the Built Environment*, 9(4): 357–359.

Quercia, R. and Stegman, M. (1992) 'Residential mortgage default: A review of the literature', *Journal of Housing Research*, 3(2): 341–379.

Ravenstein, E. (1885) 'The Laws of Migration', *Journal of the Statistical Society of London*, 48(2): 167–235.

Redfern Review (2016) *The Redfern Review into the Decline of Home Ownership*, https://britainthinks.com/pdfs/TW082_RR_online_PDF.pdf [accessed 29 November 2019].

Reinhart, C. and Rogoff, K. (2009) *This Time is Different: Eight Centuries of Financial Folly*, Princeton and Oxford: Princeton University Press.

Resolution Foundation (2018) 'Home ownership is rising, but the crisis is far from over', www.resolutionfoundation.org/media/blog/home-ownership-is-rising-but-the-crisis-is-far-from-over/ [accessed 29 November 2019].

Rhodes, D. (2015) 'The fall and rise of the private rented sector in England', *Built Environment*, 41(2): 258–270.

Rhodes, D. and Rugg, J. (2018) *Vulnerability amongst Low Income Tenants in the Private Rented Sector*. York: Centre for Housing Policy, University of York.

RICS (2019) *International Models for Delivery of Affordable Housing in Asia*, Insight Paper, London: RICS.

Riddel, M. (2000) 'Housing market dynamics under stochastic growth: An application to the housing market in Boulder, Colorado', *Journal of Regional Science*, 40(4): 771–788.

Riddel, M. (2004) 'Housing-market disequilibrium: An examination of housing-market price and stock dynamics', *Journal of Housing Economics*, 13(2): 120–135.

Rohe, W., van Zandt, S. and McCarthy, G. (2001) 'The social benefits and costs of home ownership: A critical assessment of the research', Paper LIHO-01-12, Joint Center for Housing Studies, Harvard: Harvard University.

Rose, L. (1989) 'Urban land supply: Natural and contrived restriction', *Journal of Urban Economics*, 25(3): 325–345.

Rowley, S. and Ong, R. (2012) *Housing Affordability, Housing Stress and Household Wellbeing in Australia*, AHURI Final Report No. 192, Melbourne: Australian Housing and Urban Research Institute.

Rowley, S., Ong, R. and Haffner, M. (2015) 'Bridging the gap between housing stress and financial stress: The case of Australia', *Housing Studies*, 30(3): 473–490.

Rowley, S., Leishman, C., Baker, E., Bentley, R. and Lester, L. (2017) *Modelling Housing Need in Australia to 2025*, AHURI Final Report No. 287, Melbourne: Australian Housing and Urban Research Institute.

Rowley, S., James, A., Gilbert, C., Gurran, N., Ong, R., Phibbs, P., Rosen, D. and Whitehead, C. (2016) *Subsidised Affordable Rental Housing: Lessons from Australia and Overseas*, AHURI Final Report No. 267, Melbourne: Australian Housing and Urban Research Institute.

Rugg, J. and Rhodes, D. (2018) *The Evolving Private Rented Sector: Its Evolution and Potential*, York: Centre of Housing Policy, University of York.

Ryan-Collins, J. (2019) *Why Can't You Afford a Home?*, Cambridge: Polity Press.

Sai-Fan Chan, T. (1999) 'Residential construction and credit market imperfection', *Journal of Real Estate Finance and Economics*, 18(1): 125–129.

Saiz, A. (2010) 'The Geographic Determinants of Housing Supply', *Quarterly Journal of Economics*, 125(3): 1253–1296.

Savills (2019) *Build to Rent*, London: Savills.

Scanlon, K. and Blanc, F. (2019) *The Bank of Mum and Dad: How it Really Works*, London: LSE London.

Scanlon, K. and Whitehead, C. (2004) *International Trends in Housing Tenure and Mortgage Finance*, London: Council of Mortgage Lenders.

Scanlon, K., Whitehead, C. and Fernandez Arrigoitia, M. (2014) *Social Housing in Europe*, Oxford: Wiley Blackwell.

Scanlon, K., Whitehead, C. and Williams, P. (2016) *Taking Stock: Understanding the Effects of Recent Policy Change on the Private Rented Sector and Buy to Let*, London: LSE London, www.lse.ac.uk/business-and-consultancy/consulting/assets/documents/Taking-stock.-Buy-to-let.pdf [accessed 28 November 2019].

Scanlon, K., Whitehead, C. and Blanc, F. (2017) *The Future Social Housing Provider*, Norwich: Flagship Group.

Scanlon, K., Whitehead, C., Blanc, F. and Moreno-Tabarez, U. (2017) *The Role of Overseas Investors in the London New-Build Residential Market*, London: Greater London Authority.

Schelling, T. (1971) 'Dynamic models of segregation', *Journal of Mathematical Sociology*, 1(2): 143–186.

Schmid, C. (2018) *Tenancy Law and Housing Policy in Europe*, Cheltenham: Edward Elgar.

Shelter (2019) *A Vision for Social Housing*, https://england.shelter.org.uk/support_us/campaigns/a_vision_for_social_housing, [accessed 19 November 2019].

Shi, S. (2009) 'The ripple effect of local house price movements in New Zealand', *Journal of Property Research*, 26(1): 1–24.

Shiller, R. (2005) *Irrational Exuberance*, Princeton N.J: Princeton University Press.

Simpson, H. (1933) 'Real estate speculation and the depression', *American Economic Review, Papers and Proceedings*, 23(1): 163–171.

Siodla, J. (2015) 'Razing San Francisco: The 1906 disaster as a natural experiment in urban redevelopment', *Journal of Urban Economics*, 89: 48–61.

Smith, L. (2017) *Planning for Housing*, House of Commons Briefing Note 03741, London: Parliament.

Smith, S., Searle, B. and Cook, N. (2009) 'Rethinking the risks of home ownership', *Journal of Social Policy*, 38(1): 83–102.

Smith, S., Whitehead, C. and Williams, P. (2013) *A Role for Equity Finance in UK Housing Markets?* York: Joseph Rowntree Foundation.

Stapledon, N. (2010) 'A history of housing prices in Australia, 1880–2010', University of New South Wales, School of Economics Discussion Paper: 2010/18.

Stephens, M. (2000) 'Convergence in European mortgage systems before and after EMU', *Journal of Housing and Built Environment*, 15(1): 29–52.

Stephens, M., Perry, J., Wilcox, S., Williams, P. and Young, G. (2018) *The UK Housing Review, 2018,* Coventry: Chartered Institute of Housing.

Stevenson, S. (2004) 'House price diffusion and inter-regional and cross-border house price dynamics', *Journal of Property Research*, 21(4): 301–320.

Stone, M. (2006) 'A housing affordability standard for the UK', *Housing Studies*, 21(4): 453–476.

Stone, M. (2006a) 'What is housing affordability? The case for the residual income approach', *Housing Policy Debate*, 17(1): 151–184.

Stone, M., Burke, T. and Ralston, L. (2011) *The Residual Income Approach to Housing Affordability: The Theory and the Practice* AHURI Positioning Paper, No. 139, Melbourne: Australian Housing and Urban Research Institute.

Thalmann, P. (2003) 'House poor or simply poor?', *Journal of Housing Economics*, 12(4): 291–317.

Theil, H. (1954) *Linear Aggregation in Economic Relations*, Amsterdam: North Holland.

Topel, R. and Rosen, S. (1988) 'Housing investment in the United States', *Journal of Political Economy*, 96(4): 718–740.

Travers, A. and Whitehead, C. (2013) *Creating the Conditions for Growth*, London: Berkeley Homes.

Tunstall, R. (2015) 'Relative housing space inequality in England and Wales, and its recent rapid resurgence', *International Journal of Housing Policy*, 15(2): 105–126.

Udagawa, C., Scanlon, K. and Whitehead, C. (2018) *The Future Size and Composition of the Private Rented Sector*, London: LSE London.

UK Government, Cabinet Papers (1965) *Housing Programmes 1965–70*; Draft White Paper, C. (65) 151.

UK Statistics Authority (2019) Correspondence on ONS Household Projections for England, www.statisticsauthority.gov.uk/correspondence/ons-household-projections-for-england/ [accessed 14 December 2019].

University of the West of England (undated) *The History of Council Housing*, https://fet.uwe.ac.uk/conweb/house_ages/council_housing/print.htm, [accessed 11 December 2019].

Vandell, K. (1995) 'How ruthless is mortgage default? A review and synthesis of the evidence', *Journal of Housing Research*, 6(2): 245–264.

Van Dijk, B., Franses, P., Paap, R. and Van Dijk, D. (2011) 'Modelling regional house prices', *Applied Economics*, 43(17): 2097–2110.

Van Ommeren, J. and Leuvensteijn, M. (2005) 'New evidence of the effect of transactions costs on residential mobility', *Journal of Regional Science*, 45(4): 681–702.

Vansteenkiste, I. and Hiebert, P. (2011) 'Do house price developments spillover across Euro area countries? Evidence from a global VAR,' *Journal of Housing Economics*, 20(4): 299–314.

Van Zandt, S. and Rohe, W. (2011) 'The sustainability of low-income home ownership: The incidence of unexpected costs and needed repairs among low-income home buyers', *Housing Policy Debate*, 21(2): 317–341.

Veld, J., Raciborski, R., Ratto, M. and Roeger, W. (2011) 'The recent boom-bust cycle: The relative contribution of capital flows, credit supply and asset bubbles', *European Economic Review*, 55(3): 386–406.

Voigtländer, M. (2009) 'Why is the German homeownership rate so low?', *Housing Studies*, 24(3): 355–372.

Voigtländer, N. and Voth, H-J. (2013) 'The three horsemen of riches: Plague, war and urbanization in early modern Europe', *Review of Economic Studies*, 80(2): 774–811.

Wallace, A., Rhodes, D. and Webber, R. (2017) *Overseas Investors in London's New Build Housing Market*, York: University of York.

Watkins, C. (2001) 'The definition and identification of housing submarkets', *Environment and Planning* A, 33(12): 2235–2253.

Watkins, C. (2008) 'Microeconomic perspectives on the structure and operation of local housing markets'. *Housing Studies*, 23(2): 163–177.

Webster, C. (2006) 'The battle for ideas that shaped British planning', Paper presented to an international seminar on Epistemological Understanding of Spatial Policy and Rural (Regional) Change, Seoul, Korea: Seoul National University.

Weicher, J. (1977) 'The Affordability of New Homes', *AREUEA Journal*, 5: 209–226.

Wertheimer, R. (1958) 'The miracle of German housing in the post war period', *Land Economics*, 34(4): 338–345.

White, M. and Allmendinger, P. (2003) 'Land use planning and the housing market: A comparative review of the UK and the US', *Urban Studies*, 40(5/6): 953–972.

Whitehead, C. (1979) 'Why owner occupation?', London: *CES Review*, No 6.

Whitehead, C. (1991) 'From need to affordability: An analysis of UK housing objectives', *Urban Studies*, 28(6): 871–887.

Whitehead, C. (1994) 'Economic flexibility and the private rented sector', *Scottish Journal of Political Economy*, 45(4): 361–375.

Whitehead, C. (1998) *The Benefits of Better Homes: The Case for Good Quality Affordable Housing*, London: Shelter.

Whitehead, C. (1999) 'The provision of finance for social housing: The UK experience', *Urban Studies*, 36(4): 657–672.

Whitehead, C. (2003) 'The economics of social housing' in A. O'Sullivan and K. Gibb, *Housing Economics and Public Policy*, Oxford: Blackwell.

Whitehead, C. (2010) *Shared Ownership and Shared Equity: Reducing the Risks of Home Ownership*, York: Joseph Rowntree Foundation.

Whitehead, C. (2016) 'Using projections of household numbers: Tensions between planning and economics', Sir Frederick J. Osborn Memorial Lecture 2016, London: TCPA.

Whitehead, C. (2017a) 'Breaking down the barriers to housing delivery?', *Journal of Planning and Environment Law*, 13 S. OP26-OP39.

Whitehead, C. (2017b) 'Social housing models: Past and future', *Critical Housing Analysis*, 4(1): 11–20.

Whitehead, C. (2018) 'Housing policy and the changing tenure mix', *National Institute Economic Review*, 245(1): R34-39.

Whitehead, C. and Cao, B. (2007) *Comparing Rents and User Costs 2005/6 and 2001/2*, Cambridge: Dataspring, Cambridge Centre for Housing and Planning Research, University of Cambridge.

Whitehead, C. and Kleinman, M. (1986) *Private Rented Housing in the 1980s and 1990s*. Occasional Paper No. 17, Cambridge: Department of Land Economy, University of Cambridge.

Whitehead, C. and Kleinman, M. (1992) *A Review of Housing Needs Assessments*, London: The Housing Corporation.

Whitehead, C. and Udagawa, C. (2020) *Housing Supply: Limits of the Market*, London: LSE London.

Whitehead, C. and Williams, P. (2017) 'Changes in the regulation and control of mortgage markets and access to owner occupation among younger households', *OECD Social, Employment and Migration Working Papers No.196*, Paris: OECD Publishing.

Whitehead, C. and Williams, P. (2019) *From Ideas to Reality: Longer Term Tenancies and Rent Stabilisation – Principles and Practical Considerations,* London: LSE London.

Whitehead, C., Williams, P. and Ipsos Mori (2018) *Evaluation of the Help to Buy Equity Loan Scheme*, www.ipsos.com/sites/default/files/ct/publication/documents/2018-10/evaluation-of-the-help-to-buy-equity-loan-scheme-2017.pdf [accessed 29 November 2019].

Whitehead, C., Markkanen, S., Monk, S., Scanlon, K. and Tang, C. (2012) *The Private Rented Sector in the New Century: A Comparative Approach*, Copenhagen: Realdania.

Wilcox, S. (2006) *The Geography of Affordable and Unaffordable Housing: And the Ability of Younger Working Households to Become Home Owners*, York: Joseph Rowntree Foundation.

Wilcox, S. and Bramley, G. (2010) *Evaluating Requirements for Market and Affordable Housing*, London: National Housing and Planning Advice Unit.

Willetts, D. (2010) *The Pinch: How the Baby Boomers Took Their Children's Future – And Why They Should Give It Back*, London: Atlantic Books.

Williams, P., Wilcox, S. and Whitehead, C. (2017) *Challenges for Our Home Ownership Safety Net: UK and International Perspectives*, London: UK Finance, www.ukfinance.org.uk/system/files/Home-Ownership-Safety-Net-11-December-2017.pdf [accessed 5 April 2020].

Wilson, W. (1998) *Rent Levels, Affordability and Housing Benefit*, Research Paper 98/69, House of Commons Library, London: Parliament.

Wilson, W. (2012) *The Reform of Housing Revenue Account Subsidy*, Commons Briefing Paper SNO0434, House of Commons Library, London: Parliament.

Wilson, W. (2017) *A Short History of Rent Controls*, Briefing Paper SN06747, House of Commons Library, London: Parliament.

Wilson, W. (2019a) *Rent Setting: Social Housing (England)*, Commons Briefing Paper 01090, House of Commons Library, London: Parliament.

Wilson, W. (2019b) *Stimulating Housing Supply: Government Initiatives (England)*, Briefing Paper 06416, House of Commons Library, London: Parliament.

Wilson, W. and Barton, C. (2018) *Tackling the Under-Supply of Housing in England*, Briefing Paper 07671, House of Commons Library, London: Parliament.

Wilson, W. and Barton, C. (2019) *The End of No-Fault Evictions*, Commons Briefing Paper CBP 8658, London: House of Commons Library.

Wilson, W. and Bate, A. (2015a) *Affordable Rents: England*, Commons Briefing Paper 05933, House of Commons Library, London: Parliament.

Wilson, W. and Bate, A. (2015b) *Extending the Right to Buy (England)*, Commons Briefing Paper 07224, House of Commons Library, London: Parliament.

Wilson, W., Keen, R. and Barton, C. (2016) *Housing Benefit Measures Announced since 2010*, Commons Briefing Paper SN05638, House of Commons Library, London: Parliament.

Wilson, W., Murphy, C. and Barton, C. (2017) *The New Homes Bonus (England)*, Briefing Paper 05724, House of Commons Library, London: Parliament.

Wood, G. and Ong, R. (2009) *The Dynamics of Housing Affordability: Movements In and Out of Housing Affordability Stress 2001–2006*, AHURI Final Report No. 133, Melbourne: Australian Housing and Urban Research Institute.

Wood, G., Ong, R. and Cigdem, M. (2015) *Factors Shaping the Dynamics of Housing Affordability in Australia 2001–11*, AHURI Final Report No. 244, Melbourne: Australian Housing and Urban Research Institute.

Yates, J. (2007) *Housing Affordability and Financial Stress*, AHURI Research Paper No. NRV3-6, Melbourne: Australian Housing and Urban Research Institute.

Yates, J. (2008) 'Australia's housing affordability crisis', *Australian Economic Review*, 41(2): 200–214.

Yates, J. and Gabriel, M. (2006) *Housing Affordability in Australia*, AHURI Research Paper No. NRV3-3, Melbourne: Australian Housing and Urban Research Institute.

Yates, J. and Whitehead, C. (1998) 'In defence of greater agnosticism: A response to Galster's "Comparing demand-side and supply-side subsidies"', *Housing Studies*, 13(3): 415–423.

Young, G., Wilcox, S., Leishman, C. and McCloy, S. (2017) *A Review of the Affordability of Social Rents in Northern Ireland.* Northern Ireland Housing Executive Research Unit, www.nihe.gov.uk/getmedia/2c7532ee-2310-456d-8ca6-e093cc08a04e/ni_affordability_report_2017.pdf.aspx?ext=.pdf [accessed 27 November 2019].

Zabel, J. and Paterson, R. (2006) 'The effects of critical habitat designation on housing supply: An analysis of California housing construction activity', *Journal of Regional Science*, 46(1): 67–95.

Zhang, J. (2004) 'Residential segregation in an all integrationist world', *Journal of Economic Behavior and Organisation*, 54(4): 533–550.

Zhang, J. (2004a) 'A dynamic model of residential segregation', *Journal of Mathematical Sociology*, 28(3): 147–170.

Zheng, G. (2013) *The Effects of Auckland's Metropolitan Urban Limit on Land Prices*, Wellington: New Zealand Productivity Commission.

Zhu, B., Betzinger, M. and Sebastian, S. (2017) 'Housing market stability, mortgage market structure and monetary policy: Evidence from the Euro Area', *Journal of Housing Economics*, 37: 1–21.

Zumbro, T. (2014) 'The relationship between home-ownership and life satisfaction in Germany', *Housing Studies*, 29(3): 319–338.

Index

Note: Page numbers in *italic* type refer to figures; those in **bold** type refer to tables.

Printed and bound by CPI Group (UK) Ltd, Croydon, CR0 4YY

16/04/2025

14658341-0003